Palgrave Studies in International Relations Series

General Editors:

Knud Erik Jørgensen, Department of Political Science, University of Aarhus, Denmark

Audie Klotz, Department of Political Science, Maxwell School of Citizenship and Public Affairs
Syracuse University, USA

Palgrave Studies in International Relations, produced in association with the ECPR Standing Group for International Relations, will provide students and scholars with the best theoretically-informed scholarship on the global issues of our time. Edited by Knud Erik Jørgensen and Audie Klotz, this new book series will comprise cutting-edge monographs and edited collections which bridge schools of thought and cross the boundaries of conventional fields of study.

Titles include:

Pami Aalto, Vilho Harle and Sami Moisio (*editors*)
INTERNATIONAL STUDIES
Interdisciplinary Approaches

Mathias Albert, Lars-Erik Cederman and Alexander Wendt (*editors*)
NEW SYSTEMS THEORIES OF WORLD POLITICS

Barry Buzan and Ana Gonzalez-Pelaez (*editors*)
INTERNATIONAL SOCIETY AND THE MIDDLE EAST
English School Theory at the Regional Level

Toni Erskine and Richard Ned Lebow (*editors*)
TRAGEDY AND INTERNATIONAL RELATIONS

Geir Hønneland
BORDERLAND RUSSIANS
Identity, Narrative and International Relations

Oliver Kessler, Rodney Bruce Hall, Cecelia Lynch and Nicholas G. Onuf (*editors*)
ON RULES, POLITICS AND KNOWLEDGE
Friedrich Kratochwil, International Relations and Domestic Affairs

Pierre P. Lizee
A WHOLE NEW WORLD
Reinventing International Studies for the Post-Western World

Cornelia Navari (*editor*)
THEORISING INTERNATIONAL SOCIETY
English School Methods

Dirk Peters
CONSTRAINED BALANCING: THE EU'S SECURITY POLICY

Simon F. Reich
GLOBAL NORMS, AMERICAN SPONSORSHIP AND THE EMERGING PATTERNS
OF WORLD POLITICS

Robbie Shilliam
GERMAN THOUGHT AND INTERNATIONAL RELATIONS
The Rise and Fall of a Liberal Project

Daniela Tepe
THE MYTH ABOUT GLOBAL CIVIL SOCIETY
Domestic Politics to Ban Landmines

Daniel C. Thomas (*editor*)
MAKING EU FOREIGN POLICY
National Preferences, European Norms and Common Policies

Rens van Munster
SECURITIZING IMMIGRATION
The Politics of Risk in the EU

Palgrave Studies In International Relations Series
Series Standing Order ISBN 978–0–230–20063–0 (hardback)
978–0–230–24115–2 (paperback)

You can receive future titles in this series as they are published by placing a
standing order. Please contact your bookseller or, in case of difficulty, write to us
at the address below with your name and address, the title of the series and the
ISBNs quoted above.

Customer Services Department, Macmillan Distribution Ltd, Houndmills,
Basingstoke, Hampshire RG21 6XS, England

Tragedy and International Relations

Edited by

Toni Erskine
Professor of International Politics Aberystwyth University, UK

and

Richard Ned Lebow
Professor of International Political Theory, King's College London, UK and
James O. Freedman Presidential Professor Emeritus, Dartmouth College, USA

palgrave
macmillan

First published 2012 by
PALGRAVE MACMILLAN

Palgrave Macmillan in the UK is an imprint of Macmillan Publishers Limited,
registered in England, company number 785998, of Houndmills, Basingstoke,
Hampshire RG21 6XS.

Palgrave Macmillan in the US is a division of St Martin's Press LLC,
175 Fifth Avenue, New York, NY 10010.

Palgrave Macmillan is the global academic imprint of the above companies
and has companies and representatives throughout the world.

Palgrave® and Macmillan® are registered trademarks in the United States,
the United Kingdom, Europe and other countries.

ISBN 978–0–230–23752–0

This book is printed on paper suitable for recycling and made from fully
managed and sustained forest sources. Logging, pulping and manufacturing
processes are expected to conform to the environmental regulations of the
country of origin.

A catalogue record for this book is available from the British Library.

A catalog record for this book is available from the Library of Congress.

10   9   8   7   6   5   4   3   2   1
21 20 19 18 17 16 15 14 13 12

Printed and bound in Great Britain by
CPI Antony Rowe, Chippenham and Eastbourne

*To our spouses, Michael Drage and Carol Bohmer,
for their love, inspiration and encouragement*

Contents

Acknowledgements

This volume is best described as a conversation. It brings together, as our most interesting discussions often do, subjects that may seem at first glance to be quite far removed from each other. The focus of this conversation is how (and, indeed, whether) the concept of tragedy that is revealed in Greek and Shakespearean dramas might inform, and enrich, our understanding of international relations. In approaching this conversation, the reader might, initially, imagine a couple of scholars engaged in a lively – and amicable – debate. This is, in fact, how this conversation actually began. Mervyn Frost and James Mayall started interrogating their respective understandings of tragedy in a diner in Chicago in 2001, between panels at the annual International Studies Association (ISA) conference – each questioning whether the other could adequately account for the tragic dimension of international relations in his work.

A year later, when one of us, Toni Erskine, heard Mervyn present the paper that had resulted from that earlier discussion with James, she was sceptical of the claims he was making about an appreciation of tragedy helping us to think about specifically ethical questions in international relations. Toni was concerned that an appeal to tragedy would somehow obfuscate notions of moral agency and responsibility. Another debate ensued. The fortunate consequence was that she challenged Mervyn to elaborate on his argument and submit it as a short 'debate' piece for the journal at which she was then Associate Editor, *International Relations*. Toni also invited James to revisit the objections he raised in the Chicago diner and provide a response. The interest generated by this initial debate prompted Toni to invite two other scholars, Nicholas Rengger and Richard Ned Lebow, to write on the theme of tragedy and international relations. These invitations brought both Nick's provocative denial of the usefulness of tragedy for understanding international relations (a position that usefully incited further responses) and Ned's passion for a theme on which he had just completed a substantial monograph to bear on the conversation.

In 2006, Toni organized and chaired a panel at ISA in San Diego with Mervyn, James, Nick and Ned presenting papers. Peter Euben had generously accepted her invitation to attend his first ISA conference and act as discussant. Future participants in the project, Chris Brown, Richard

Beardsworth and Tracy Strong, were in the audience in San Diego. The panel was a great success and a number of members of the audience suggested that the papers be collected together in a book. Toni commissioned a few more pieces for *International Relations* as a result of the panel discussion, and Toni and Ned took the audience's comments to heart and decided to edit a book based on revised versions of these articles. We are very grateful to Sage, the publisher of *International Relations*, for sponsoring the 2006 ISA panel in San Diego and for providing permission to print revised versions of essays by Mervyn Frost, James Mayall, Nicholas Rengger, Richard Ned Lebow, Chris Brown and Peter Euben, which were originally published in the journal. We would like to express particular thanks to David Mainwaring at Sage who worked with Toni on the journal, was instrumental in sponsoring the 2006 panel and has been a great source of support since the project's inception.

We not only asked the authors of the journal articles to elaborate and develop their pieces for our book, but, at Palgrave Macmillan's suggestion, we extended invitations to additional scholars to participate. We were lucky to have Robbie Shilliam, Tracy Strong, Kamila Stullerova, Catherine Lu and Ben Schupmann follow the existing contributors in cutting across theoretical perspectives and disciplinary boundaries to join the discussion. Commissioning these pieces over an extended period of time, so that each new contribution could respond to those before them – and approaching a group of outstanding and original scholars who were each willing to engage carefully and critically with the others – has, we think, resulted in a unique project. The book is, indeed, a conversation. Each chapter offers a new argument, and a new perspective on tragedy and international relations, while at the same time variously challenging, extending, rejecting, or correcting particular points from the preceding chapters. If the reader begins reading the chapters by Mervyn and James with the image of two scholars engaged in heated discussion in a diner or coffee shop, it would be apt, as the book progresses, to imagine the diner gradually filling up, with each new arrival listening intently to the on-going conversation, and then making his or her own passionate intervention.

We are very grateful to Knud Erik Jorgensen, Audie Klotz, Christina Brian, Liz Blackmore and Alison Howson at Palgrave Macmillan for their unfailing support of this project, for allowing us to experiment with an unconventional format, and for encouraging us to take it beyond what we had initially envisaged. We also owe a debt of gratitude to Susanna Karlsson for her meticulous and incredibly efficient editorial assistance. Most of all, we wish to thank those who have participated in this conversation: for embracing the project with such enthusiasm, for responding to a stream of requests and comments that must have seemed unending, and for making us think about tragedy and international relations in ways that we had not even conceived of when we began this book.

Toni Erskine and Richard Ned Lebow

Earlier versions of the chapters by Mervyn Frost, James Mayall, Nicholas Rengger, Richard Ned Lebow, Chris Brown, J. Peter Euben and Richard Beardsworth appeared in *International Relations:* Frost (2003) 'Tragedy, Ethics and International Relations', *International Relations* 17/4, 477–95; Mayall (2003) 'Tragedy, Progress and the International Order: A Response to Frost', *International Relations* 17/4, 497–503; Rengger (2005) 'Tragedy or Scepticism? Defending the Anti-Pelagian Mind in World Politics', *International Relations* 19/3, 321–8; Lebow (2005) 'Tragedy, Politics and Political Science', *International Relations* 19/3, 329–36; Brown (2007) 'Tragedy, "Tragic Choices" and Contemporary International Political Theory', *International Relations* 21/1, 5–13; Euben (2007) 'The Tragedy of Tragedy', *International Relations* 21/1, 15–22; and Beardsworth (2008) 'Tragedy, World Politics and Ethical Community', *International Relations* 22/1, 127–37.

Notes on Contributors

Richard Beardsworth is Professor of Political Philosophy and International Relations and directs the Research Center in the division of International Politics, Economics and Public Policy at the American University of Paris. Having worked extensively in the domain of critical theory, he moved more recently to the domains of international political theory and applied international theory. His research interests lie in the relation between value and power in world politics, global and regional governance, and state responsibility. His new book, *Cosmopolitanism and International Relations Theory*, was published in 2011 by Polity Press. He is also the author of *Derrida and the Political* (Routledge, 1996), *Nietzsche* (Les Belles Lettres, 1998), numerous articles on German and French theory, and was general editor of *Tekhnema: Journal of Philosophy and Technology* (1994–2001).

Chris Brown is Professor of International Relations at the London School of Economics. He is the author of *International Relations Theory: New Normative Approaches* (Harvester Wheatsheaf and Columbia University Press, 1992), *Understanding International Relations* (Palgrave Macmillan, 1997; 4th edn 2009), *Sovereignty, Rights and Justice* (Polity, 2002), and most recently *Practical Judgment in International Political Theory: Selected Essays* (Routledge, 2010) as well as numerous book chapters and journal articles in international political theory. He is also editor of *Political Restructuring in Europe: Ethical Perspectives* (Routledge, 1994) and (with Terry Nardin and Nicholas Rengger) *International Relations in Political Thought: Texts from the Greeks to the First World War* (Cambridge, 2002).

Toni Erskine is Professor of International Politics at Aberystwyth University in Wales, United Kingdom. She is also currently Honorary Professor of Global Ethics at RMIT University in Melbourne and Visiting Scholar at Sydney University, Australia. She is past Chair of the International Ethics Section of the International Studies Association (2008–10), and was Lurie-Murdoch Senior Research Fellow in Global Ethics at RMIT University (2008–11) and British Academy Postdoctoral Fellow at Cambridge University (1999–2002). She is author of *Embedded Cosmopolitanism: Duties to Strangers and Enemies in a World of 'Dislocated Communities'* (Oxford, 2008), and editor of *Can Institutions Have*

Responsibilities? Collective Moral Agency and International Relations (Palgrave Macmillan, 2003), and *Responding to 'Delinquent' Institutions* (forthcoming). She is currently working on a monograph titled *Who is Responsible? Institutional Moral Agency and International Relations*.

J. Peter Euben is Research Professor of Political Science, Research Professor of Classical Studies, and the Kenan Distinguished Faculty Fellow in Ethics at Duke University. He specializes in ancient, modern and contemporary political thought; literature and politics; political education; democratic culture and politics; and the politics of morality. He is the author of *The Tragedy of Political Theory* (Princeton, 1990), *Corrupting Youth* (Princeton, 1997) and *Platonic Noise* (Princeton, 2003); editor of *Greek Tragedy and Political Theory* (California, 1987); and co-editor of *Athenian Political Thought and the Reconstitution of American Democracy* (Cornell, 1995), *Debating Moral Education* (Duke, 2009) and *When Worlds Elide: Classics, Politics, Culture* (Lexington Books, 2010). He is presently working on a book titled, *The Necessities of Utopia and the Prospects for Rationality*.

Mervyn Frost is Head of the Department of War Studies at King's College, London. His research interest is in the field of ethics in international relations. His publications include: *Towards a Normative Theory of International Relations* (Cambridge University Press, 1986), *Ethics in International Relations* (Cambridge University Press, 1996), *Constituting Human Rights: Global Civil Society and the Society of Democratic States* (Routledge, 2002), and *Global Ethics: Anarchy, Freedom and International Relations* (Routledge, 2008). He edited *International Ethics* (Sage, 2011), a four volume set of reprints on ethics and international relations. He has published in *Political Studies*, *The Review of International Studies*, *International Relations*, *Cambridge Review of International Affairs*, *Theoria* and *Millennium: Journal of International Studies*.

Richard Ned Lebow is Professor of International Political Theory, King's College London and James O. Freedman Presidential Professor Emeritus at Dartmouth College. His *A Cultural Theory of International Relations* (Cambridge 2008) won the Jervis-Schroeder Prize from the American Political Science Association for the best book in international relations and history and the Susan Strange Award of the British International Studies Association for the best book of the year. Subsequent publications include *Why Nations Fight* (Cambridge 2010), *Forbidden Fruit: Counterfactuals and International Relations* (Princeton 2010) and *The Politics and Ethics of Identity: In Search of Ourselves* (Cambridge 2012).

Catherine Lu is Associate Professor of Political Science at McGill University. She is the author of *Just and Unjust Interventions in World Politics: Public and Private* (Palgrave Macmillan, 2006; paperback with new Afterword, 2011). She has also published in *The Journal of Political Philosophy*, the *European Journal of Social Theory*, the *Journal of International Political Theory*, the *Journal of International Law and International Relations*, *International Studies Review*, *Review of International Studies* and *International Relations*. She has been a Faculty Fellow at the Edmond J. Safra Center for Ethics at Harvard (2004–5), and an Alexander von Humboldt Foundation Research Fellow at the Freie Universität Berlin (2010–11). Her research interests include international political theory; ethical challenges of humanitarianism, intervention and the use of force; justice and reconciliation after violence, oppression and atrocity; cosmopolitanism and its critics; and literature and philosophy. She is currently working on a book manuscript, *The Idea of Settling Accounts in World Politics*.

James Mayall was Sir Patrick Sheehy Professor of International Relations and Director of the Centre of International Studies at Cambridge University from 1998 until his retirement in 2004. He is now Emeritus Professor at the Centre and Academic Advisor to the Royal College of Defence Studies in London. He has written and published widely on North-South relations, international theory and the impact of nationalism on international relations. His more recent research has concentrated on the resurgence of ethnic, national and religious conflicts since the end of the Cold War. His publications include (with Krishnan Srinivasan) *Towards the New Horizon: World Order in the 21st Century* (Standard Publishers, New Delhi, 2009); (as editor) *The Contemporary Commonwealth, An Assessment, 1965–2009* (Routledge, 2009); *World Politics: Progress and its Limits* (Polity, 2000; second and expanded Japanese edition 2009); *The New Interventionism 1991–1994: United Nations Experience in Cambodia, former Yugoslavia and Somalia* (Cambridge, 1996); and *Nationalism and International Society* (Cambridge, 1990), which won the Political Studies Association's prize for the best monograph of the year. He was elected a Fellow of the British Academy in 2001.

Nicholas Rengger is Professor of Political Theory and International Relations at St Andrews University in Scotland. His scholarly interests range widely across political philosophy, intellectual history, international relations, philosophy and theology. He has just finished a study of the just war tradition and contemporary thought, titled *State of War: Teleocratic Politics, The Just War and the Uncivil Condition in World Politics*, and is currently completing a collection of his essays to be called *Dealing in Darkness: Essays in Political Theory and International Relations*.

Benjamin A. Schupmann is a Ph.D. candidate in Political Science at Columbia University, New York. His dissertation will look at the place of state theory in the writings of Carl Schmitt. In 2008 he completed his *dottorato di ricerca* in political philosophy at Luiss Guido Carli in Rome, Italy with a dissertation entitled *Morgenthau mal compris: The Philosophical Roots of Hans Morgenthau's Political Realism*. His research interests include state and constitutional theory, philosophy of science, political realism and rule-following in the philosophy of language.

Robbie Shilliam is Senior Lecturer in International Relations at Queen Mary, University of London. He has published on the history of political thought in International Relations in journals such as *Millennium*, *European Journal of International Relations* and *History of Political Thought* as well as on slavery and race in *Thesis Eleven, Review of International Studies* and *Comparative Studies in Society and History*. He is author of *German Thought and International Relations* (Palgrave Macmillan, 2009); editor of *International Relations and Non-Western Thought* (Routledge, 2010); and co-editor of *Silencing Human Rights* (Palgrave Macmillan, 2008).

Tracy B. Strong is Distinguished Professor of Political Science at the University of California, San Diego. His publications include *Friedrich Nietzsche and the Politics of Transfiguration* (California, 1975; 3rd edn Illinois, 2000), *The Idea of Political Theory: Reflections on the Self in Political Time and Place* (Notre Dame, 1990), *Jean-Jacques Rousseau and the Politics of the Ordinary* (Sage, 1994) and (with Marcel Hénaff) *Public Space and Democracy* (Minnesota, 2000). He is currently working on music, language and politics in the period that extends from Rousseau to Nietzsche and on American political thought. His *Politics without Vision: Thinking without a Banister in the Twentieth Century* will appear from the University of Chicago Press in early 2012.

Kamila Stullerova is Lecturer in Security Studies in the Department of International Politics at Aberystwyth University, Wales. Her research interests include realist and *modus vivendi* liberal approaches to political and International Relations (IR) theory and the crossroads between social and political theory with special focus on IR theory. She is currently finishing a monograph on Judith Shklar's liberalism of fear and developing a project in political theory of security.

1
Understanding Tragedy and Understanding International Relations

Toni Erskine and Richard Ned Lebow

Tragedy is one of the oldest conceptual lenses of Western culture. Indeed, it would not be an exaggeration to say that tragedy is constitutive of Western culture itself. Writing more than two millennia ago, Thucydides thought that tragedy was an appropriate lens through which to view international relations.[1] We interrogate this assumption. Does tragedy offer a plausible framework for examining international relations? If so, in what ways can the concept of tragedy revealed in ancient Greek, Shakespearean, and later dramas inform and enrich our understanding of international relations today? And, perhaps most importantly, if the lens of tragedy *does* illuminate aspects of international relations for us, can this knowledge enhance our chances of avoiding or reducing tragic outcomes in the future? The contributors to this volume by no means agree on the answers to these questions. We do, however, agree that these are crucial points of enquiry.

Importantly, we also share a common conceptual starting-point. When we invoke the idea of tragedy, we all refer to a particular genre and set of constitutive concepts – albeit sometimes sceptically or critically, and often with subtle differences of interpretation. In this chapter, we, the editors, comment on this understanding of tragedy and say something about its genesis – a move that takes us back to Athens in the fifth century BCE. We suggest that this understanding of tragedy remains relevant to us today, even though we are steeped in profoundly different circumstances than the audiences of Euripides or Aeschylus, Sophocles or Shakespeare. Tragedy, we contend, continues to offer prescient and important insights into international relations, a proposition that is thoroughly explored and debated in subsequent chapters.

Understanding tragedy

The most frequent associations between tragedy and international relations involve the everyday, English-language use of the word tragedy as connoting, quite simply, horrible things happening to generally innocent people. 'Tragedy' and 'tragic' are routinely used to describe circumstances of seemingly inexplicable suffering. It should perhaps not be surprising then to find that these terms are regularly invoked in commentaries on international relations to punctuate declarations of grief and disbelief in the face of cataclysmic events. Earthquakes and floods, wars and famines, epidemics and environmental disasters are all described as 'tragic' in this sense. Standard shorthand for the 1994 genocide in which approximately 800,000 people were murdered is the 'Rwanda tragedy'; the 2010 *Deepwater Horizon* oil spill in the Gulf of Mexico has been branded the 'BP tragedy'. We acknowledge this colloquial use of tragedy, but explore a different, more specific, historical understanding of the term; one that we argue has particular purchase for analysing international relations.

Our conception of tragedy has roots in ancient Athens where it was associated with a form of theatre that not only had a profound impact on the *polis* but also on the subsequent development of European philosophy and culture.[2] Attempting to reduce our understanding of tragedy to a single definition would be difficult and counterproductive. Stephen Booth observes that '[t]he search for a definition of tragedy has been the most persistent and widespread of all nonreligious quests for definition'.[3] This is not a quest we wish to join. Tragedy is a multi-faceted genre whose many faces tell us different and not always compatible things about life – and about international relations. While abstract and spare in its presentation, tragedy revels in complexity. We want to highlight this complexity rather than forcing tragedy into a conceptual straightjacket.

Our understanding of tragedy can be traced back to fifth-century Athenian plays that the Greeks called '*tragōidia*'. These plays flourished in a short-lived moment – the second half of the fifth century BCE in Athens – when drama, politics, and philosophy were intimately connected. The Athenian Dionysia, a large festival held every year in late March in honour of the god Dionysus, was its venue. Tragedies and other plays were performed in a large, open-air amphitheatre on the southern slope of the Acropolis before an audience of citizens and non-citizens, Athenians and foreigners, of all classes. The generals (*stratēgoi*) poured the libations to open the festival, and this was followed by a public display of allied tribute, an announcement of the names of the city's benefactors (including those who underwrote the cost of producing the plays), and a parade of state-educated boys, now men, in full military panoply provided by the city. The plays themselves were organized as a contest (*agōn*) in which playwrights competed with words in the same way that personal and political disputes were transformed into verbal contests in the law courts and assembly.

Despite these very specific origins, tragedy was not limited to ancient Greece. As a genre, tragedy survived and assumed a variety of forms and features in different historical and social contexts. Our understanding of tragedy has evolved and broadened to accommodate these latter examples. Playwrights and scholars alike have stretched and reinterpreted the parameters of the genre. Recognizing this evolution and diversity is critical to understanding not only tragedy but also the changing circumstances to which it has been adapted. It nevertheless makes sense to begin our overview with the account of tragedy provided by Aristotle, our most impressive secondary Greek source and near-contemporary of the great fifth-century playwrights. Aristotle established formal categories that have remained central to contemporary understandings of tragedy, even though, as John Drakakis and Naomi Conn Liebler observe, 'their discursive force has been transformed over time'.[4] These categories are adopted and discussed throughout the volume, whether or not individual contributors invoke Aristotle explicitly.

For Aristotle, tragedy is a type of 'imitation' (*mimesis*), which is distinct from other modes of imitation such as music, comedy, and epic poetry.[5] 'A tragedy, then', Aristotle famously extols in the *Poetics*, 'is the imitation of an action that is serious and also, as having magnitude, complete in itself ... with incidents arousing pity and fear, wherewith to accomplish its catharsis of such emotions'.[6] Central to the Aristotelian interpretation is the audience's emotional response to the suffering of the hero and the release (*katharsis*) this ultimately engenders. Aristotle maintains that only a particular type of plot is capable of eliciting these emotions.[7] The structure of the drama is accordingly also a fundamental attribute of tragedy.[8] To qualify as a tragedy, the plot must contain some great miscalculation or error of judgement (*hamartia*) on the part of the protagonist. In 'complex tragedies', this miscalculation sets in motion a chain of events that lead to a reversal of fortune (*peripeteia*) and recognition (*anagnorisis)* in the sense of a transformation from ignorance to knowledge as the protagonist realizes his error.[9] Aristotle describes the protagonist as being 'one like ourselves' (and thereby eliciting fear of our own vulnerability), but also as being of 'great reputation and prosperity' who is, in some respects, better than the average man (and thereby having farther to fall).[10] This tragic hero makes choices – and invariably arrives at the 'wrong' decisions in that they ultimately but ineluctably lead to disastrous outcomes. The agent is often presented to us as someone who has considerable free choice but is deeply affected by forces and structures beyond his control.[11] Alternatively, the *hamartia* arises from an inflexible and unyielding commitment to an otherwise laudable value like honour, family, or civil order. The pity and fear of the members of the audience is a response to what they understand, at least in part, to be 'undeserved misfortune' by the protagonist.[12] The fact that people of noble character can make profound and consequential mistakes drives home the realization that fortune is precarious for the mighty and powerless alike. We too can take wrong turns, antagonize the gods or our fellow human beings, and stumble into adversity.

Greek tragedies flourished for less than a century. Jean-Pierre Vernant suggests that tragedy could only exist when the distance between the heroic past and its religious values was great enough to allow new values based on the *polis* and its juridical structure to have emerged, but close enough for the conflict in values to have been painfully real.[13] For tragic man to appear, the concept of human action must have emerged but not yet acquired too autonomous a status. By the first decade of the fourth century BCE that moment had passed. Athenians had lost a war and an empire, and, perhaps, the inner strength and confidence necessary to confront, let alone relish, critical portrayals of *polis* life and the human condition.[14]

Most classicists encourage us to consider tragedy a culturally specific phenomenon. For classicists, tragedy must be situated in context, and is a vehicle for helping us understand fifth-century Athens and Greek life more generally. We respect this focus, but insist that just as texts take on meanings beyond those intended by their authors, so do genres. Moreover, by analysing these genres we can ask and perhaps answer questions that could not have been framed in fifth-century Greece.

Tragedy was revived during the Renaissance, and the tragedies of William Shakespeare arguably reached an artistic level equal to those of ancient Athens. There can be little doubt that Greek tragedy was a model for Shakespeare. *Romeo and Juliette* addresses the same theme as Aeschylus' trilogy, the *Oresteia*: how private feuds threaten the city. To suggest the link between the two dramatic representations, Shakespeare names the prince of Verona 'Escalus', a thinly veiled reference to Aeschylus. The prince's name is perhaps also a play on the word 'escalation', and may convey Shakespeare's greater pessimism, evident in the contrasting outcomes of the two tragedies.[15] Not only did classical Greek tragedy provide inspiration for Shakespeare, but the genre of tragedy has been strongly influenced by the Elizabethan playwright – an influence that is apparent in the attention paid to Shakespearean dramas in a number of the chapters that follow. Of course, as Chris Brown notes in his contribution, Shakespearean tragedies differ in significant ways from their classical predecessors.[16] In his acclaimed analysis of Shakespearean tragedy, A. C. Bradley observes that Shakespearean tragedies have, 'up to a certain point, a common form or structure' that distinguishes them from Greek tragedies.[17] Bradley characterizes Shakespearean tragedy as 'the story ... of human actions producing exceptional calamity', thereby rejecting the role of fate found in Greek tragedy and highlighting the challenging theme of moral responsibility that we will return to in our concluding chapter.[18] Another difference that is frequently noted is the interiority of Shakespearean characters in contrast to their Greek counterparts. The characters of Greek tragedy are distinguished by a particular combination of traits, skills, and commitments and are presented as universal archetypes, not as unique individuals.[19] Yet, these and other differences between Greek and Shakespearean tragedy should not detract our attention from their many common features that have led generations of critics to categorize them within a single genre. Indeed, Bradley repeatedly refers to the defining capacity of Shakespearean tragedy to evoke fear and pity, thereby aligning it with the Aristotelian understanding of Greek tragedy, even though the means by which Shakespearean tragedies evoke these emotions sets them apart.[20] Both variations on tragedy, according to our contributors, yield important insights for international relations.

Moreover – and importantly for a volume that looks at the relationship between tragedy and politics – the genre attracted the attention of a number of prominent eighteenth- and nineteenth-century European philosophers who have exerted a significant influence on contemporary political thought. David Hume, G.W.F. Hegel, Karl Marx, and Friedrich Nietzsche, among others, either use tragedy to establish theoretical frameworks or employ their own frameworks to reflect on the relationship between tragedy and political life. Hegel, for example, reflecting on Greek tragedy, but breaking from the focus on human suffering and purgation of the Aristotelian tradition, reads tragic plots as explorations of conflicting conceptions of duty, 'the collision of equally justified powers and individuals'.[21] Such conflicts are at their core identity conflicts, which, for Hegel, reflect a particularly modern dilemma. Nietzsche rejects

Hegel's valorization of the 'rational' in Greek tragedy and celebrates the 'Dionysian' irrational element of tragedy, which he compares to the spirit of music.[22] Nietzsche remains focused on suffering, but maintains, optimistically, that it can be transcended: 'despite every phenomenal change, life is at bottom indestructibly joyful and powerful'.[23]

If Shakespeare's borrowing from Greek tragedy can enrich his dramas and encourage us to find in them deeper levels of meaning, and if philosophers such as Hegel and Nietzsche can draw on the same source to enhance their own work, we lesser mortals can mine the rich trove of tragedy and reflections about it to help us interrogate contemporary realities. Of course, defending such a project requires that we anticipate the concerns of those who might question our move of transposing the genre of tragedy from the time and place in which it originally flourished, to our own, markedly different, circumstances.

Contemporary relevance

A critic might object to our attempt to view today's world through a lens borrowed from a radically different time and context and argue that any image produced by it would necessarily be blurred and distorted. In the second half of the fifth century BCE, Greek city states shared a common culture and relations among them were considered an extension of interpersonal and family relations. There was not even a word for foreign policy, and *xenia*, or guest friendship, was most often invoked to describe inter-polis relations. Greeks expected these relations to be governed by the same pattern of mutual obligation, generosity and self-restraint that applied to relations between households. Fifth-century Greeks never thought that *xenia* could be extended to non-Greeks, whose cultures and values were different from their own. Few contemporary countries remotely resemble city states, and even those few existing city states have much larger populations than Athens, which was the largest Greek polis. Face-to-face relations among citizens who come together collectively to make (or at least debate and ratify) policies are no longer possible. A critic of our comparative enterprise might also point out that even countries that comprise reasonably robust regional political systems differ significantly in their cultures, making modern day regional relations, let alone international relations, much closer to relations between Greeks and their non-Greek neighbours, than to inter-polis relations. Not only have we left the specific setting of the Greek tragedy, but, more importantly, we lack the kind of political and civic structure in which it thrived – and made sense.

To underline this point, our critic might note the decline and all but disappearance of tragedy at the end of the fifth century BCE. At a certain moment, tragedy was no longer regarded as an appropriate vehicle for Athenians to work through contemporary political and ethical issues and consolidate civic identity. No great Greek tragedies were written after the death of Euripides in about 406. If tragedy is so culturally specific that it was no longer an appropriate trope in fourth-century Athens, what possible relevance can it have today? In our twenty-first-century world of climate change and clones, 'medical miracles' and weapons of mass destruction, cyberspace, and international courts, what can works intended to negotiate and sustain civic culture in pre-industrial settings possibly teach us? Many of the ethical choices and dilemmas that face us now could not have been conceived of in ancient Greece, or in Elizabethan England for that matter. Arguably, the way we perceive life and death has changed irrevocably; our capacity to understand and manipulate our environment has been enhanced; our conceptions of obligation, human agency, nature, and religion would be foreign to the audiences who attended tragedies in Greek or Elizabethan times. We bear radically different moral burdens and are heirs to distinct cultural legacies and political problems. The questions posed by Greek and Shakespearean tragedies, our sceptic would challenge, are no longer *our* questions.

Finally, our critic might, with reason, doubt our ability to experience tragedies in the ways their authors intended. The performance and role of tragedies in fifth-century Athens and Elizabethan England were phenomena whose significance and meanings are elusive to us. Adrian Poole contends that '[t]he theatre itself does not occupy for us the kind of cultural centrality that it did for the Greeks or for Shakespeare' and '[w]hether one reads [tragedy] in Greek or English translation, what we have to play with are the shadows of what was once the substance of an occasion, a performance'.[24] With specific respect to Greek tragedy, Vernant emphasizes that this spectacle was not merely an art form, but a 'social institution that the city, by establishing competitions in trag- edies, set up alongside its political and legal institutions'.[25] Tragedy no longer fills this role, nor can it for us.

We acknowledge all of these differences, but then we do not intend to use tragedy as political theatre to negotiate change and build legitimacy. Tragedy served additional purposes in Athens and these ends may be more relevant to our world. As we shall see, tragedy was also used to understand and challenge foreign policy at the moment when competi- tion between hegemons became sufficiently acute that neither felt any longer restrained by considerations of *xenia* or the responsibilities of *hēgemonia*. In addition, Greek tragedies conveyed ethical insights; they were an important source of moral guidance. The ethical questions that we face differ from those of the past, yet broad tragic themes endure, such as human limitation and fallibility, painful deliberation in the face of conflicting ethical commitments, and the ambiguity of evolving norms and values. Tragedies were written at a time when values were in flux.[26] These works have achieved particular resonance during instances of upheaval. If, as Poole suggests, '[t]he very substance of these plays is the rejection of precedent, or the need to break new bounds, to move into uncharted territory', then tragedies have the potential to outlive the particular context in which they were first written and performed.[27] Tragedies offer people broader understandings of themselves and their place in the world rather than socializing them to specific beliefs or behaviours. They might be said to impart a tragic view of life and politics which, some of our contributors maintain, transcends time and culture because it describes fundamental verities of human existence. Indeed, one of our key assumptions in editing this volume is that the insights achieved through an appreciation of tragedy are as relevant today as they were in the very different circumstances that inspired the emergence of this genre.

Two insights for international relations

Of the many insights revealed by tragedy, two seem particularly relevant to contemporary international relations: its enduring capacity to warn us of the dangers of power and success and its problematization of all conceptions of justice. The first of these two insights has to do with hubris and its likely consequences. The more powerful and successful an actor becomes, the greater the temptation to overreach in the unreasonable expectation that it is possible to predict, influence, or control the actions of others and by doing so gain more honour, wealth, or power. Hubris for the Greeks is a category error; powerful people make the mistake of comparing themselves to the gods, who have the ability to foresee and control the future. This arrogance and overconfidence leads them to embrace complex and risky initiatives that frequently have outcomes diametrically opposed to those they seek. In Greek tragedy, hubris leads to self-seduction (*atē*), serious miscalculation (*hamartia*) and, finally, revenge of the gods (*nemesis*). In the case of Oedipus, the tragic hero of the three remaining plays that make up Sophocles' celebrated Theban storyline (*Oedipus Tyrannos, Oedipus at Colonus* and *Antigone*), *nemesis* produces an outcome the reverse of what the actor expected to achieve.[28] Oedipus brings his fate upon himself by a double act of hubris: he refuses to back off at the crossroads when confronted with a stranger's road rage, and he trusts 'blindly' in his ability to reason his way to a solution to the city's infertility, despite multiple warnings to the contrary. In *Antigone* (chronologically, the third of these Theban plays), Creon, who succeeds Oedipus as the ruler of Thebes, refuses to bury the traitor Polynices in order to assert his power as the undisputed ruler of the city, and, for the same reason, sentences Antigone to a live burial for attempting to give her brother the proper rites in violation of his edict.[29] After being warned by Tiresias, the same blind prophet who warned Oedipus, Creon tries in vain to save Antigone, but she has taken her own life, as do Creon's wife and son after learning of her death. Creon's actions were intended to save the city, but brought disorder and the downfall of his house. We all have a dangerous propensity for overestimating our capacities. By making us confront our limits and recognize that chaos lurks just beyond the fragile barriers we erect to keep it at bay, tragedy can help keep our conceptions of ourselves, and our societies, from becoming infused with hubris.

As far as we know, Herodotus was the first to reveal this important insight by applying the tragic plot line to history in his account of the Persian Wars. Xerxes' decision to invade Greece is portrayed as an act of hubris and the defeat of his fleet at Salamis in 480 BCE as his fitting nemesis. Thucydides tells a similar tale in his account of the Peloponnesian War, with Athens cast as Persia, the decision to ally with Corcyra and the Sicilian Expedition as a double *hamartia*, and the destruction of the Athenian fleet and army in Syracuse, defeat by Sparta and loss of empire as a fitting *nemesis*.[30] In modern times, hubris has been found a useful and revealing framework to explain Louis XIV's drive for hegemony, Germany's expectation of a limited war in the east in 1914, Hitler's invasion of the Soviet Union in 1941, and the behaviour of the US after the end of the Cold War. The 2003 Anglo-American invasion of Iraq arguably revealed all the hallmarks of hubris. The invasion of Iraq was expected to be a short-term, low-cost operation that would replace Saddam Hussein's regime with a pro-American one and make Iran, North Korea and the Palestinians more compliant.[31] It turned into a costly, open-ended commitment that undermined British and American prestige and may have emboldened Iran and North Korea to accelerate their nuclear programs. Analysts – including the editors of this volume and three of our contributors – are not shy about attributing this outcome to the hubris of the Bush administration, which led its senior officials to assume the presence of weapons of mass destruction, a quick victory with minimal forces, a joyous welcome by 'liberated'

Iraqis, and, given their power and popularity, no need to plan their occupation of the country beyond occupation of the oil ministry.[32] A tragic understanding has the potential to make us more cautious in formulating foreign policy goals in recognition of the self-defeating outcomes of excesses of power and confidence.

A second insight for contemporary international relations revealed through tragedy has to do with our understanding of justice. Tragedies often present the audience with contrasting and equally valid conceptions of justice, as in, again, *Antigone*, where Creon and Antigone are absolutely unyielding in their respective commitments to civil and religious authority. In Aeschylus' *Oresteia*, which tells the tragic tale of the house of Atreus, the audience confronts the moral dilemma caused by Orestes murdering his mother, Clytemnestra. The Furies, who pursue him, insist that it is wrong to murder a parent, while Orestes maintains that he was fulfilling his duty as a son by avenging his father's murder at the hands of his mother and her lover. The killing by Orestes is only the last of a series in his family and the trilogy. Each murder is conceived as necessary, even just, and each provokes more violence in return – violence carried out, as was the murder of Clytemnestra and her lover, in the name of justice. There is no clear villain and no discernible or 'just' solution, which is reflected in the deadlocked jury when Orestes is brought to trial. Such tragedies demonstrate that our conceptions of justice are parochial, not universal, and are readily undercut by too unwavering a commitment to them.

Many prominent students of IR who consider tragedy to be central to international relations emphasize this second insight, among them the classical realist thinkers Hans Morgenthau and Reinhold Niebuhr, and Herbert Butterfield, a theorist of what is widely known as the English School within IR.[33] They associate the potential for tragedy with ethical, religious, and cultural diversity. Any effort to impose one's own code on other actors in such a world will encounter resistance because it threatens the identities of these others and not merely their interests. Also drawing on tragedy's depiction of multiple and often competing conceptions of justice, Brian Orend advocates introducing the notion of what he calls 'moral tragedy' to the just war tradition, a prominent body of thought within normative IR theory.[34] When Orend proposes that just war theory would gain from hitherto neglected 'reflection on war's tragedy', he is urging us to appreciate situations in which one is confronted with competing demands of both justice and obligation, so that, sometimes, one has no choice but to commit a wrong. For Orend, '[a] moral tragedy occurs when, *all things considered*, each viable option you face involves a severe moral violation. It is a moral blind alley: there is no way to turn and still be morally justified'.[35] The same course of action can be seen as morally required and prohibited – and one is left with no solution to the dilemma regarding what is the right action. The specific dilemma upon which Orend focuses is one in which a particular community faces certain massacre or enslavement, and can only be saved if sacrosanct norms of restraint against its enemy – such as non-combatant immunity – are temporarily disregarded. This is the situation that Michael Walzer, taking a phrase from Churchill, described as a 'supreme emergency'; that is, an instance in which extreme and otherwise prohibited measures might legitimately be taken to ensure the survival of one's political community.[36] It thereafter became the subject of heated debate within the ethics of war. For Orend, the paramount point is the direct and irreconcilable conflict between the obligation to protect one's community and the obligation to respect principles of restraint in war. The most accurate way to describe the inescapable resulting violation of one of these obligations, he reasons, is in terms of 'moral tragedy'. Orend maintains that such a violation is unavoidable and can be excused, but can never be morally justified.

Orend's example of a seemingly intractable moral dilemma is important. Yet, in the spirit of ethical, religious, and cultural pluralism highlighted by Morgenthau, Niebuhr, and Butterfield, we might take an additional lesson for the ethics of war from tragedy's depiction of justice. An appreciation of tragedy not only has the potential to inform our thinking about the perceived dilemmas that arise in war when there appear to be multiple, conflicting obligations and, therefore, no obvious right course of action. It also provides a valuable check on the equally consequential wartime ethical considerations that we make when we are confident both that there *is* an obvious legitimate course of action – and, indeed, only *one* legitimate course of action – and that we know what this is. In the context of just war judgements, a tragic understanding might encourage us to question the robustness of our seemingly unassailable claims to just cause and reflect before acting, perhaps precipitously, on policies we believe can be justified in their name.[37] The lack of readily discernable external evaluative criteria to adjudicate between competing conceptions of what is morally permissible, or indeed required, means that our conviction in the justness of our cause needs to be tempered with knowledge of both our own limits and the difficulty of championing one set of principles over another.

Tragedy, as we suggest above, makes us aware and more respectful of competing conceptions of justice. This is not a concession to moral relativism, according to which any conception of justice would necessarily be rendered undecipherable when transmitted beyond its specific context. There is a crucial distinction to be made between denying that standards of good and evil and right and wrong exist, and acknowledging our own limits and fallibility in definitively discerning what these standards are. Tragedy teaches the latter without assuming the former – and warns that the blind pursuit of one conception of justice is self-defeating. The insight that we presume our conceptions of justice to be absolute at our peril has the potential to contribute to a more sophisticated treatment of international conflict. Specifically, this insight might foster an understanding of why certain conflicts appear intractable, the dynamics by which they escalate, and the importance of restraint. To the extent that relevant actors are able to learn lessons from tragedy and see it as an appropriate frame of reference, it might also foster an understanding of the means by which the frequency and intensity of conflicts can be reduced.

This account of two insights that we contend are particularly relevant to international relations is by no means exhaustive. Further examples are explored in the chapters that follow. Moreover, our contributors debate and adopt different stances on the points that we have just proposed. Our dual purpose has simply been, first, to illustrate how adopting the lens of tragedy has the potential, retrospectively, to enhance our understanding of international relations, and, second, to intimate that such a lens might also offer guidance, prospectively, on how to avoid repeating and perpetuating past mistakes. The lively conversation that follows builds on our preliminary examples and fleshes out these broader themes.

Structuring the conversation

The contributions to this conversation are grouped under three headings. In Part I, 'Recovering the Tragic Dimension of International Relations', Mervyn Frost, James Mayall, Richard Ned Lebow, and Nicholas Rengger discuss why, how, and – in Rengger's case – whether insights from tragedy can help us to understand international relations as a field of study and realm of politics. What would it mean to recover the tragic dimension of international relations? Frost initiates the discussion with a provocative set of proposals about what tragedy can tell us about ethics in international relations. Each subsequent contributor weighs in on the preceding arguments while forcefully setting out his own position. Frost and Mayall spar over the possibility of progress and reform at the international level. Rengger, in alliance with Michael Oakeshott – who debated the relevance of tragedy to politics over 60 years ago in correspondence with Morgenthau – insists that art and politics are distinct domains. Lebow concludes this section by offering a counter-argument to Oakeshott and Rengger. All four contributors introduce themes that become central points of discussion and debate throughout the volume.

In Part II, 'Tragedy and International Relations as Political Theory', Chris Brown, Peter Euben, Richard Beardsworth, and Kamila Stullerova demonstrate the utility of using political theory to interrogate international relations theory and practice – and, moreover, lend support to the claim that international relations can just as effectively be used to evaluate political theory. Brown begins by arguing that tragedy also has political purchase outside debates over classical realism, where, he observes, it receives the most attention both within IR circles and (either implicitly or explicitly) in the first section of this volume. He focuses instead on international political theory (IPT), and specifically on cosmopolitan theorists in the analytical tradition, who, he laments, have neglected the notion of tragedy to their detriment. Euben agrees with Brown that poetry and drama, ambiguity and unresolved dilemmas, 'better capture the rhythms of actions and so of politics' than closely-reasoned, unbreakable chains of analytical reasoning.[38] Yet, he cautions, the lessons of tragedy remain elusive. Tragedy is not something that one can hope to master. In the context of a final reading of Thucydides through the lens of tragedy, Euben extols the challenges and necessary ambiguity, but also the value and enduring relevance, of looking to tragedy to better understand politics. In his correspondence with Oakeshott, Morgenthau insisted that tragedy 'is a quality of existence, not a creation of art'.[39] Beardsworth offers a very different reading of tragedy. Ethics, he insists, is always immanent to politics and tragedy explores this recognition. Art and politics are distinct practices but tragedy is inherent in both. Stullerova advances a comparable argument; tragedy is distinct because of its focus on suffering and death that cannot be explained as just or, at times, even as meaningful. IR seeks to explain similar phenomena and does so by looking for patterns of behaviour. Tragedy is one of these patterns.

In Part III, 'On the Nature of Tragedy in International Relations', Benjamin Schupmann, Tracy Strong, Catherine Lu, and Robbie Shilliam reflect on and challenge the understandings of tragedy invoked to this point. Strong and Schupmann introduce a new perspective on tragedy by joining the conversation via their respective readings of Nietzsche. According to Schupmann, Nietzsche understands tragedy as an imitation of human affairs and a better vehicle than science for understanding social reality. Tragedy can serve as an antidote for hubris. Schupmann, in effect, makes a powerful claim for the relevance of tragedy to political action. Strong reminds us that tragedy was a political practice even before it was theatre. The Greek word *tragōidia* is a contraction of *tragos* (goat) and *aeidein* (to sing). Its initial reference was to a ritual conducted to benefit the city as a whole at which a goat was sacrificed while being sung to. In its dramatic form, tragedy stays faithful to its roots and is an expression of politics, and of life more generally. Lu and Shilliam both suggest that other contributors envisage tragedy too narrowly and in a way that unnecessarily circumscribes its potential to contribute to political analysis. For Lu, while moral incoherence and human vulnerability are central to all tragedies, it is important to acknowledge that the sources of such incoherence differ. For Shilliam, the symbolic association of Ancient Greece with European (and colonial) modernity prevents tragedy from including people standing elsewhere from European civilization as both subjects and objects of the drama. Lu calls for a recognition of 'tragic visions' rather than a single 'tragic vision'; Shilliam implores the reader to engage in geo-cultural travel and view the tragic drama from 'elsewhere'. Together they highlight the diversity and potential dynamism of this genre – both of which we submit make tragedy a particularly valuable and challenging lens through which to interrogate international relations.

In this volume we draw on a particular yet multifaceted and dynamic conception of tragedy and ask how such a conception might help us to better understand international relations. Perhaps even more provocatively, we also question whether it is possible to learn from tragedy in ways that would allow us, practically, to avoid future tragedies, and, conceptually, to rethink prominent assumptions within IR. We focus on these latter points of enquiry in the final chapter of this volume in light of the varied and sophisticated arguments of our contributors. Both how tragedy can help us to understand international relations and whether we can learn from tragedy in a way that positively informs future policies and intellectual pursuits pose important problems. This collection is the result of our joint conviction that attention to them can make us better scholars and practitioners of international relations.

Notes

1. Thucydides, *The Landmark Thucydides: A Comprehensive Guide to the Peloponnesian War* (revised edition of the Richard Crawley translation), ed. by Robert B. Strassler (New York: Free Press (1996)).

2. For useful introductions to this genre, see the following: 'Tragedy', in M. Banham (ed.) (1995) *Cambridge Guide to Theatre* (Cambridge: Cambridge University Press), pp. 1118–20; S. L. Feagin (1998) 'Tragedy', in E. Craig (ed.) *Routledge Encyclopedia of Philosophy* (London: Routledge), vol. 9, pp. 447–52; M. Weitz (1967) 'Tragedy', in P. Edwards (ed.) *The Encyclopedia of Philosophy* (London: Collier-Macmillan), pp. 155–61; J. Drakakis and N. Conn Liebler (1998) 'Introduction', in J. Drakakis and N. Conn Liebler (eds) *Tragedy* (London: Longman), pp. 1–20; and J. Wallace (2007) *The Cambridge Introduction to Tragedy* (Cambridge: Cambridge University Press). For an introduction to this genre and its constitutive concepts in the specific context of international relations, see R. N. Lebow (2003) *The Tragic Vision of Politics: Ethics, Interests and Orders* (Cambridge: Cambridge University Press).
3. S. Booth (1983) *King Lear, Macbeth, Indefinition and Tragedy* (New Haven: Yale University Press), p. 81.
4. Drakakis and Liebler (1998) 'Introduction', p. 3. For a more critical account of the esteem given to these Aristotelian categories in analyses of tragedy, see Booth (1983) *King Lear, Macbeth, Indefinition and Tragedy*, p. 82: 'we still use Aristotle's dicta on tragedy *in the way* we use a source of truth that, like the revealed truth of the Bible, is not available to human beings first hand.'
5. Aristotle, *Poetics*, in J. Barnes (ed.) (1984) *Complete Works of Aristotle, Volume 2: The Revised Oxford Translation* (Princeton: Princeton University Press), 1447a 15–18. (With Aristotle we follow the standard numbering procedure, which refers back to Immanuel Bekker's 1931 edition of the Greek text and consists of a page number, column and line. Thus, *Poetics* 1447a 15–18 refers to lines 15 to 18 of the first column of page 1447 of Bekker's edition.)
6. Aristotle, *Poetics*, 1449b 23–7.
7. Aristotle, *Poetics*, 1452a 2–10; See also the discussion in Feagin (1998) 'Tragedy', p. 448.
8. Wallace highlights both the 'functional' and 'formal' aspects of Aristotle's definition of tragedy along these lines in Wallace (2007) *The Cambridge Introduction to Tragedy*, p. 118.
9. Aristotle, *Poetics*, 1452a 10–1452b 10. Aristotle defines both 'simple tragedies' and those that distinguish themselves as superior, 'complex' examples.
10. Aristotle, *Poetics*, 1453a 1–20.
11. We have put scare quotes around 'wrong' simply as a reminder of the complex understanding of outcomes as the result of both actions (and misjudgements) of agents and forces and circumstances beyond the control of these agents. It would be misleading to present this conception of tragedy as involving the protagonist choosing a course of action that is clearly wrong over one that is unambiguously right. As Drakakis and Conn Liebler note, the drama would then be devoid of the Aristotelian understanding of dilemma and, instead, take on 'the shape of simple melodrama, pitting forces clearly identifiable as 'good' and 'evil' respectively against each other, and not tragedy'. Rather, '*hamartia*, "missing the mark", is understood not as an optional or avoidable "error" resulting from some inadequacy or "flaw" in the "character" of the protagonist but as something that *happens* in consequence of the complex situation represented in the drama'. See Drakakis and Liebler (1998) 'Introduction', p. 9. Mervyn Frost makes a similar point in Chapter 2 of this volume, pp. 21–43.

12. Aristotle, *Poetics*, 1453a 1–5.
13. J. -P. Vernant (1990) 'Tensions and Ambiguities in Greek Tragedy', in J.-P. Vernant and P. Vidal-Naquet (eds) *Myth and Tragedy in Ancient Greece* (New York: Zone Books), pp. 29–48.
14. J. -P. Vernant (1972) 'Greek Tragedy: Problems of Interpretation', in R. Macksey and E. Donato (eds) *The Structuralist Controversy: The Languages of Criticism and the Sciences of Man* (Baltimore: Johns Hopkins University Press), pp. 273–88, and Vernant (1990) 'Tensions and Ambiguities in Greek Tragedy'; C. Segal (2001) *Oedipus Tyrannus: Tragic Heroism and the Limits of Knowledge*, 2nd edn (New York: Oxford University Press), pp. 15–18, 20–2; S. Goldhill (1986) *Reading Greek Tragedy* (Cambridge: Cambridge University Press), and Goldhill (1990) 'The Great Dionysia and Civic Ideology', in J. J. Winkler and F. I. Zeitlin (eds) *Nothing to Do with Dionysos?: Athenian Drama in Its Social Context* (Princeton: Princeton University Press), pp. 97–129; J. J. Winkler (1990) 'The Ephebes' Song: *Tragōidia and Polis*', in Winkler and Zeitlin (eds) *Nothing to Do with Dionysos?*, pp. 20–62; F. I. Zeitlin (1986) 'Thebes: Theater of Self and Society in Athenian Drama', in J. P. Euben (ed.) *Greek Tragedy and Political Theory* (Berkeley and Los Angeles: University of California Press), pp. 101–41; J. P. Euben (1990) *The Tragedy of Political Theory: The Road Not Taken* (Princeton: Princeton University Press), pp. 50–9.
15. Athena's intervention saves Orestes in Aeschylus' trilogy, putting an end to the feud that has all but destroyed the house of Atreus and making the city and its courts the proper venue for dispute resolution. By contrast, Escalus' intervention, which takes the form of imposing the death penalty on dueling, compels Romeo to flee Verona and sets in motion the chain of events that culminates in his and Juliette's suicides.
16. C. Brown, 'Tragedy, "Tragic Choices" and Contemporary International Political Theory', Chapter 6, this volume, 75–85 (p. 75).
17. A. C. Bradley ([1904] 2007) *Shakespearean Tragedy*, 4th edn (London: Palgrave Macmillan), p. xlviii.
18. For this definition of tragedy, see Bradley ([1904] 2007) *Shakespearean Tragedy*, p. 9; for Bradley's analysis of the role of fate in Shakespearean tragedy, see Bradley, pp. 16–20. It should be noted, however, that the degree to which Greek tragedy relies on fate, and the degree to which it allows for the influence of agency, are open to debate. We return to these questions in Chapter 14 and note that although outcomes in Greek tragedies may seem preordained, the audience retains the impression that these outcomes also rely on the decisions and actions of individual agents.
19. Lebow makes this point in *In Search of Ourselves: The Politics and Ethics of Identity* (forthcoming).
20. It is interesting to note that Aristotle's categories frequently seem very well-suited to Shakespearean as well as Greek tragedy. Not only does A. C. Bradley (implicitly) draw on Aristotelian concepts in his *Shakespearean Tragedy*, but Walter Kaufmann notes in *Tragedy & Philosophy* (New York: Anchor (1969)), p. 317, that 'it is one of the great ironies of history that some of Aristotle's ideas about tragedy seem to apply rather better to Shakespeare than to Aeschylus or Sophocles'.
21. Hegel, *Hegel's Aesthetics: Lectures on Fine Art*, trans. by T. M. Knox (Oxford: Clarendon Press (1975)), vol. II, p. 1213.

22. Wallace (2007) *The Cambridge Introduction to Tragedy*, p. 124.
23. F. Nietzsche, *The Birth of Tragedy*, trans. by Douglas Smith (Oxford: Oxford University Press (2000)), p. vii. Benjamin Schupmann and Tracy Strong offer valuable analyses of Nietzsche's account of tragedy in Chapters 10 (pp. 129–143) and 11 (pp. 144–157) of this volume, respectively.
24. A. Poole (1987) *Tragedy: Shakespeare and the Greek Example* (New York: Basil Blackwell), pp. 5, 7.
25. Vernant (1990) 'Tensions and Ambiguities in Greek Tragedy', pp. 29–49 (pp. 32–3).
26. We have been particularly influenced on this point by Vernant. See his (1990) 'The Historical Moment of Tragedy in Greece: Some of the Social and Psychological Conditions', in Vernant and Vidal-Naquent (eds) *Myth and Tragedy in Ancient Greece*, pp. 23–8, and 'Tensions and Ambiguities in Greek Tragedy'. In 'Tensions and Ambiguities', p. 33, Vernant observes that 'although tragedy, more than any other genre of literature … appears rooted in social reality, that does not mean that it is a reflection of it. It does not reflect that reality but calls it into question'. For a similar argument that 'tragedy's point … was the breaking of conventional boundaries,' see J. P. Euben, Chapter 7, this volume, pp. 86–96 (p. 92).
27. Poole (1987) *Tragedy: Shakespeare and the Greek Example*, p. 12.
28. We have avoided the label 'trilogy' here simply because the plays were not written as such, but, rather, are what remain of three different sets of plays, written by Sophocles for three separate competitions.
29. Sophocles did not compose these plays in chronological order. Rather, they were written in the order of *Antigone*, *Oedipus Tyrannos* and *Oedipus at Colonus*.
30. F. M. Cornford (1907) *Thucydides Mythistoricus* (London: Arnold), pp. 176–82; G. Crane, *Thucydides and the Ancient Simplicity*, pp. 241–6; T. Rood (1999) 'Thucydides' Persian Wars', in C. Shuttleworth Kraus (ed.) *The Limits of Historiography: Genre Narrative in Ancient Historical Texts* (Leiden: Brill), pp. 141–68; Lebow (2003) *The Tragic Vision of Politics*, pp. 126–41.
31. R. N. Lebow (2008) *A Cultural Theory of International Relations* (Cambridge: Cambridge University Press), Ch. 9 for an analysis of the Bush administration's motives.
32. B. Woodward (2004) *Plan of Attack* (New York: Simon & Schuster); M. R. Gordon and B. E. Trainor (2006) *Cobra II: The Inside Story of the Invasion and Occupation of Iraq* (New York: Pantheon); M. Isakoff and D. Corn (2006) *Hubris: The Inside Story of Spin, Scandal and the Selling of the Iraq War* (New York: Crown); T. E. Ricks (2006) *Fiasco: The American Military Adventure in Iraq* (New York: Penguin). Also, see the contributions to this volume by James Mayall, Richard Beardsworth, and Tracy Strong, in Chapters 3 (pp. 44–52), 8 (pp. 97–111) and 11 (pp. 144–157) respectively.
33. See, for example, H. Morgenthau (1958) *Dilemmas of Politics* (Chicago: Chicago University Press), R. Niebuhr (1938) *Beyond Tragedy: Essays on the Christian Interpretation of History* (London: Nisbet and Company), and H. Butterfield (1931) *The Whig Interpretation of History* (London: Bell). As cited by Mervyn Frost in Chapter 1 of this volume, pp. 1–18; H. F. Gutbrod provides an analysis of each theorist's account of tragedy in (2001) *Irony, Conflict, Dilemma: Three Tragic Situations in International Relations* (University of London: unpublished dissertation). For a concise account of IR's classical

realism, with particular attention to its relationship with the notion of trag-
edy; See R. N. Lebow (2010) 'Classical Realism', in T. Dunne, M. Kurki, and
S. Smith (eds) *International Relations Theories: Discipline and Diversity*, 2nd edn
(Oxford: Oxford University Press), pp. 58–76.

34. See B. Orend (2006) *The Morality of War* (Peterborough, ON: Broadview
Press), pp. 154–7. 'Normative IR theory', 'international political theory', and
'international ethics' are broadly interchangeable labels for a field of study
within IR that variously draws on moral philosophy and political theory to
explore moral expectations, decisions and dilemmas in world politics. For
an introduction to this field, see T. Erskine (2010) 'Normative IR Theory', in
Dunne, Kurki, and Smith (eds) *International Relations Theories: Discipline and
Diversity*, 2nd edn, pp. 37–57.

35. Orend (2006) *The Morality of War*, p. 155 (Emphasis in the original). Note
that this type of tragic moral dilemma is addressed in Chapters 2, 6 and 12 of
this volume by Mervyn Frost, Chris Brown and Catherine Lu respectively.

36. M. Walzer ([1977] 2006) *Just and Unjust Wars: A Moral Argument with Historical
Illustrations*, 4th edn (New York: Basic Books), pp. 251–68. Note that Walzer
does not present this as a 'moral tragedy'; this is Orend's unique contribution. Walzer, Orend would maintain, overlooks the tragic dimension of this
situation. Nevertheless, as we note below, Walzer's rationale for the division between *jus in bello* and *jus ad bellum* considerations – for which his
"supreme emergency" argument is a controversial exception – is an excellent
illustration of one of the insights that we have taken from tragedy.

37. The same insight into the dangerous repercussions of assuming that one has
exclusive access to interpreting *the* just course of action in cases of conflict
underlines the call of Walzer and other just war theorists to separate *just ad
bellum* from *jus in bello* considerations, thereby preventing subjective understandings of the justness of going to war from lending legitimacy to evading
principles of just conduct; See Walzer ([1977] 2006) *Just and Unjust Wars*.
See also F. de Vitoria, 'On the Law of War', in *Political Writings* (Cambridge:
Cambridge University Press (1991)), pp. 306–7 [2.1], for his argument that
one of the reasons for waging a just war with restraint is that one can never
be sure of the ultimate justice of one's cause. Indeed, the difficulty of discerning the justice of any war should make us both humble in our claims
to justice and moderate in our use of force. We are very grateful to Cian
O'Driscoll for drawing our attention to this passage.

38. J. P. Euben, 'The Tragedy of Tragedy', Chapter 7, this volume, pp. 86–96.

39. H. J. Morgenthau, letter to Michael Oakeshott, 22 May 1949, Morgenthau
Papers, Library of Congress.

Part I
Recovering the Tragic Dimension of International Relations

2
Tragedy, Ethics and International Relations

Mervyn Frost

Is the notion of tragedy one that students of international ethics ought to take seriously? I pose the question against the following background: Some time ago James Mayall, now Emeritus Professor of International Relations (IR) at Cambridge University, challenged my general approach to international ethics as being too progressive, optimistic and teleological. He claimed that constitutive theory, a position within normative IR theory on which I have been working for some years now, failed to take account of the tragic dimensions of international relations and that this was a weakness of the theory. I took him to be making a point about normative IR theory more generally. In this chapter I wish to evaluate these charges. What I wish to explore in this chapter is not merely the narrow charge against constitutive theory, but the wider question about the pertinence of tragedy for those concerned with ethics in international relations.

In this chapter then, I wish to consider whether the failure to deal explicitly with tragedy is a weakness of present day approaches to international ethics in general. The same question may be raised in a number of different ways: Ought those who confront ethical issues in international relations, whether as practitioners or theorists, to take account of tragedy? Is there a case to be made that books on ethics in international relations should include, as a central component, a section on tragedy? Should key decision-makers in international relations (presidents, foreign secretaries, diplomats, citizens) be given an education that includes in it the study of tragedy?

Friedrich Gutbrod completed a doctoral dissertation in 2001 titled *Irony, Conflict, Dilemma: Three Tragic Situations in International Relations* in which he made out a case for the importance of tragedy for the discipline of IR.[1] He pointed out that several of the great scholars in IR explicitly maintain the importance of an appreciation of tragedy for

21

those seeking to understand and act in the field of world politics. Those whom Gutbrod discusses are Herbert Butterfield, Reinhold Niebuhr and Hans Morgenthau.[2] I believe that many in the so-called English School (like Mayall) would support this position, as would most realists.

The potential for tragedy in international relations, according to these authors, arises from the fact that we live in a plural world in which different states (and the nations and peoples they contain) are guided in what they do, internally and externally, by a wide range of different ethical, religious and cultural codes. In this plural world there is no overarching set of values to which all subscribe. There is also no clear goal towards which these diverse states, nations and peoples are moving. Where any particular state sets out to implement its preferred set of values in the world, it is likely to come up against resistance. It will encounter a world in which its own power confronts that wielded by other actors. The reality of power politics might in turn bring about consequences far removed from those originally sought; it might bring about tragic consequences. E. H. Carr warned of the dangers of attempting to impose our own ideas of how the world ought to be on the world as it really is. On his view we require some 'utopian' ideas about how the world ought to be, but these need to be tempered by a close study of power relations as they exist. Underlying these and determining them is a human nature that is unchanging, one which is, among other things, fuelled by egoism and the passions. It is not wholly governed by reason. Given this, we need to take note of the essential tension between realism and idealism.[3] A failure to do this may have tragic consequences.

Hans Morgenthau, for whom 'all foreign policy is a struggle for the minds of men',[4] put it as follows:

> Political realism refuses to identify the moral aspirations of a particular nation with the moral laws that govern the universe ... The light-hearted equation between a particular nationalism and the counsels of Providence is morally indefensible, for it is that very sin of pride against which the Greek tragedians and the Biblical prophets have warned rulers and ruled. That equation is also politically pernicious, for it is liable to engender the distortion in judgement which, in the blindness of crusading frenzy, destroys nations and civilizations – in the name of moral principle, ideals or God himself.[5]

For realists such as Morgenthau, tragedy is what follows from a 'blindness to the realities of international affairs'.[6] He claims that there is a 'tragic presence of evil in all political action'.[7] For Reinhold Niebuhr, human action in both the public and private spheres is often both tragic and worthy of pity. Any analysis which did not take note of this he would consider flawed.[8]

Before I turn to consider the worth of the notion of tragedy, let me make some general points about ethics in IR. In recent years there has been a resurgence of interest in the academic study of ethics in international relations. Where once the discipline eschewed ethics and focused on the study of power in world politics, since the end of the Cold War there has been a remarkable growth in what has come to be known as normative IR theory. A host of books have been written, new journals have emerged, and most departments that teach IR have at least one or two modules that deal with ethical issues.[9] Typical topics which are covered in the literature and in the specialized modules are: justice in international relations, human rights in a world of states, intervention, the right to self determination, secession, justice in war, governance, democratization of international institutions and many others. A quick glance through some of the module outlines, journal articles and monographs will reveal that 'tragedy' has not been a focus of attention in any of this work. Ought it to have been?

Typically scholars and practical politicians concerned with ethical issues in international relations have sought answers to the general question: What from an ethical point of view would we be justified in doing under the circumstances? The kinds of circumstances in which this question comes to the fore might include those where a decision has to be made whether it would be ethical to go to war or not, whether it would be ethical to intervene in the domestic affairs of a sovereign state, whether power should be deployed to promote human rights in cultures and places where they have not traditionally been respected. A full list of ethical questions that face actors in international relations today would be much longer. This is but a small sample from a long list. Is there reason to suppose that those seeking answers to these questions should devote time and energy to the study of tragedy?

Many people have devoted considerable effort to the study of tragedy. Their work is part of a tradition that spans two-and-a-half-thousand years. Those in this tradition have not primarily been concerned with 'tragedy' understood in its colloquial sense in which it is used as a synonym for 'disaster'. The writers in this tradition focus on tragedy as a specialized notion, which is both complex and contentious. The focus of the tradition has been on a set of plays. This is the art form which has been used to exemplify tragedy and which has provided the material for much of the philosophical discussion surrounding it.

Prima facie tragedy as it has come down to us in the plays of the Greek playwrights such as Aeschylus, Sophocles and Euripides, and subsequently and most famously in the plays of Shakespeare, seems to be directly pertinent to ethics and pertinent to those seeking answers to the questions mentioned. This would seem to be the case because the very stuff of tragedy is ethics. In the great tragedies the audience is always presented with a set of ethical problems of a certain kind. At the core of every tragedy is an ethical struggle. There are many forms that the ethical drama in tragedy takes, but there can be no doubting that the tragedies turn on ethical matters. In the great tragedies the audience is presented with protagonists such as Oedipus, Antigone, Agamemnon and Hamlet, who are shown to be enmeshed (whether they know it or not) in ethical webs that are particularly excruciating for the characters and, of course, for the audience insofar as it empathizes with what is being presented. The same applies to the romantic tragedy *Romeo and Juliet*.

At a very abstract level one may say that in these plays 'tragedy' identifies a dramatic rendering of a story in which the audience is confronted with protagonists, portrayed as worthwhile and praiseworthy people, who, when confronted with a particular problem, act in accordance with what for them are core ethical principles. Yet by so doing, they bring about consequences that cause great suffering both to themselves and others and which undermine key ethical principles which they themselves hold dear. What makes the action in the plays 'tragic' is that the protagonist is shown in situations where doing the ethically right thing brings about harm and suffering to himself (or herself) and those affected by the deed. In tragic stories what was done was not a mistake. The audience is invited to appreciate how actors with moral stature cannot but do what is ethically required of them; to do otherwise would be perfidious indeed. But in doing what is required of them they bring about painful consequences. In some cases the protagonist only comes to see with hindsight how his/her own action, which he/she had thought ethical, was the cause of great suffering. Here the protagonist does not see the tragic consequences at the moment of action, but the audience sees them (or anticipates them). In others, the tragic dimension may be seen at the moment of decision and action.

The background against which tragedies emerge is one in which we the audience can see the protagonists embedded in a world of conflicting and contradictory ethical practices. This is a world in which actors are simultaneously participants in different practices that are contradictory from an ethical point of view. Choosing to follow the ethic of one practice brings the actor into conflict with the ethic of another practice to which he/she is also committed. Doing the right thing in the one involves doing wrong in the other.

If the very stuff of tragedy is ethics, it seems puzzling, to say the least, that normative IR theorists have not paid more attention to it. This puzzling *lacuna* is not only to be found in the field of ethics in IR, but is also found in the wider field of Political Studies (within which IR is a constituent subfield). Undergraduates in the English-speaking world who have read Politics at university are not required to cover the topic of tragedy. Typically they will be required to have studied some of the works of Plato, Aristotle, Machiavelli, Hobbes, Kant, Hegel, Locke, Bentham, Mill and Rawls. The key concepts which students are required to analyse include, among others, justice, equality, liberty, democracy and human rights, but tragedy does not feature on their curriculum. Why not? Is this a shortcoming in Political Studies as it is presently taught?

In what follows I shall be considering whether the absence of an interest in tragedy has indeed been a flaw in Political Studies and IR.

Tragedy: What is it?

As indicated above, the idea of tragedy has been the subject of a long and distinguished scholarly tradition. I am not intending to make a substantive contribution to this literature (and I am also not qualified to do so). What I aim to do is to set out in a crude form some of the main features of tragedy as they have emerged from the tradition. Having done this I shall then attempt to determine how, if at all, knowledge of this specialized tradition could make a contribution to those seeking answers to the pressing ethical questions in contemporary international relations.

What are the identifying features of tragedy? I take this question to be applicable to tragic plays, novels, films and, of course, to tragedy as it occurs and is told of in everyday life whether it be at the micro level of the family or the macro level of world politics. Of course not all the things we refer to as 'tragic' exhibit exactly the same features. Not all the events we would label 'tragic' exhibit all the characteristics that I mention below. The term is flexible and evolving. Cataloguing the details is, and always will be, an ongoing task as new forms of tragedy appear. Nevertheless, there is a core set of meanings to our use of this term. There are family resemblances between the different uses and definitions of the term. Many of the core meanings derive from the ancient Greek tradition of tragic drama.

In order to bring the features of tragedy into focus let me set out a tragedy in the realm of international relations that never occurred but which might well have. The characters are real, but the particular tragic event I recount is hypothetical. In the time of *apartheid,* Breyten Breytenbach was one of South Africa's internationally acclaimed authors. He was a radical critic of the regime and as such became a member of a secret opposition movement that aimed to destabilize the government. His account of his efforts in this direction is presented in his book *The True Confessions of an Albino Terrorist.*[10] His brother Jan Breytenbach was a General in the South African Defence Force (SANDF) operating in Angola. He was a charismatic leader seen by right wing whites as a hero of the struggle against communism. It might well have happened that the General's forces came face to face with a group of insurgents lead by his brother, the 'Albino Terrorist'. One or both brothers might have faced the choice to advance 'the cause' and risk killing his brother or to protect his brother and undermine 'the cause'.[11] For the sake of this illustration let us suppose that Jan, the General, ordered his helicopter gunships to locate and destroy a 'terrorist' column in transit through the bush of Angola without knowing at the time that his brother was in it. In this action his brother is killed. Or we can imagine the other brother, Breyten, setting off a landmine to destroy a column of soldiers without knowing that his brother was leading it. What marks out both these accounts of an act and its consequences as tragic? It seems to me that the following cluster of features is crucial. In looking at this what must be kept in mind at every point is that we are discussing representations (plays as written or performed, stories as told or written) and what ethical configurations these present to us, the audience, of such representations.

I have presented to you, the audience, an account (a tale, a story, a description of a set of events) which shows the protagonists (Jan and Breyten) each acting for the strongest of ethical reasons, but bringing about consequences which are painful to them (and us) when judged by a rival ethic which itself has a claim on the protagonists in question. In this story as I have set it up, we take it that both brothers are bound by the ethic of family life. But each is also linked to a military organization (the SANDF in Jan's case and The Liberation Movement in Breyten's). The story indicates that in the circumstances portrayed, each brother would have had to choose to act in accordance with *either* the ethic embedded in that social practice we know as the family *or* in accordance with the ethic embedded in their respective military institutions. No compromise was possible. What the military institutions demanded of each was diametrically opposed to what the family demanded of them. For Breyten the choice was between what was required of him as fighter for a liberation movement and what was required as a brother. For Jan it was the competition between what was required of him as a soldier in a standing army and as a brother.

What makes the story tragic is the conjunction of the ethical choice made with the consequences of that choice. The particular link that 'tragic' accounts make between act and consequence is to show, with the benefit of hindsight, that the protagonists were in a 'lose/lose' predicament. If General Jan Breytenbach had decided to uphold the ethic of family life by not attacking the enemy he would have dishonoured himself as a soldier and citizen of the *Apartheid State*. He would have lost something that was valuable to him. Given that he was constituted as a soldier in the SA Defence Force this loss would have been an ethically painful thing for him to suffer. But in the event, as we have imagined it, he chose to uphold the military ethic. This too was a losing manoeuvre, for by doing this he undercut the ethic associated with the other institution he valued, the family. A similar set of permutations can be constructed for Breyten, the freedom fighter. In this imaginary example we see both actors situated in circumstances in which each would have had to decide what to do, and whichever choice he made it would have consequences that would have been painful in terms of the ethic not chosen.

As indicated in the previous point, 'tragedy' is a term used to refer to a special relationship between an act undertaken for ethical reasons and its negative/painful consequences. A tragic account is thus a consequence-driven one. It invites an ethical evaluation of a series of events consisting of an act and its consequences. This kind of thinking is to be distinguished from forms of consequentialist thought, such as standard utilitarianism, however. Unlike utilitarian thought, the negative consequences we encounter in tragedies are not read as showing the original act to have been a mistake. For writers in the tragic tradition, the original act, even though it might have resulted in negative consequences, is still judged to have been an ethical thing to have done given the circumstances. For a utilitarian, in contrast, a set of negative consequences would show that the original action was based on a miscalculation. The original act would be judged to have been a mistake, in that it was not utility maximizing, and thus not ethical.

At the heart of all tragedy is an ethical *agon* (the metaphor refers to a duel or competition). In our example the *agon* is between the ethic associated with the social practice we refer to as the family, on the one hand, and the ethic associated with the practices of military life, on the other. Another example might have as the *agon* the tension between family life and the ethical requirements of a polity such as a state. A famous example of this dilemma is to be found in Sophocles' play *Antigone*. Antigone's brother turned against his own state, Thebes. He was killed beyond the walls of the city. His sister Antigone says that the ethics of family life demand that she bury him. The ruler of Thebes, Creon, who is also Antigone's uncle, insists that the ethics of the polity demand that, as a traitor, Antigone's brother be left unburied outside the walls of the city. In the play the audience is exposed to the arguments of Antigone giving primacy to the ethics of the family, and to those of Creon spelling out the duties citizens owe to the state. The protagonists and the audience agonize about the conflicting require-ments of each of these social practices. As always, a key feature of the *agon* is that no compromise is possible. In this case either one obeys the ethic of the family or that of the polity. There is no middle way. No harmonization of the ethics is thought possible. There is simply a tragic conflict between the two.

The *agon* reveals the element of *conflict* that is central to tragedy. The conflict with which tragedy concerns itself is that between two ethical forms both of which have a valid claim on the actor or actors involved.

In tragedy the conflict in the *agon* is not between a protagonist who is taken to be good and an antagonist who is understood to be the ethi-cally unacceptable 'other'. These are not fights between good and evil, between the foreigner and us, or between friends and enemies. What gives tragedy its edge is the way in which the ethical positions in con-flict are positions understood and endorsed by both the parties involved and by the audience. Tragedy, one might say, involves a conflict within our own ethical space. 'To agonize' is to be engaged with an internal ethical conflict.[12]

In some tragedies, at some point it dawns on the actor, the audience, or both, *post hoc*, that the deed which was done brought about *unan-ticipated consequences* which reveal the *agon* involved in the sequence.[13] In such cases the unanticipated consequences that resulted from the course of action taken are a source of great and ongoing sorrow to the actor(s) in question. Aristotle referred to this moment of recognition as *anagnorisis*.[14]

In those series of events that are construed as tragic there is often an element of *irony*. What the actors intend does not come about and quite often their acts cause an outcome antithetical to their own judgement about what would constitute a good ethical result. If it could be shown that General Breytenbach's military campaign in Angola hastened the end of *apartheid* instead of protecting it (which had been the original ethical justification for it), this would be a tragic irony. This indeed was the tragic irony for those many staunch Afrikaner nationalists who gave their lives for the ethic of 'separate development'. The *preipeteia* of tragedy shows how people, through actions performed with the best of intentions, destroy that which they would have protected.

At the heart of the tragic tradition is the belief that our ethical commitments cannot always be brought into harmony with one another in some overarching ethical architecture at the point of action, and that they do not result in the emergence of an ethically harmonious whole over time. Often we, just like the Breytenbach brothers in the example, find ourselves, embedded in ethical arrangements that are contradictory, conflictual and ambiguous. In the tradition of tragedy this is taken to be part of the human condition.

At a fundamental level those who write on tragedy (whether they be playwrights or IR scholars) wish to make it clear to us that it would be wrong to think that were people to act ethically, humankind's condition would progress or improve. For tragedy teaches us that even good people acting in ethically sound ways cannot be assured good outcomes, and, indeed, may themselves cause negative consequences through their ethical acts. If such tragic outcomes are possible among those close to us in our own families, churches, states and so on, it follows that the chances of progress will be even slighter when we encounter people with ethical systems sharply opposed to ours. 'For it is the perpetual tragic irony of the Tragedy of Life that again and again men do thus laboriously contrive their own annihilation, or ill the thing that they love.'[15]

In summary then, what we encounter in tragic accounts are good people striving to act ethically but discovering, either at the point of decision or after the event, that they are located in an ethical *agon* that shows their own deeds to have been ethically hurtful to them and to those to whom they feel themselves ethically accountable. With hindsight the actors or the audience might come to see ironic results flowing from the protagonists' deeds. A modern example in international relations is the United States (US) intervening in Somalia (operation 'Restore Hope' December 1992) for the best of ethical reasons, only to find that the consequences of this action were such that the war took on new and more destructive forms. The *agon* in this case would be between a view which advocated the primacy of the system of sovereign states governed by the non-intervention rule, and a view which stressed the primacy of international civil society with its embedded ethic about individual human rights. The latest US intervention (with Britain) into Iraq started out with the best of ethical intentions, but turned into a tragedy.

Tragedies also occur when international organizations, like the United Nations (UN), set up structures to provide humanitarian aid to people in need and find that these structures themselves become central to elements in an escalating conflict. The UN attempted to create safe havens in Bosnia. Far from providing safety, these ended up trapping people in locations within which they could easily be targeted by the Serbian forces. Here again the *agon* would be between intervention and non-intervention. A final example might refer to the refugee camps in Zaire, set up for the soundest of ethical reasons to cope with the refugees fleeing conflict in Rwanda and Burundi in 1994, themselves becoming safe havens for the training of Interahamwe soldiers committed to continuing the genocide in Rwanda.

Possible benefits which the study of tragedy might provide for normative theorists

In this chapter I am exploring whether or not the study of tragedy is important/useful for those having to make difficult ethical decisions in the domain of international relations. For example, I have in mind those citizens who are trying to decide whether on ethical grounds they would be justified in participating in some specific war, or, whether they should refuse to do so. I am addressing statesmen and women who have to decide whether to commit resources to an intervention in a sovereign state with a view to protecting individual human rights there, or who have to make decisions about how to treat migrants, and so on through the many examples of ethical questions which confront all of us in international relations today. What has the tradition of tragedy to offer that may be of use to us in thinking about such matters?

There is a plausible response to the question that would bring this chapter to a speedy conclusion. This is that tragedy has nothing whatsoever to contribute to answering ethical questions, because ethical questions are about what to do in the future, whereas, tragedy is always a tale told about what happened in the past. The tragedian always uses hindsight to link an ethical act with a set of negative, often ironic, consequences. As we have seen, the punch in tragic stories, plays and real-life dramas comes from the link made between an actor's deeds, their consequences and an *agon* (a conflict between rival ethics both considered to be binding on the protagonist(s)). Crucial to the tragic view is the conviction that even if the actor had had full knowledge of the consequences of his action, he or she would still have had to make an agonizing choice between the practices concerned. In some strong sense the negative consequences could not have been avoided, given the ways in which the actors in question were constituted in the conflicting practices. Thus, from the point of view of the tragic tradition it could not be useful for a person on the point of a decision to be told: 'Before making your decision be careful to avoid tragedy.' Those who argue from the tradition of tragedy do not believe that it is something that can be eradicated by simply taking more care about one's decisions. For it is precisely the consequences which an actor does *not* have in mind which could turn what seems to him or her an ethically sound course of conduct into a tragedy. It is precisely the unavoidable aspect of the ethical conflict (or *agon*) that besets the protagonists which produces the series of events (act and its consequences) as tragic. Another way of making this point is to note that it is precisely not the point of tragic accounts to highlight how the protagonist failed in his or her estimation of the consequences which would flow from a given course of action or to highlight how he or she failed to appreciate a way out of the *agon* confronting them. Aeschylus, Euripides, Sophocles and Shakespeare were not writing accounts which could be read as criticisms of their protagonists for failing to predict the likely consequences of their actions. In these plays the protagonists are not shown up as hapless social scientists. Quite the contrary, they are shown as having done their best to anticipate the future. But in spite of their best efforts, ironically, their ethical conduct backfires on them in unintended ways. This is what makes a tragedy of this particular series of acts and sequences. Furthermore, even had the protagonists known what the outcome of their action would be, they would still have regarded themselves as ethically bound to do what they did. In *Hamlet*, Shakespeare is not to be understood as criticizing Hamlet for not making what was clearly the right choice. Instead, in the great tradition of tragic writers, he shows in this play how complex and contradictory the ethical imperatives that make their demands on us are. For these writers there is something tragic about the human condition both at the individual level and at the political one.

The conclusion indicated in the previous paragraph must be that if the writing of tragedy, and writing about it, is a backward looking enterprise, then it clearly cannot have anything to offer those worried about forward looking questions such as, 'What is to be done?'. Knowledge of past tragedies cannot prevent new ones from happening. The injunction 'Act so as to prevent a tragedy' is nonsensical. It displays a misunderstanding of what tragedy is about. The only way in which tragedies could be avoided would be if actors had perfect information about the future, and if all the social practices within which we participate could be shown to be in perfect harmony with one another. Neither of these is plausible or even possible. Therefore, tragedy is always a possibility. 'Act so as to avoid tragedy' is a pointless command. It might even be a comic one.

In the light of the above, it would seem as if we must conclude that the study of tragedy is useless to those facing decisions with an ethical dimension. This conclusion is not warranted. For although the injunction 'avoid tragedy' cannot guide us to ethically sound decisions, there are ways in which knowledge of tragedy may have something to contribute to the solution of ethical problems. *An education in the tragic tradition can help us identify ethical problems and may help us understand certain key features of these problems.* It alerts us to the relationships that hold between an actor, the wider society within which he or she is constituted as an actor of a certain kind, ethics and the consequences of his or her acts.

By reading, watching and studying tragedies what is brought home to us are the ways in which the protagonists are constituted as the people they are within specific social practices, each of which has an ethic embedded in it. Thus, in the hypothetical example that I deployed above, we saw how each of the Breytenbach brothers was constituted in two social practices.[16] Each was located in the family and in a military formation. In like manner in the play *Antigone* that I outlined above, we understand Antigone's decision as one that is guided by principles that are internal to the structure of family life within which she understands herself (and is recognized by others) as a daughter who has certain obligations to her brother. Similarly, we understand that Creon in his capacity as ruler within the polity has certain obligations which both he and others in the polity expect him to honour.

Tragedy reveals to us how being an actor under a certain description requires of us that we take the ethic of the practice in which we are established as such seriously. In reading tragedies (or watching them) we come to see that what is to count as ethical behaviour is not a free choice for the actors concerned. It is imposed on them by the practice within which they are constituted as the actors they are – brother, daughter, general, freedom fighter or king. For example, in *Antigone*, the play makes it clear that *qua* daughter and *qua* King, Antigone and Creon are not free to choose whether or not to obey the ethical principles of family life and of the polity, respectively. Insofar as they occupy these roles, each is required to obey the dictates of the ethic embedded in these practices. This is not to deny that a specific interpretation of the ethic might be a contentious one arrived at only after much struggle. But this in no way diminishes the central point which is that as actors of a certain description they are required to attempt an interpretation of the ethic embedded in the constituting practice in question. Failure to do so would result in their having their status as actors of this kind put into question. The threat of being de-constituted, expelled or excommunicated from the practices in question acts as the imperative that forces actors to be in earnest about the ethic embedded in the practice.

Tragedy reveals to us how we are constituted as actors in a whole range of different social practices, each with its own ethic. It is this fact that makes tragedy possible. For a tragedy is what occurs when, through our simultaneous participation in several different social practices with conflicting ethics, a set of consequences arises which, from an ethical point of view, is extremely painful for us. Thus tragedies occur through our being simultaneously participants in families and in military formations, churches and states, nations and states, and so on. Antigone was a sister and a subject at the same time. Creon was King and an uncle. Tragedy reveals how each of the practices within which we are constituted as actors of a certain kind imposes on us a set of ethical imperatives. It shows how it often happens that these come to clash with one another. It shows how we as actors can be torn apart by this kind of ethical clash within, as it were, our own plural, contradictory and conflictual ethical universe.

Tragic stories demonstrate how certain kinds of ethical dilemmas do not merely involve a decision-maker choosing between rival ethical principles – do not merely involve him or her choosing whether to commit to this or that principle – but involve a decision which, either immediately or in its consequences, causes the decision-maker to undermine his or her own ethical standing in some practice which was/is important to him or her. For example, a state may choose to intervene in the domestic affairs of another in order to protect human rights. If it does so, it undermines its standing in the practice of states, which has as a central component the non-intervention rule. If it fails to do so, it undermines its standing within the international practice of rights (global civil society). Another way of putting this is to say that tragedy reveals to us how by acting in terms of the ethic internal to one practice an actor undermines his or her ethical standing in another. For what tragedy purports to show is that our ethical commitments sometimes do not cohere, and, sometimes, positively conflict. The tragic view throws doubt on any suggestion that our ethical commitments can be brought into harmony.

Central to the tradition of tragedy is the importance which writers in it attach to the unanticipated consequences that may follow even the most ethical of actions. The tradition shows how unexpected consequences can thoroughly thwart the intention of the actor(s). These unexpected results arise because there are so many forces operative in the world in which we live. In the natural world our scientific expertise is simply not good enough to enable us to predict everything that will come about. In the social world, though, things are far more difficult in that what we do often causes reactions from other actors. How they will react to what we have done depends on their interpretations. Different actors will interpret what we have done in different ways. It is difficult if not impossible to predict them all. What someone does in the belief that it was the ethically right thing to do, might, in some broad sense, cause misinterpretations of the act in question that in turn bring about tragic consequences. Thus, for example, where the US intended to get aid to those who needed it in Somalia, what they did was (mis)interpreted by many in Somalia who saw the 'aid' as a strategic resource to be used in the political struggles within the region. The outcome was tragic – not at all what the US had intended.

Tragic accounts reveal the complexity of our own ethical practices and the relationships that hold between them. In much recent writing on ethics in international relations, attention has been paid to the problem of 'other cultures' with their associated ethical commitments that are different from ours. There is no doubt that this is a very real problem for ethical theory. But the tragic tradition highlights an equally important and possibly even more difficult class of ethical problem which is the one we encounter *within* ourselves as individuals, and *within* those social practices (families, churches, states and international organizations) that constitute who we are.

What emerges from the foregoing discussion is that *an education in the tradition of tragedy makes explicit the form* of some of the more intractable ethical problems we encounter in the course of our lives. But making explicit the shape of a problem is still far removed from solving it. As an actor with an understanding of tragedy stands before an ethical problem, he or she will know that, through no fault of his or her own, it may come about that his or her action could bring about what he or she specifically seeks to avoid. The actor knows that were this to happen this would cause him or her long lasting unhappiness. Furthermore, he or she knows that he or she might at some future stage in life be forced to make a tragic choice in the context of some *agon* that has not yet occurred to him or her.

In the previous paragraphs I have outlined some of the features of the circumstances of ethical choice that are highlighted in the tradition of tragedy. But while knowing what these are gives us a sense of the social circumstances in which our ethical decisions will have to be made, this knowledge still does not guide us to any particular ethical decision.

Tragic accounts reveal to us how actors from time to time become victims of the complex ethical arrangements within which they (and we) live. Besides revealing these to us, accounts of tragic events also put major ethical questions to us. This, I wish to argue, is the greatest contribution which the tradition of tragedy has to make to contemporary normative IR theory. Those who produce tragic texts challenge us (the audience) to consider whether the ethical arrangements that gave rise to the tragedies ought to be reformed or whether they ought to be changed. In other words they invite us to consider the overall ethical architecture of the multiple social practices within which we are constituted as the actors we are. They invite us to consider the relationship between the social practices that produced the *agon* which led to the tragedy. This level of ethical evaluation is, of course, not available to the protagonist(s) in any particular tragedy. The Breytenbach brothers, Antigone, Oedipus, Agamemnon, Creon, Hamlet, Romeo and Juliet and all the other famous victims of tragedy had to make difficult decisions within the practices within which they were constituted as brothers or sisters, generals, freedom fighters, kings, princes or princesses. Given that these practices were constitutive of whom they were, they had no option *qua* brothers, sisters, generals, kings or princes but to take the ethic embedded in these practices seriously. But we as the audiences of such tragic stories are not faced with this imperative. In the light of what we have seen and heard, we can, at our leisure, consider the practices which produced the *agon* and can give careful consideration to the relationships which hold between them and between the ethical codes embedded in them. We do this with a view to the consideration of the eradication of the antagonistic relationship between them through institutional reform.

In traditional societies where the institutional structures are thought to have been put in place by gods (or a god), by nature, or are thought of simply as 'the given' which cannot be changed, it may well have been the case that viewing tragedy did not lead to thoughts about institutional reform. But we no longer think of social practices as being static, stable and given for all time. Instead, we are well aware of the possibilities of transformation. In short we are well aware that existing social practices are in a broad sense social constructs. This point is a constant refrain of almost all post-positivist approaches to social theory.

How might a tragic account lead us to consider social transformation? Let us consider Breyten Breytenbach, the freedom fighter. We have seen how a conflict between what was required of him as a brother and what was required as a member of the liberation movement might have led him to make a tragic choice. We can see how, for him, his simultaneous membership of both practices might have landed him in the classic tragic lose/lose position. But we the audience are in a position to evaluate the *agonistic* practices in their interrelationship to one another. Are the ethics of these two practices fundamentally at odds with one another, such that people who participate in both will inevitably find themselves in tragic circumstances? Or are they related to one another in such a way that a tragic outcome will be the rare exception? How important is membership of these practices for our own sense of ourselves? From our point of view, do the claims of family always trump those of liberation movements? It might be thought that a liberation movement is a public institution designed to pursue a just cause and that claims made in its name should prevail over those made in the name of a private institution such as the family. Others might argue that a liberation movement that did not take family values seriously would not be one for which it would be worth fighting. In the audience of the original tragedy we might find some who would argue one way and others who would put forward the contrary point of view. I am not concerned with taking sides on this matter. All I wish to point out is that for many people in the contemporary world tragic stories raise the possibility of changing, reforming or transforming the social institutions under consideration. At its most general, the question posed to us by all tragic stories is: Are there good reasons to maintain and nurture the social institutions that produced this tragedy? In answer to this question some Marxists have argued that the family is not an institution worth preserving (or not in its present form) because it is a patriarchal and bourgeois institution. They would advocate reconstituting our social institutions to do away with the family in its bourgeois form. Others might take the family as the primary social institution and argue that only those institutions that protect and nurture it should be preserved. On this view, liberation movements and armies that do not have as a primary goal the preservation of family life do not deserve our support. Such people would argue that military organizations should be so organized that the soldiers in them always recognize the primacy of family loyalties. The Mafia and some of the ruling families in the Middle Eastern states make just such a case. Where there is a conflict of loyalty between state and family, family wins. Here again I do not wish to enter into this particular debate. My concern once again is to point out that all tragic stories raise such questions for modern audiences. Let me discuss in more detail one contemporary *agon* which is global in scale and which creates the conditions for any number of tragedies. I shall briefly indicate some of the questions about social transformation that it raises.

A modern tragedy and the constitutional questions it raises

Many of us have found ourselves to be the tragic victims of what appears to be an agonistic relationship between the two most powerful global practices of our time. We consider ourselves to be rights holders in the global society of rights holders. For the purposes of this chapter let us call this 'global civil society'. In this society, we regard ourselves as rights holders and recognize all other people as holding equal sets of rights to those that we claim for ourselves. Quite often we refer to this set of rights as 'natural rights' in order to indicate that having these rights does not depend on the *largesse* of the state within which one finds oneself. As members of global civil society, we criticize all individual and collective actors who do not respect people's civil society rights like the right to life, the right not to be assaulted, tortured, imprisoned without a fair trial, the right to freedom of association, freedom of speech, conscience and the right to academic freedom. But, and here the potential for tragedy emerges, all of us who consider ourselves to be rights holders in global civil society simultaneously consider ourselves to be the bearers of citizenship rights within the society of democratic and democratizing states. As such, we expect others to respect the rights of the sovereign states within which we are constituted as citizens. We expect others to recognize our state's right to non-interference in its domestic affairs and so on.

Our simultaneous membership of these two social practices regularly puts us into predicaments in which whatever we do will have tragic consequences. For example, as members of global civil society we recognize other people as holders of the same set of fundamental human rights that we claim for ourselves. Within global civil society we, as individual rights holders, ought to be free to make use of our basic rights as we see fit. We ought to be free to move about seeking our fortunes, making friends, studying, praying together, participating in sport, and so on, at will. In this social formation we ought to be constrained only by the general rule that in what we do we should not abuse the rights of others. However, as citizens of sovereign states we are often called upon to put impediments in the way of rights holders who are not members of our own state. We are called upon to do this in order to secure advantages for our own state and our own fellow citizens. In pursuit of national self-interest we are asked to agree to policies which hinder the free movement of migrants across our borders, to policies which tax goods produced abroad, and to many other kinds of regulations which discriminate against outsiders with a view to benefiting our own people. In every case in which we are confronted with a choice that asks us to choose either in favour of our state or in favour of individual human rights, we are confronted with what is at base a tragic choice. We find ourselves in the classic 'lose/lose' dilemma. If we choose to support our fellow citizens, we undermine the ethical commitments we have as members of global civil society, whereas, if we choose to uphold the individual rights which civilians have as members of global civil society, then we may rightly be criticized for ignoring the best interests of our fellow citizens. Governments and the citizens that support them regularly have to make decisions about policies imposing tariffs on foreign imports (thus supporting their fellow citizens) or opposing the imposition of tariffs (thus letting down their fellow citizens, but standing up for rights holders everywhere in the global free market). This is a classic tragic choice. Whichever way an individual chooses he or she ends up undermining his or her commitment to a set of values embedded in the other institution involved in this particular *agon*.

There are many different policy areas in contemporary international life in which individuals are finding themselves plunged into this particular tragic dilemma, a dilemma in which they confront an *agon* between the ethic embedded in global civil society on the one hand and the society of democratic states on the other. Let me briefly list a few of these.

This tragic dilemma is encountered with regard to problems associated with refugees in many different parts of the world. As members of global civil society, refugees have the same rights and freedoms as anybody else and ought to be able to move about freely. But wearing our hats as citizens of this or that state we come to see refugees as foreign invaders who threaten the national interest of our state. The tragic dilemma is also encountered with regard to free trade issues. As members of global civil society we recognize that all people everywhere have the freedom to own property and to trade with it as they see fit. But as citizens of particular states we consider ourselves bound to curtail foreign traders insofar as they disadvantage our fellow citizens.

A similar tragic dilemma confronts us with regard to the intervention/non-intervention debate. As members of global civil society we recognize that all people everywhere have the same set of basic rights. Where these are infringed, as fellow members of global civil society, we ought to do what we can to protect their rights. This might require of us that we intervene in certain conflicts where rights are being abused. But doing this might require of us that we undermine the 'respect the borders of sovereign states' norm that is fundamental to the practice of sovereign states within which we enjoy citizenship rights. Whichever side we choose to support in this debate will require of us that we do things contrary to the requirements of the other practice. We shall be required to take a tragic choice.

Yet another tragic choice faces us when contemplating issues to do with distributive justice in international affairs. Here, a fundamental part of the *agon* is once again as follows: our membership of global civil society requires of us to regard all people everywhere as having the same basic set of individual rights. This has huge implications for questions to do with international distributive justice. But opposing this is the requirement imposed on us as citizens of a sovereign democratic and democratizing state which requires of us that we do what we can to advantage our own state even where this has to be done at the expense of other states (and at the expense of the citizens in them).

My central point raised in all the examples mentioned above is that in the modern world we repeatedly come up against many different forms of one specific modern *agon* that generates tragedies again and again. The basic form of this tragedy-inducing social conflict turns, we might say, on an ongoing *agon* between what is required of us by the ethic underpinning global civil society, on the one hand, and the ethic underpinning the society of democratic and democratizing states, on the other. We repeatedly have to choose on which side of this *agon* we wish to stand. Having chosen we then have to suffer the consequences of having undercut our commitment to the practice on the other side of the divide. We have to suffer the remorse involved in being the victim of a tragedy. But as I have already pointed out, once we characterize the relationship between these two practices as one that has already led to tragic outcomes and which will continue to do so, this is not the end of the matter. For we, as modern men and women, no longer consider the social formations within which we live to be given for all time. These practices are not, metaphorically speaking, 'set in stone'. We do not have to shrug the dilemma off with, 'It cannot be avoided, life just is tragic'. Instead, we can consider changing them.

I find it difficult to find any reason for not asking big questions about the relationships which hold between major social practices which we, with hindsight, can see as practices that repeatedly produce tragic outcomes (that is, outcomes where protagonists end up having to act against what is required of them in one social practice by obeying the ethical imperatives of another). If it were the case that transformation of one practice (or the other) was not possible, then, by definition, our response to tragedy would simply have to be a stoic one. We would have to say to ourselves, 'This is just how the world is, it is filled with conflict and contradictions which we simply have to accept.'

But this is not how matters stand. Today we are well aware of the possibilities of transformation and we devote a lot of time and energy to thinking about it. Here are two recent examples of transformations successfully completed. For more than 40 years, the Republic of South Africa was constituted according to the principles of *apartheid*. The juxtaposition of this social form with Christian religious formations worldwide and with the global practice of human rights placed many people in the position of tragic victims. The articulation of such tragedies in books such as Alan Paton's *Cry the Beloved Country*, and in many other books, films, plays and poems, over time, brought people to question the constitution of South Africa.[17] The questioning of the ethics of this practice led people to political action that in turn led to a political transformation. There are no longer new tragic victims of that particular tragedy-producing *agon*.

In a similar vein, the conditions for tragedy that prevailed in Europe during the two World Wars of the twentieth century produced tragic victims who had to choose between an ethic of nation and one of European civil society. Tragic instances of these times have been written about in countless texts. These in turn led to a re-evaluation of these practices and to a process of transformation that has produced the European Union. The particular kinds of tragedy that the earlier institutions produced are no longer likely in Western Europe although they have arisen in a vigorous way in Central and Eastern Europe. It seems to me that nowadays people who are confronted with tragic accounts of acts and their consequences must proceed to the next step. This step requires an evaluation of the practices that produced the tragedies in the first place, with a view to transforming them in ways that will avoid these particular tragic outcomes in the future. The Balkan states have been engaged in just such an exercise.[18]

Concluding remarks

I set out to find an answer to the following question: Is the study of tragedy useful to those seeking to answer pressing ethical questions in international relations today? In order to do this I produced a rough and ready account of certain core features of tragedy as it has been used in the tradition of writing on tragedy. I argued that tragic accounts display for an audience an actor who is enmeshed in a specified social context, who confronts an ethical conflict, and who acts out an ethical imperative that leads (often ironically) to an outcome that from an ethical point of view is hurtful to the actor him- or herself. At the heart of the tragic sequence – from ethical struggle, to act, to negative consequences – is an *agon* which is a conflict between the ethical values embedded in rival practices, both of which are fundamentally constitutive of the protagonist as he or she values him- or herself to be. In what followed, I argued that in a world in which we are all constituted as actors under any number of descriptions, in a range of different social practices, in a world in which we cannot possibly foresee all the consequences of our actions, it is always possible that what we do will have tragic consequences. But knowing this does not provide us with any guidance when we seek to answer the question: What would be ethical for us to do in these circumstances? This is the first major conclusion of this chapter. Tragedy does not offer any direct guidance to those seeking answers to ethical questions.

However, later in the chapter I argue that although the tradition of tragedy is not directly of use to those interested in international ethics, it is indirectly useful, in that tragic stories (what I have called 'tragic accounts') highlight the social constitution of actors in a diverse range of social practices. They make it plain how within such social practices the participants are compelled to comply with the internal ethics of the practices in question, and they make it plain how actors who are located in multiple practices will have to wrestle with conflicts and contradictions as they emerge. In a sense then tragic tales present us with a useful picture of the circumstances of ethical choice within which individuals find themselves. More important though is the way that tragic accounts bring to the attention of those who are the audience of such tales (in other words, bring to *our* attention) questions about the ethical *raison d'etre* of the social practices which give rise to the tragedies presented to us. For we are nowadays constituted as people who can contemplate the transformation of the social institutions within which we live. (As an example, I have offered what is arguably the greatest tragedy-producing conflict in our contemporary world: that between global civil society on the one hand and the society of democratic and democratizing states, on the other).[19] Tragedy asks us to consider the possible transformation of the social formations that provided the *agon* that produced the tragedy. Tragedy does not solve ethical problems, but, rather, poses them to us.

Notes

1. H. F. Gutbrod (2001) 'Irony, Conflict, Dilemma: Three Tragic Situations in International Relations', Unpublished Dissertation, London School of Economics.
2. H. Butterfield (1931) *The Whig Interpretation of History* (London: Bell); R. Niebuhr (1938) *Beyond Tragedy: Essays on the Christian Interpretation of History* (London: Nisbet and Company); H. J. Morgenthau (1958) *Dilemmas of Politics* (Chicago: Chicago University Press).
3. E. H. Carr (1946) *The Twenty Years Crisis*, 2nd edn (London: Macmillan), p. 12.
4. H. J. Morgenthau (1948) *Politics among Nations* (New York: Alfred Knopff), p. 341.
5. Morgenthau (1948) *Politics among Nations*, p. 11.
6. H. J. Morgenthau (1948) 'The Political Science of E. H. Carr', *World Politics*, 1 (127), 127–34.
7. H. J. Morgenthau (1946) *Scientific Man Versus Power Politics* (Chicago: Chicago University Press), p. 203.
8. Niebuhr (1938) *Beyond Tragedy*.
9. To mention but a few books in this area: K. Booth, T. Dunne and M. Cox (eds) (2001) *How Might We Live? Global Ethics in the New Century* (Cambridge: Cambridge University Press); J. H. Rosenthal and C. Barry (eds) (2009) *Ethics in International Affairs: A Reader*, 3rd edn (Washington, DC: Georgetown University Press); M. Lensu and J. -S. Fritz (2000) *Value Pluralism, Normative Theory and International Relations* (London: Macmillan in Association with *Millennium: Journal of International Studies*); K. Hutchings (1999) *International Political Theory: Rethinking Ethics in a Global Era* (London: Sage); C. Brown (1992) *International Relations Theory: New Normative Approaches* (Hemel Hempstead: Harvester Wheatsheaf); M. Cochran (1999) *Normative Theory in International Relations: A Pragmatist Approach* (Cambridge: Cambridge University Press).
10. B. Breytenbach (1985) *The True Confessions of an Albino Terrorist* (London: Faber).
11. 'The Cause' for the one would have been national liberation and for the other the maintenance of the Afrikaaners' right to self-determination.
12. In the account that I gave above, had I left out the Breytenbach brothers, it would simply have been a standard story about an encounter between

enemies. What changed the account into a tragic one was the introduction of an *agon*.

13. This would have happened in our example had Jan Breytenbach unwittingly had his brother killed. When this unanticipated consequence came to light it would have caused him sorrow in terms of the ethic associated with family life.

14. F. L. Lucas (1981) *Tragedy* (London: Chatto and Windus), p. 110.

15. Lucas (1981) *Tragedy*, p. 112.

16. In what follows I am taking it as given that we are always constituted as actors of a certain kind (soldier, lecturer, husband, president) in the context of social practices/institutions the rules of which specify what is to count as appropriate conduct by those constituted as actors of the specified kind. The relevant practices for the examples I have given are, of course, armies, universities, marriages and states.

17. A. Paton (1958) *Cry the Beloved Country: A Story of Comfort and Desolation* (Harmondsworth: Penguin).

18. I shall not, in this chapter, go into what might be involved in the ethical evaluation of practices that give rise to tragic outcomes; I have attempted this elsewhere. See M. Frost (1996) *Ethics in International Relations: A Constitutive Theory* (Cambridge: Cambridge University Press).

19. I have written more about this elsewhere; See M. Frost (2002) *Constituting Human Rights: Global Civil Society and the Society of Democratic States* (London: Routledge).

3
Tragedy, Progress and the International Order

James Mayall

It is a familiar axiom that many of the best ideas for writing and research are generated after hours, over a drink or a meal away from the formality of the seminar room or conference panel. Mervyn Frost's powerful contribution to this volume is a case in point. It had its genesis in a Chicago diner during the 2001 International Studies Association (ISA) Conference. According to him, I challenged him by suggesting that his constitutive approach to international ethical theory was 'too progressive, optimistic and teleological'. The occasion was a convivial one and in truth I cannot remember the exact terms of my challenge. In the cold light of day I think his claim is partly right and partly wrong.

He is right in thinking that I believed then, and continue to believe, that much of the writing about international relations since the end of the Cold War – and, in the early years, much of the practice also – was unduly optimistic. In particular, the willingness of the United Nations (UN) Security Council, strongly supported by many intellectuals, to will liberal ends was not matched by an equal willingness to provide the means of delivering them. I am not sure that I had constitutive theory particularly in my sights, although it is true that the favoured post-Cold War liberal project – the protection of human rights, democratization and the rule of law – corresponds closely to what he describes as the core values of a 'global civil society'.

He is wrong to infer that my emphasis on the tragic dimension of international relations implies opposition to the idea of progress or to efforts to improve the quality of international life. Indeed, the immediate background to my late night challenge was a conclusion that I had reached in *World Politics: Progress and its Limits*:

> The modern world cannot easily escape its historical mode of thought; it follows the arrow of time wherever it leads and despite its

problematic and, under some circumstances, ominous implications for international relations. We are stuck with the idea of progress because it is the coin of democratic politics. It provides its underlying ethic, as tragedy provided it when the fate of peoples was subsumed in the fate of their leaders, whose humanity had to play second fiddle to their role.[1]

As Frost so effectively demonstrates, tragedy is not the outcome of mistakes or the failure to calculate accurately the consequences of particular policies. On the contrary, tragedy is the outcome of a confrontation of two conceptions of the right, only one of which can prevail. It is tragic partly because the defeat of one conception of right does not automatically turn it into a wrong, even if this is how the victor will try to represent it, and partly because, nonetheless, the loser has no alternative than to endure the outcome. This is why – to follow Frost's etymological deconstruction – we typically describe tragic choices as *agonizing*.

In most respects, it seems to me, his analysis of the relevance of the study of tragedy for an understanding of international relations is exemplary. I agree in particular that the injunction 'act so as to avoid tragedy' makes no sense. But while I agree also with his explanation of why, nonetheless, an awareness of the tragic possibilities of the human condition is valuable – in that 'it can help us identify ethical problems and help us understand certain key features of these problems' – I would put the case more strongly. An awareness of the possibility of tragic outcomes is a necessary antidote to the hubris of progressive thought and the constant liberal temptation to avoid accepting responsibility for well-intended actions that go wrong.

There are two points on which I think we might still disagree. The first is Frost's insistence that membership of global civil society represents one prominent form of contemporary social practice just as membership of 'the society of democratic and democratising states' represents another with which it may come in conflict, with possibly tragic consequences. The examples that he provides of the possibility of progressive reform as a way out of the vicious circle within which history seemed condemned to repeat itself, the peaceful overthrow of the *apartheid* regime in South Africa and the transformation of European rivalries within the institutional framework – are indeed impressive.

Still, these achievements do not, in my view, provide evidence of an uncontested evolution towards a global human rights culture. It is true that the only coherent position on human rights is one that maintains that they derive from our humanity and not from a particular culture or way of life. In this sense, they cannot be tied in time or space. Indeed, I am not even sure that it is helpful to describe global civil society, assuming such a society exists, as a social practice: respect for human rights is not like bingo, gardening or multi-party politics. Although, theoretically, human rights have as little respect for international boundaries as the tsetse fly, in practice, as his examples testify, the securing of rights is always the result of a specific historic struggle to establish a state of affairs that did not previously exist.

The appeal to a universal standard in such struggles is useful and at certain stages may be important, but it remains secondary. If, as I have argued, international relations continue to respond more closely to a tragic than to a democratic political idiom, it is not because such battles are not worth fighting. They obviously are. Nor would I contest Frost's argument that those involved are able to evaluate 'the practices that produced the tragedies in the first place [i.e., *apartheid* and the repetitive cycle of European wars] with a view to transforming them in ways that will avoid these particular tragic outcomes in the future'. It is because, modern ideas and the global traffic in ideas notwithstanding, the international environment remains radically different from, and presents obstacles of a different kind (or at least of so large a degree that it amounts to almost the same thing), to those that occur within a single country or political culture. In other words, even if one pattern of behaviour with tragic consequences can be transcended, another is always likely to loom up from beyond the horizon.

My second point of potential disagreement with Frost's position, then, turns on the different weight that we appear to attach to the impediments to progress imposed by the external world. Frost is right in suggesting that the ethical problems faced by decision-makers are ultimately the same, whether they arise at home or abroad. Environments are not moral actors. But, neither are all international environments equally hospitable to progressive policies. For Pascal, what was true on one side of the Pyrenees was false on the other; and in relations across cultural boundaries it can be notoriously difficult to reach a common understanding – for example about standards of decency – with regard to the meaning of progress. Even among allies who share the same broad aims and fundamental values, the pitfalls are greater than at home where the government is generally in control both legally and politically. Harold Macmillan described his failure to persuade Eisenhower to make a gesture towards Khrushchev in order to save the 1960 Paris summit following the U-2 incident as 'the most tragic moment of his life'.[2] The pitfalls facing those who wander further afield are likely to be more numerous and deep.

In the remainder of this chapter I will attempt to illustrate my own position, which I have suggested diverges from Frost's in a number of respects. I will do this by sketching, albeit in an abbreviated and schematic fashion, the difficulties that confront current Western efforts to democratize the international order.

Promoting democracy?

One colourful interpretation of international events since September 2001 is that Western policies to promote democracy are merely a facade, masking a resurgent Western imperialism. On this view, international politics is, as it has always been, power politics in which ambition is constrained only by prudence, and moral men are forced to respond to the imperatives of immoral states. If there is an international morality in such a world, it is the original morality of the duel. In a duel both contestants accept that in a conflict over fundamental values and vital interests only one can prevail. It is possible to salvage honour in defeat, for example, by showing courage, but there is no point in pretending that both sides can win.

In this kind of world the weaker side will always have an incentive to employ irregular methods. In his day, the English national hero, Sir Francis Drake, was as enthusiastic an exponent of the art of asymmetrical warfare as Osama bin Laden has been in ours. Drake was a devout Protestant, but he was also a pirate and a terrorist who preyed on Spain, the superpower of the day. His hatred of Spain and the ruthlessness with which he pursued his Spanish targets conveniently combined faith and material interest. The fact that he was honoured by England need not surprise us. At the time, at least as viewed from Madrid, England was a terrorist state, a paid up member of the early-seventeenth-century axis of evil.

To the extent that this comparison shows that militant Islam does not have a monopoly on 'righteous' terror, and that the view of moral absolutes is likely to shift over time, such comparisons are useful. But because they ignore changes in the institutional, legal and moral parameters within which the two sets of events occurred, they prejudge the question of international progress. And because they reduce all political behaviour to a violent clash of interests, they also rule out any serious consideration of the tragic element in international life.

To evaluate international relations, one must first specify the order within which they are conducted. There are three possibilities, although the first two are not necessarily mutually exclusive. These possibilities are (a) an imperial order, for example, the Pax Romana, Pax Britannica and possibly now the Pax Americana; (b) a society of states based on respect for sovereignty, non interference in domestic affairs, territorial integrity and a balance of power; (c) a cosmopolitan community of mankind based on equal rights and either the abolition of separate states and governments, or the adoption by all states of parallel constitutions and values.

Only under this last order is progress as it is understood in liberal democracies a credible possibility, that is, the protection of fundamental human rights and the continuous improvement in the quality of life of the population. Even then, international order would be vulnerable to attack by the supporters of eschatological progress, but this would be a minor and remote danger because by definition the international order would reflect an overwhelming consensus. We presumably have to assume that, in such a world, a wide variety of cultures could coexist peacefully under the umbrella of a common civic loyalty.

In reality, the attempt to establish a liberal international community has always faced formidable obstacles. The first arises because evolution is unreliable – and anyway takes too long! Consequently, while the aim is to replace power politics with rule-based diplomacy and an international community based on a commitment to common political values, success depends on the efforts of the most powerful states. These states may try to make the others an offer they cannot refuse, but even when accepted, it is likely to be resented. Western governments who openly seek to pursue an ethical foreign policy (e.g., the Carter Administration in the 1970s or the Blair government in the 1990s) invariably find themselves accused of double standards whenever they subordinate their allegedly universal principles to their national interests.

The problem is compounded by the implausibility of the democratic formula as a solution to the political problems of many divided societies. Kant's perpetual peace assumed a union of like-minded and similarly structured republics. Republican citizens are first and foremost emancipated individuals; their familial, ethnic and religious affiliations have no political significance. It is not merely the Islamic world that cannot easily be poured into this mould. If democracy is to be re-branded as a doctrine of genuinely universal appeal, it will have to be grounded not merely in a human rights culture but one that is more sensitive to group rights than is presently the case.[3]

This need was recognized in theory in Boutros Boutros-Ghali's 1992 *Agenda for Peace*, but it has made little progress with governments, whether they are attempting to export democracy, or are under pressure to import it.[4] This is partly because governments of all kinds are more willing to sign up for human rights conventions than to support an international regime that will police their implementation, but it is even more because they fear that recognition of group rights will fuel separatist sentiment. The reluctance of governments to grapple with the issue of group rights is understandable, but it fatally feeds into the alienation of religious and other minorities from the institutions of established democracies, and often undermines at source the process of democratization. There is an important paradox here: liberal political theory promises an escape from the claustrophobic enchantment of customary society; but disenchantment – in the current idiom it is more often referred to as empowerment – can only be achieved by respecting its power and legitimacy. There may be occasions when the paradox can be resolved with the aid of outside intervention – as in Japan after 1864 and 1945 – but there is no evidence that the experiment can be replicated at will.

An age of empire

Well before 11 September 2001, Western arguments that sovereignty had to be qualified by respect for the international human rights regime, and Western selectivity in humanitarian intervention had fuelled African and Asian suspicions of the West's real motives and objectives. The truly appalling nature of the 11 September attacks allowed the Americans to build a broad based coalition against terrorism, but the single-minded ferocity of the response seemed more like a revenge tragedy than the upholding of universal principles through due process of law.

The unveiling of American's pre-emptive strategy in the Bush Doctrine,[5] followed by the controversial conquest of Iraq without the authority of the UN Security Council, inevitably further fuelled fears of US imperial ambitions. Indeed, the decision to invade Iraq is an almost perfect example of the kind of tragic dilemma that Frost examines – the US government had to decide whether to uphold the multilateral principles, of which it was originally the chief architect, or to overthrow a tyrannical regime that it had helped to create, but which it was believed possessed weapons of mass destruction that would one day be turned against the West. If these were the opening moves in a new imperial campaign, the omens did not look promising at the outset.

Has the decision to invade Iraq had tragic consequences? Nine years on it is still too early to say. Recent years have witnessed a gradual improvement in security, principally as a result of General Petraeus's surge, which massively increased the number of troops on the ground in Bagdad and the Sunni triangle. The insurgency that was triggered by the occupation may be losing steam, with potentially positive effects for the elected but beleaguered Iraqi government. But a separatist civil war between Shia, Sunni and Kurds, now that the American troops have been withdrawn, with all the tragic consequences that this implies, cannot be ruled out. In that event the implications for the Iraqi people, the wider Middle East and indeed for international society more generally are impossible to calculate, but seem unlikely to be positive.

From a moral standpoint, the age of empire had two features. First, because there was no world empire, several imperial powers co-existed within a society of states. Towards the end of this period, the most powerful imperial states were also democracies. One consequence was that, in their own eyes at least, they were able to pursue progressive and/or modernizing policies. They were accountable for these policies at home, rather than in the colonies themselves, but until well after decolonization the tragic consequences of this democratic oversight were not apparent. The second feature was that within international society (from which colonial possessions were banished except at the margin as in Princely India), the traditional morality of honour and competition persisted. The nationalization of the state under democratic pressures merely reinforced the inevitably tragic outcome. The xenophobic patriotism to be found on all sides at the outbreak of the First World War, and its linking to absurdly inflated civilizational claims, is perhaps the most obvious example.

One must conclude, therefore, by asking what has changed. Imperial powers notoriously employ double standards. They may use various techniques of indirect rule to purchase a measure of legitimacy and to reduce the costs of empire, but they invariably arrogate rights and privileges denied to their subject populations. There is now only one power in the world that can aspire to imperial status (China arguably has the potential over the long term, but not in the immediate future). However, the US is deeply schizophrenic in relation to its exercise of world leadership. On the one hand, US political culture is deeply exceptionalist, probably more significant in this context than its periodic isolationism, a characteristic that invites direct comparison with the former European imperial powers. On the other, the American ideology is universal democracy. During the Cold War, they could seek regional clients to police the frontiers of the informal empire they deemed to be 'the free world', without concerning themselves with their democratic credentials and human rights records. The Cold War was novel in that nuclear weapons meant that the two superpowers could not reasonably confront one another on the battlefield. Had they done so (and despite deterrence this was always a possibility), it would have transformed into the hottest of hot wars. The danger existed because ultimately what was at stake was honour. The Cold War was a conflict about fundamentals (not between fundamentalists) and because victory was not assured a tragic outcome remained a possibility.

Future tragedy

An imperial and uncontested democracy – roughly what we have now – is quite different. Its claims are progressive, not just at home but everywhere. But it now matters that the regional policemen should be democrats. The danger is that the empire will collapse under the combined force of cynical hypocrisy abroad, and savage attack from the unassimilated at home. Vulnerability to terrorism will destroy the capacity for irony, on which democratic freedoms ultimately depend.

We must hope that this prognosis is unnecessarily apocalyptic. Its plausibility is a consequence of the mixed regime in which we currently live. As I suggested at the beginning of this chapter, the idiom of contemporary politics is democratic and, therefore, progressive, although international relations are still conducted in many – admittedly not in all – contexts according to the tragic idiom of the traditional society of states. Liberals too often rely on the hidden wiring of a constitution of liberty that simply does not exist at the international level.

The consequences of such over-optimism were made brutally clear in the chaos of post-war Baghdad, described to me by a friend as a modern equivalent of the barbarian sack of Rome. It is clear that President Obama's Democratic Administration has tried to pull back from the grandiose and universalist ambitions of its predecessors. But, while it is not clear what other options were available to Obama, the fact that the price of withdrawal from Iraq has involved a reinforced military engagement with both Afghanistan and Pakistan perhaps increases rather than reduces the likelihood of a tragic outcome. Contra Frost's argument in the previous chapter, invoking the dilemmas that arise within the global civil society of rights holders when they confront the practices of the society of democratic and democratizing states, will not, I fear, save us from either future folly or future tragedy. With Frost's important insights – and those of the other contributors to this volume – however, it may mean that we are better placed to understand them.

Notes

1. J. Mayall (2000) *World Politics, Progress and Its Limits* (Cambridge: Polity Press), p. 153. This book has been recently updated and revised for publication in Japan (translation by Masayuki Tadokoro, Tokyo (2009)).
2. Quoted in N. Ashton (2002) *Kennedy, Macmillan and the Cold War: The Irony of Interdependence* (Basingstoke: Palgrave Macmillan), p. 131.
3. See G. M. Lyons and J. Mayall (eds) (2003) *International Human Rights in the 21st Century, Protecting the Rights of Groups* (Lanham, MD: Rowman and Littlefield).
4. B. Boutros-Ghali (1992) *Agenda for Peace* (United Nations), para 18. For text, see A. Roberts and B. Kingsbury (eds) (1993) *United Nations, Divided World: The UN's Role in International Relations* (Oxford: Clarendon Press), Appendix A, pp. 468–98.
5. *National Security Strategy of the United States*, National Security Council, 20 September 2002.

4
Tragedy or Scepticism? Defending the Anti-Pelagian Mind in World Politics

Nicholas Rengger

In the previous two chapters, James Mayall and Mervyn Frost rehearse a debate which (they tell us) began over dinner at the International Studies Association (ISA) annual convention in Chicago in 2001. The substance of the debate was initiated by Mayall's claim (as reported by Frost) that Frosts 'constitutive' approach to international political theory was 'too progressive, optimistic and teleological'.[1] Frost's response is to investigate how we might understand tragedy and suggest that, of course, we should be aware that the possibility of tragedy always lurks in the undergrowth of international relations, but that the awareness of this possibility 'can help us identify ethical problems and may help us understand certain key features of these problems'. He chides Mayall with allowing his sense of tragedy to lead him to oppose progress and efforts to improve the quality of international life.

However, Mayall rejects this charge. While he certainly thinks that an awareness of tragedy 'is a necessary antidote to the hubris of progressive thought', he does not 'give up' on progress as such, rather he simply thinks that the obstacles to the kind of progress that Frost's work lays out as desirable and morally worthwhile are rather greater than Frost supposes, though he adds the rider that 'the idiom of contemporary politics is democratic and therefore progressive' and that this is where we are, and must remain.

It might be said, then, that Mayall's response to Frost is to lay out the dimensions of the 'tragedy' that truly faces us now: a mode of political being that requires a belief in progress, but (as Mayall argues at greater length elsewhere)[2] a world that is powerfully recalcitrant and remains locked in the modes of being that deny this, in form or in fact. In this portrayal, a growing chorus of others, it seems, joins him. It is a commonplace, after all, that realist accounts of politics depict the political realm as a realm of 'recurrence and repetition'[3] where the dichotomy between human moral self-understanding and the necessities of success-ful political action is unavoidably confronted to the detriment of the former or the collapse of the latter. The recognition of this permanent tension in human experience is one of the aspects of realist thinking that gives it its real intellectual, indeed also moral, power; and without denying that there is considerable variety within the realist tradition of political thought,[4] the word that is often used to refer to this condition, by many realists, in many different contexts, is tragedy.[5]

Of course, the sense of the world as *essentially* tragic is not unique to realism; many other thinkers from a wide variety of assumptions and in a wide variety of historical periods have shared it – including some who have been deeply influential on realism, such as Thucydides,[6] but also many who have not, for example Hamann.[7] Nonetheless, in the twentieth – and now twenty-first – century, and at least in connection with politics, it is the realist version of this argument that has been most important.

This makes the exchange between Mayall and Frost even more inter-esting; for neither of them – and especially not Frost – can be convinc-ingly seen as a realist. So what is it, then, that Frost and Mayall might be said to share with realists in the context of the idea of tragedy? To make this clear I want to turn for a moment to Richard Ned Lebow's remarkable and powerful restatement of the realist tradition, *The Tragic Vision of Politics*. In this book, Lebow seeks to recast realist thinking, or, rather, to recover the insights of classical realist thinkers and use them to offer an understanding of the interlinked aspects of order, interests and ethics. The bulk of the book is taken up with a detailed (and at times bravura) reading of three thinkers Lebow sees as archetypical classical realists, Thucydides, Clausewitz and Morgenthau. However, he opens and closes the book with an appreciation of the character of tragedy and an assessment of its implications for political life. His basic claim is that the classical Greek idea of tragedy, which for him lies at the heart of the insights of classical realism, 'can help keep our conceptions of ourselves and our societies from becoming infused with hubris' by forcing us to 'confront our limits and recognize that chaos lurks just beyond the fragile barriers we erect to keep it at bay'.[8] For Lebow, 'tragedy and classical realism do not so much solve problems as they deepen our understanding of them by engaging our intellect and emotions' and he quotes the classicist Charles Segal to the effect that '[t]he kind of intellect tragedy encourages is one mindful of incoher-ence, respectful of the contradictions of experience and conscious that questions about justice and politics do not yield their significance to terse hypotheses'.[9] Of course, it might be said that at the beginning of the twenty-first century the sense that *international* politics, at least, is such a realm of 'recurrence and repetition', is stronger than it has been for some time and for obvious reasons. Conflict and war seem to be everywhere in the ascendant; the optimistic assumptions of the early 1990s have been revealed as facile and deluded; Hobbes' famous twins 'Force and Fraud' seem once more to be in the driving seat of international affairs. And this, realists will chorus, is what we have always told you. Only by accepting this tragic reality do we have any hope of really being able to deal with it.

Some, such as Frost, would want to dissent from aspects of this picture. In his chapter, he is certainly more optimistic about the prospects for global civil society and the idea of progress than Mayall is; yet he seems nonetheless to agree with both Mayall and Lebow that the real importance of tragic vision is that it allows us to understand our situation better *and learn from this so that we can make it better still.*

In the rest of this chapter, I want to offer two thoughts about this. First, I want to suggest that the connection between understanding and action is more problematic than Frost, Mayall or Lebow suggest, and that, in this respect, the notion of tragedy that they deploy seems a somewhat attenuated one, especially if one compares it with the way Morgenthau for example, understands it. And secondly, and perhaps more radically, I want to suggest that perhaps, in any event, it is better to do without the notion of tragedy (in world politics) altogether.

First, then, let me turn to the issue of understanding and action. The point I want to emphasize here is that the notion of tragedy as deployed by Frost and in some respects Mayall and Lebow, emphasizes the possibility that in using tragedy to understand the world better, we can also use it to act better in the world. This it seems to me is not necessarily how Morgenthau – at least in *Scientific Man Versus Power Politics*[10] – understood the relation. Of course, he certainly believed that human experience in the world of affairs was tragic and that we needed to confront this truth if we wished to develop a sound basis for conduct, either in our own lives or those of our polities. This view was implicit in everything he wrote from his early writings on international law to his later writings on Vietnam and on the uses of American power.[11]

As is now well known, thanks in large part to Christoph Frei's biographical research,[12] *Scientific Man versus Power Politics* emerged from both Morgenthau's immersion in the European jurisprudential debates that had dominated his intellectual life in the late 1920s and early 1930s and his confrontation with American thought during his first nine years in the United States. Morgenthau had come to believe that American ideas, indeed in important respects the American mind itself, gave systematically wrong answers to the most fundamental of questions, those questions which (as Frei has shown) Morgenthau had taken over from his reading of Nietzsche and Kant: What may I hope for? What can I know? What is man? As a result, American thought is characterized by Morgenthau as being in the advanced state of a disease, 'an intellectual, moral and political disease' with its roots in 'basic philosophical assumptions'.[13] The essence of this disease, Morgenthau felt, was a 'historical optimism' that was rooted in the belief that human beings could always master any problem thanks to their capacity for rationality. This belief, however, systematically neglects what, for Morgenthau, is the central reality of the human condition. As he puts it towards the end of the book, 'suspended between his spiritual destiny which he cannot fulfil and his animal nature in which he cannot remain (man) is forever condemned to experience the contrast between the longings of his mind, and his actual condition as his personal, eminently human tragedy'.[14] For Morgenthau this is a theme to which he returns again and again in this book and which echoes and re-echoes across the rest of his work. Human beings are necessarily and always imperfect and can *never* overcome this.

From this basis Morgenthau develops a twin critique. One prong of the assault was on the belief, which stems from ignoring the reality of the human condition, that knowledge can be acquired, deployed and used in a scientific manner to resolve *any* potential problem. This was the problem he called 'dogmatic scientism'. As a number of commentators have pointed out,[15] Morgenthau's move to Chicago in 1943 brought him into contact with the leading representatives of the fledgling 'science of politics' and indeed the wider community of social scientists (sociologists and economists prominently among them) who held an unshakeable belief in historical optimism and a progressive view of science and politics. Morgenthau emphasized, both in *Scientific Man* and elsewhere, his complete repudiation of these views (though in *Scientific Man* his explicit opposition to the 'School of Merriam' was muted since his position at Chicago was hardly assured).

The other prong to Morgenthau's critique was a critique of liberalism itself. It is perhaps in this realm, more than any other, that Morgenthau's old jurisprudential foe Carl Schmitt had an influence on him, though, of course, Nietzsche and Weber are also prominent influences.[16] As Frei points out, what irritates Morgenthau most of all is the liberal 'repudiation of politics', the attempt to replace the necessarily

messy clash of interests and power that is the political realm with something else; Morgenthau's examples include legalism, moralism, pacifist
liberalism and democratic nationalism. Morgenthau seeks to recall for
liberals the centrality of an autonomous political sphere; if they forget this they forget everything that the history of liberal thought and
practice should have taught them. Morgenthau, unlike Schmitt, was no
opponent as such of a liberal society; quite the contrary. But liberals,
he believed, had to see the reality of their predicament squarely and
that, fundamentally, meant confronting the tragic in all its forms: the
'tragic sense of life, the tragic presence of evil, the tragic antinomies of
human existence' and so on. This does not mean that there is no *sense*
of the good in politics but rather 'there is no progress toward the good,
noticeable from year to year, but undecided conflict which sees today
good, tomorrow evil prevail'.[17]

While, of course, there is a good deal that Lebow and Morgenthau
share, it seems to me that this way of seeing the 'tragic vision' is far less
amenable to the hopes of 'social learning' that animate the last part of
Lebow's book, and which link him in certain respects at least to Frost
and Mayall. For Lebow, as he puts it in the final chapter of his book,
'tragedy suggests ... that all knowledge is local, temporally bound and
quickly negated ... [such] knowledge can feed back into our theoretical
inquiries and help create a positive, reinforcing cycle of discovery'.[18]
I find it hard to see the Morgenthau of *Scientific Man Versus Power Politics*
agreeing with that. For him the law of unintended consequences,
human malfeasance and sheer brute luck would, more often than not,
get in the way. While this view certainly evolves in his later writings, he
never repudiates it and in his later writings, particularly on Vietnam, it
comes once more to the fore.[19] Yet, if Morgenthau is right about this,
then even the relatively modest hopes entertained by Mayall or Lebow
might well turn out to be mistaken.

But even if this is not so, it might perhaps be better to avoid the
invocation of tragedy altogether. This thought is in part inspired by an
argument of Michael Oakeshott, found in his review of *Scientific Man
Versus Power Politics*, which appeared first in the *Cambridge Journal* in
1947.[20] Oakeshott wrote approvingly of the main argument of the book
(though not without some rather arch sideswipes at Morgenthau's style)
and, in fact, picks up clearly the main target of Morgenthau's critique,
especially in the context of international politics. As he remarks,

[p]erhaps it is in the sphere of international relationships that the
project of a science of politics [that Morgenthau was criticizing]

has made itself most clear ... From Grotius to the United Nations a continuous attempt has been made to demonstrate Bentham's proposition that 'nations are associates not rivals in the grand social enterprise', and to elaborate the principles of a science of peace. And Professor Morgenthau is an acute ... guide for anyone wishing to follow the trail of this enterprise: he does not distinguish real moral achievements (such as they are) from rationalist aspirations and projects, but he knows an illusion when he sees one.[21]

Oakeshott moves from this point to an exposition of Morgethau's reasons for rejecting historical optimism. Morgenthau's argument about the inevitably fragmented character of human action, the *animus dominandi* and so on, is, Oakeshott thinks, the strongest argument Morgenthau makes. As Oakeshott says, '[i]t is central to the book, and it owes something to both Augustine and Hobbes: since the faith which is being condemned is the modern successor to that of Pelagius, the argument which exposes it is a new anti-Pelagianism'.[22] Oakeshott puts Morgenthau's argument here as follows:

[t]he assumption of rationalism is that the conflict which springs from the human *animus dominandi* can be resolved, and the *animus* itself expelled ... But this, if we have followed Professor Morgenthau's argument, is absurd; the *animus* is inherent in the nature of man and human activity and nothing whatever can abolish it.

He adds that he does not 'propose to offer any criticism of this argument. Its main principles belong to a tradition of European thought many centuries old; and, if it is no more, it is at least a cogent criticism of the neo-Pelagian assumptions of "scientism"'.[23]

This, however, leads on to the most fundamental difference between Morgenthau and Oakeshott. Where Morgenthau suggests we should understand the tragic sense of life and the role that it can play, Oakeshott says,

[t]his is all very well; we know what he is trying to say, but it is an unfortunate way of expressing it. Human life is not 'tragic', either in part or as a whole: tragedy belongs to art, not to life. And further, the situation [Morgenthau] describes – the imperfectability of man – is not tragic, nor even a predicament, unless and until it is contrasted with a human nature susceptible of a perfection which is in fact foreign to its character, and rationalism rears its ugly head

once more in any argument which assumes or asserts this contrast. To children and to romantic women, but to no one else, it may appear 'tragic' that we cannot enjoy Spring without Winter, eternal youth, and passion always at the height of its beginning. And only a rationalistic reformer will confuse the imperfections which can be remedied with the so-called imperfection which cannot, and will think of the irremovability of the latter as a tragedy. The rest of us know that no rationalistic justice (with its project of approximating people to things), and no possible degree of human prosperity, can ever remove mercy and charity from their place of first importance in the relations of human beings, and know also that this situation cannot properly be considered either imperfect or a tragedy.[24]

It is worth pointing out that, while appreciative of the review in general, this point was one that Morgenthau, in private correspondence with Oakeshott, refused to concede. The tragic, he insisted, 'is a quality of existence, not a creation of art'.[25] But this I think rather misses the point of Oakeshott's scepticism. Oakeshott is sceptical about tragedy as a public category partly for philosophical reasons (it was part of Oakeshott's conception of philosophy, of course, that different modes of human experience – as for example practical life and aesthetics – could not directly blend with one another),[26] but also because he thought that it simply misstated the reality. Human beings, and human actions, are simply what they are. The greatest problem of modern political thought, Oakeshott thought, was the increasingly dominant attempt – or rather attempts, for there are many different versions – to make them something else. It is in this respect, of course, that Oakeshott agreed with Morgenthau about the problems and the errors in rationalism and scientism – both attempt to do this – and their baleful consequences for modern thought. But Oakeshott was equally sceptical about the idea that this situation was in any sense 'tragic'.

Both Oakeshott and Morgenthau are anti-Pelagians, in that they do not believe that there is a man-made short cut to heaven and that the beginning of political wisdom is to see this and accept it. This sensibility is shared, at least to some extent, by Lebow, Mayall and Frost. However, for *these* writers, the human condition must be seen – in rather different ways – as tragic. Oakeshott suspects, I think, that this way of seeing the situation will do more harm than good. While perhaps preferable to the unwarranted optimism that characterizes much rationalism and scientism – whose influence has hardly waned since Morgenthau's time, as Lebow's acute discussion of modern social science in the last chapter of *The Tragic Vision* makes engagingly clear – it carries with it its own risks. First, that it becomes almost a mirror image of the Pelagian case – as I think for example it does in *Scientific Man Versus Power Politics* – running the risk so to speak of throwing the reasonable baby out with the rationalist bathwater. Second, that it confronts those who perhaps do not go this far – as neither Frost nor Mayall, nor indeed Lebow, do – with the awkward task of trying to square an almost impossible circle by arguing on the one hand that recognizing the reality of 'tragedy' in human life should make us more aware of the precariousness of our situation and should discourage us from hubris, and on the other that we can learn from this – somehow – ways of making the world a better or a safer place. Oakeshott's injunction to remember charity and mercy is his oblique way of saying that the best ways of dealing with the dissonances of the world depend upon us accepting human life and its vicissitudes as it is and they are, trying neither to wish them out of existence, as Pelagians do, nor to overly romanticize them, as some other anti-Pelagians do by talking of the 'tragic' character of existence.

Given the increasing encouragement our own time has given to various contemporary versions of modern Pelagianism, I think a robust anti-Pelagianism is both a necessary corrective and the best way of trying to deepen our understanding of the character and trajectories of modern political thought, in international relations as elsewhere. My hunch, however, is that it is better to go with Oakeshott's scepticism than with Morgenthau's sense of the tragic in order to develop it. In this respect, and notwithstanding my broad agreement in many areas with Frost, Mayall and Lebow, I submit that it is right to be sceptical as to the value of seeing the world as a 'tragic' place. George Steiner once wrote of the 'death' of tragedy.[27] I would not be so bold, but perhaps might share his suspicion that the world as it is now is incongruent with the possibilities of the tragic as it was born, all those years ago, 'on the plains of Argos'. The search for a robust anti-Pelagianism in political thought must, I think, reckon with that fact as much as with its scepticism towards the claims of Pelagius.

Notes

For discussions on themes related to Pelagian and anti-Pelagian moral and political thought, I am very grateful to Michael Bentley, Chris Brown, John Burrow, Peter Euben, Mervyn Frost, Ian Hall, Stephen Halliwell, Trevor Hart, Renee Jeffery, Ned Lebow, Andrew Linklater, James Mayall, Noel Malcolm, Ian Markham, Terry Nardin, Mitchell Rologas, Noel O'Sullivan, David Owen, Tracy Strong, and Mike Williams. Moreover, I would like to thank Toni Erskine for suggesting that some of these ideas might be profitably aired first in the pages of *International Relations* and subsequently in this volume, and Ned Lebow for being happy to continue our amicable differences on these topics in print.

1. M. Frost 'Tragedy, Ethics and International Relations', Chapter 2 in this volume, pp. 21–43 (p. 21).
2. J. Mayall (2000) *World Politics: Progress and its Limits* (Cambridge: Polity Press).
3. This phrase is, of course, Martin Wight's. See his essay 'Why is there no International Theory?' in H. Butterfield and M. Wight (eds) (1966) *Diplomatic Investigations* (London: George Allen and Unwin).
4. For excellent illustrations of just how diverse readings of realism can be, see M. J. Smith (1986) *Realist Thought from Weber to Kissinger* (Baton Rouge: Louisiana State University Press); J. Rosenthal (1992) *Righteous Realists: Responsible Power in the Nuclear Age* (Baton Rouge: Louisiana State University Press); A. J. H. Murray (1997) *Reconsidering Realism: Between Cosmopolitan Ethics and Power Politics* (Edinburgh: Keele University Press); R. N. Berki (1981) *On Political Realism* (London: Dent); and M. Williams (2004) *The Realist Tradition and the Limits of International Relations* (Cambridge: Cambridge University Press). Although its overall subject is much wider, the two final chapters of Thomas Pangle and Peter Ahrensdorf (1999) *Justice among Nations: The Struggle for Power and Peace* (Kansas: University of Kansas Press) – on Morgenthau and Kenneth Waltz – are also very good.
5. R. N. Lebow (2003) *The Tragic Vision of Politics: Ethics, Interests and Orders* (Cambridge: Cambridge University Press), on which more in a moment, and J. Mearsheimer (2002) *The Tragedy of Great Power Politics* (New York: Norton).
6. The extent of Thucydides' influence on realist scholarship is considerable, though whether Thucydides himself can be considered a 'realist' of any sort himself is far more contestable. I incline to the view that political realism as a self-conscious tradition of thinking is, in fact, a creature of the late-nineteenth and early-twentieth century and so none of the usual suspects to be found in standard texts on realism – Thucydides, Augustine, Machiavelli, Hobbes – can be seen as a realist on this view, though to say this does not, of course, deny their influence on those who can be so described. The most impressive and judicious treatment of Thucydides' political thinking that I know of, Clifford Orwin's *The Humanity of Thucydides* (Princeton; Princeton University Press (1994)), argues convincingly (to me) that Thucydides is not a realist in the modern sense, but does not deny some quite close affiliations.
7. See, for perhaps the best general treatment of Hamann, I. Berlin (1999) *The Magus of the North* (Oxford: Oxford University Press).
8. Lebow (2003) *The Tragic Vision*, p. 364.
9. Lebow (2003) *The Tragic Vision*, p. 59.
10. H. J. Morgenthau (1946) *Scientific Man versus Power Politics* (Chicago: University of Chicago Press).
11. See the essays gathered together in H. J. Morgenthau (1970) *Truth and Power: Essays from a decade 1960–1970* (New York: Praeger).
12. See C. Frei (2001) *Hans J Morgenthau: An Intellectual Biography* (Baton Rouge: Louisiana State University Press).

13. Morgenthau (1946) *Scientific Man*, p. 6.
14. Morgenthau (1946) *Scientific Man*, p. 221.
15. Frei (2001) *Hans J Morgenthau*, pp. 190–4; Smith (1986) *Realist Thought*, Chapter 6; Rosenthal (1992) *Righteous Realists*. See also Chapter 2 of M. Rologas (2001) *Hans Morgenthau: Intellectual in the Political Sphere* (Ph.D. thesis, St Andrews).
16. In addition to Frei, see especially Williams (2004) *The Realist Tradition*, Chapter 2 on this point.
17. Morgenthau (1946) *Scientific Man*, p. 205.
18. Lebow (2003) *The Tragic Vision*, pp. 360–1.
19. See again, for example, the essays collected in Morgenthau (1970) *Truth and Power*.
20. And now collected in M. Oakeshott (1996) *Religion, Politics and the Moral Life* (ed. Tim Fuller) (New Haven: Yale University Press). Hereafter referred to as *Religion*.
21. Oakeshott (1996) *Religion*, p. 101.
22. Oakeshott (1996) *Religion*, p. 103.
23. Oakeshott (1996) *Religion*, p. 105.
24. Oakeshott (1996) *Religion*, pp. 107–8.
25. Morgenthau, letter to Oakeshott 22 May 1948, *Morgenthau Papers*, B 44.
26. For the two most developed (and subtly different) versions of this argument see M. Oakeshott (1933) *Experience and Its Modes* (Cambridge: Cambridge University Press) and 'The Voice of Poetry in the Conversation of Mankind' in M. Oakeshott (1962) *Rationalism in Politics* (London: Methuen).
27. G. Steiner (1961) *The Death of Tragedy* (London: Faber).

5
Tragedy, Politics and Political Science

Richard Ned Lebow

My reading of Frost, Mayall and Rengger indicates a broad area of agreement concerning the likelihood that complicated policies, domestic or foreign, have unintended, largely negative consequences. These authors believe that such problems are more likely in a world characterized by competing ethical perspectives. Frost is more optimistic than either Mayall or Rengger that a transformation of the international system is nevertheless possible. Drawing on Oakeshott's rejoinder and correspondence with Morgenthau, Rengger questions the utility of tragedy to transcend the arts and make a useful contribution to the practice and study of international relations. My own position is closest to Frost's, and the reasons for this will be apparent in the course of 'unpacking' this debate.

Let us begin with the broad areas of agreement. Frost tells us that many highly regarded students of international relations (e.g., Morgenthau, Niebuhr, Butterfield and most of the 'English School') consider tragedy central to international relations. They associate the potential for tragedy with ethical, religious and cultural diversity. Efforts to impose one's own code on other actors in these circumstances will almost certainly encounter resistance because it threatens their identities as well as their interests.[1] As all political behaviour is 'a struggle for power over men', and 'degrades man by using him as a means to achieve fundamentally corrupt ends', the potential for tragedy is omnipresent.[2] For Morgenthau, tragedy has another broader cause: the 'sin of pride', which blinds us to the realities of international affairs.[3]

Building on Aristotle's reading of Greek tragedies, Frost offers a more precise and useful definition of tragedy. It describes 'a special relationship between an act undertaken for ethical reasons and its negative or painful consequences'. Tragic accounts are narratives that illustrate a chain of events linking an ethical decision to an unintended negative consequence by means of an *agon*, or contest between actors. Their dénouement comes when surviving actors recognize what has happened and are overwhelmed by grief. In their efforts to protect what is important to them, they end up destroying it. This reversal, called a *peripeteia* by Aristotle, is the irony that deepens the sense of tragedy. Tragedy arises, Frost and Aristotle agree, because the world is full of actors not only with clashing ethical perspectives, but with strong, unyielding commitments to them.[4]

Frost's description of tragedy is accepted by neither Mayall nor Rengger. Morgenthau's evocation of 'the sin of pride' nevertheless directs our attention to an important component of tragedy for the Greeks: the idea of hubris.[5] For tragedians, and Greeks more generally, hubris is a category error. People commit hubris when they confuse themselves with the gods in their belief that they can transcend human limitations. The tragic playwrights understand hubris as the result of otherwise commendable character traits and commitments. Thucydides associates it with cleverness, self-confidence, forethought, decisiveness, initiative and risk taking, the very qualities that lead to political success. For Pericles and the citizens of Athens, success stimulates the appetite for further successes while blinding them to the attendant risks. Hubris is manifest as over-confidence in one's own judgement and ability to control events. It encourages leaders and followers to mistake temporary ascendancy for a permanent state of affairs.

Hubris leads us back to Frost's description of tragedy through the mechanisms responsible for policy failure. The kind of bad judgement and irrational risk taking that hubris encourages angers other actors because it most often finds expression in efforts to control and impose one's values on them. Such conflicts presuppose the prior existence of the clashing ethical perspectives that lie at the core of Frost's understanding of tragedy. Invoking an understanding of hubris that harks back to the *Iliad*, Aristotle defines it as 'the serious assault on the honor of another, which is likely to cause shame, and lead to anger and attempts at revenge'.[6]

Hubris leads us beyond Frost's characterization of tragedy by focusing our attention on the role of agency, and, more specifically, on the kinds of actors most likely to succumb to hubris. For Homer and the tragedians, those most likely to succumb are invariably the powerful: kings and warriors like Agamemnon, Ajax and Creon, who lose their self-control and respect for the *nomos* that legitimizes their power and fame. Oedipus is an interesting variant on this theme. He remains respectful of the laws of humankind, but loses sight of the limits of human knowledge and power. He gains a kingdom and queen by winning two contests: the first with his father Laius at the crossroads, and then with the Sphinx outside of Thebes. He loses his wife and throne by 'winning' another contest, this time with himself. Against the advice of his wife and chief advisor, he uses his authority and formidable intellect to prove to himself that he can discover the cause of the Theban plague. *Oedipus* reflects the Greek understanding of the human dilemma. Tragedy is inescapable, and efforts to circumvent it by power and intellect risk making it more likely.

Mayall and Rengger pick up on this aspect of tragedy. Mayall agrees with Frost that awareness of tragedy is 'a necessary antidote' to the hubris of progressive thought and its unwillingness to accept responsibility for initiatives carried out in its name that fail to produce their intended outcomes. Mayall acknowledges that progress has been made in some regions towards banishing war and enhancing human rights, but denies that it constitutes 'uncontested evolution towards a global human rights culture'.[7] He questions the existence of a global civil society and the appeal of a universal standard on which it is based. International environments are not always hospitable to progressive projects, he warns. And agreement about core values and strategies – so essential to cooperation – is even difficult among actors who share common 'lifeworlds'.[8] More fundamentally, he doubts the ability of human beings to transcend the tragic dimension of politics. 'Even if one pattern of behavior with tragic consequences can be avoided, another is always likely to loom up from beyond the horizon.'[9] Rengger concurs, observing that such a pessimistic outlook is common to realists, who view the political world as one of 'recurrence and repetition'. They consider the tension between moral self-understanding and the imperatives of political life as unavoidable and insurmountable.[10] Greek tragedians, Thucydides included, were undeniably realists in this sense. They believed that the cycle of *hubris* (arrogance), *atē* (seduction) *hamartia* (missing the mark, miscalculation), and *nemesis* (catastrophe) would repeat itself as long as humans stride the earth.

It is useful to distinguish two levels of coping with tragedy. First, and least visionary, is an attempt to finesse some tragedies by knowledge of their existence and general causes. Sensitivity to ethical dilemmas, knowledge of one's own and others' identities, self-restraint in the pursuit of goals, efforts to gain support for them by persuasion instead of coercion, and tentative rather than all-out commitments to goals may have the potential to reduce vulnerability to tragedy. There is also the more ambitious goal of altogether transcending the tragic condition. Enlightenment philosophers, liberals and socialists have all shared this vision, which rests on the ability of reason to construct an order that will harmonize human interests and allow general fulfilment of human needs.

Morgenthau fits comfortably in the first category, and Rengger believes that Frost, Mayall and I do, too. Rengger represents my position accurately, quoting lines from *Tragic Vision of Politics* to the effect that immersion in tragedy can encourage conceptions of self and order that act as antidotes to hubris.[11] Hubris, of course, is only one cause of tragedy, and the possibility remains of tragedies arising from clashing ethical imperatives.

Frost is primarily interested in tragedy as a normative theory that allows us to frame and understand ethical dilemmas and their consequences more clearly. With respect to policy, he draws largely pessimistic conclusions. Well-intentioned people acting ethically can produce negative outcomes. If such outcomes are possible in interactions among people in the same family, church or state, 'the chances of progress will be even slighter when we encounter people with ethical systems sharply opposed to ours'.[12] He follows with strong arguments against the beneficial consequences of awareness and learning. Central to the dynamics and dramatic power of tragedy is the assumption that full knowledge of the consequences of their actions would not have dissuaded actors from making the same agonizing choices. Their choices are constrained because they flow from their identities; they act as they must, making the ensuing conflicts unavoidable. Their choices are generally responsible ones. Aeschylus, Sophocles, Euripides and Shakespeare's characters carefully consider the likely consequences of their behaviour and are blindsided by possibilities they did not, or could not have predicted. Tragedy cannot be prevented by knowledge of past tragedies or more careful decision-making.[13]

Frost is a great believer in the benefits of global civil society, but recognizes that it poses ethical dilemmas with possibly tragic outcomes. As citizens of states and global society, we routinely confront 'lose-lose' dilemmas that force us to choose between the individual rights of global citizens and the seeming interests of our national units. Tragedy nevertheless has a transformative potential because of its ability to bring these dilemmas to our attention, intensify our dissatisfaction with the conditions responsible for them, prompt us to search for the most just arrangements, and commit us to their realization in practice. The interaction of reason and emotions in this way was an underlying cause of the transformation of the Republic of South Africa and post-war Western Europe.[14]

Mayall agrees that the peaceful overthrow of *apartheid* in the Republic of South Africa and the institutionalization of peaceful inter-state relations in Europe are impressive achievements, but denies that they are evidence of an 'uncontested evolution towards a global human rights culture'.[15] In his view, current efforts by Western powers to promote democracy are as much rhetorical as real, and provoke opposition by would-be losers to the extent they are taken seriously. They are also unrealistic – as Kant recognized – in the absence of a universal, cosmopolitan culture and one, moreover, that recognizes group as well as individual rights. Such a culture would require serious constraints on sovereignty, which are simply not in the offing. The more feasible alternative is an imperial democracy imposed by the United States, which, like other empires, demands the rights and privileges it denies subject people. Rather than promoting a global civil society, such an informal empire is more likely to collapse 'under the combined force of cynical hypocrisy abroad and savage attack from the unassimilated at home'.[16]

Rengger is just as pessimistic. Realist thinking, he reminds us, derives its intellectual and moral power from its recognition that that political necessity almost always trumps ethical considerations. Nothing has changed in this respect since the end of the Cold War. Conflict and war 'seem to be everywhere ascendant', aspirations for a new world order have been exposed as 'facile and deluded', and Hobbes' famous twins – force and fraud – 'seem once more to be in the driving seat of international affairs'.[17] Rengger also doubts that knowledge about tragedy can make the world less tragic. He cites Morgenthau in support. In *Scientific Man Versus Power Politics*, where Morgenthau discussed his understanding of tragedy, he argued that human beings are flawed and can never overcome their imperfections.[18] If Morgenthau is right, Rengger insists, 'then even the relatively modest hopes entertained by Mayall or Lebow might well turn out to be mistaken'.[19]

Rengger's reading of *Scientific Man Versus Power Politics* is unimpeachable, but this work does not represent Morgenthau's final position on human fallibility. Morgenthau wrote the book in the immediate aftermath of the worst irruption of barbarism spawned by Western civilization. His marginal life in Germany, academic humiliation in Geneva, loss of position and possessions in Madrid, anxious wanderings in Europe in search of a visa to a safe haven, struggles to survive economically in New York and Kansas City, and loss of grandparents in the Holocaust darkened his mood and sapped his faith in human

reason. Morgenthau was nevertheless too intellectually curious, reflective and open-minded to allow his *Weltanschauung* to ossify. His intellectual growth did not stop with his early post-war books, but continued
throughout his career. By the 1970s, he became convinced that the Cold
War had been resolved de facto by mutual acceptance of the post-war
political and territorial status quo in Europe. He regarded with interest
and approval Western European efforts to build a more peaceful conti-
nent on the twin foundations of parliamentary democracy and suprana-
tional institutions. Both transformations, he explicitly recognized, were
based on learning and reason.[20]

Even more than Frost and Mayall, Rengger doubts the normative
value of tragedy. He draws on the fascinating exchange between Hans
Morgenthau and Michael Oakeshott following the publication of
Scientific Man Versus Power Politics. Oakeshott was favourably impressed
by Morgenthau's book, but not by his invocation of tragedy. He insisted
that tragedy was art, not life.[21] Morgenthau stuck to his guns and wrote
back that tragedy was 'a quality of existence, not a creation of art'.[22] The
two men came out of different intellectual traditions. For Morgenthau,
steeped in German literature and philosophy, tragedy was a natural discourse, and a language he found useful to frame his opposition to the
liberal and idealistic assumption that reason and good will could construct institutions that would promote more or less harmonious social
relations at every level of interaction. Oakeshott thought and wrote in
a highly idiosyncratic framework. Both discourses serve their purposes
admirably, and there may be some intellectual payoff to having parallel
ways of authoring critiques. A relevant analogy is to the damaging
consequences of hyper-individualism. Sophocles and Thucydides have
much to say about this subject, and use the tropes and forms of Greek
tragedy to examine the causes and destructive effects of such behaviour
at the family, state and inter-polis levels. Tocqueville, drawing on the
writings of Montesquieu and Condorcet, has made a similar argument
by using the concept of 'self-interest well understood'.[23] Once again,
we benefit from multiple discourses, which are more reinforcing than
cross-cutting, and enrich our understanding of a phenomenon by framing it differently.

None of our authors argues that knowledge of tragedy has much
practical value. Such a claim is, however, implicit in Thucydides, just
as it is explicit in the later Morgenthau. Why would Thucydides have
invested decades in researching and writing his history and offer it as
a 'possession for all time' if he thought human beings and their societies were prisoners of circumstance and fate? He must have believed

that people possess at least some ability to control their destinies. Psychotherapy assumes that people will repeatedly enact counterproductive scripts until they confront and come to terms with the experiences that motivate this behaviour. This can only be achieved through regression; people must allow themselves to relive painful experiences they have repressed and come to understand how they shape their present behaviour. Sophists relied on a somewhat similar process. Their works were offered as courses of study that engage the emotions and mind. By experiencing the elation, disappointment, anguish and other emotions a story provoked, and by applying reason to work through its broader meaning and implications, readers could gain enlightenment. Neither sophists nor analysts *tell* readers or analysands what lessons to learn; both believe that lessons can only be learned and come to influence behaviour when they are the result of a process of cathartic self-discovery. Thucydides' account of the Peloponnesian War encourages Athenians and other Greeks to relive traumatic political experiences in the most vivid way and to work through their meaning and implications for their lives and societies. I believe he harboured the hope that such a course of 'therapy' could help free people of the burdens of the past and produce the kind of wisdom that could enable some societies to transcend their scripts.[24]

Frost believes that civil society in the West is the product of this kind of learning. He is hopeful that a global civil society will emerge that will promote human rights and peaceful inter-state relations. Mayall insists that an effective global civil society requires preconditions which are not present in today's world. He may be right, but cultural diversity and lack of democracy in China, many Muslim countries and much of Africa do not preclude the possibility of making some progress towards global civil society. Movement towards democracy in many Pacific Rim countries over the course of the last two decades is convincing evidence of precisely this kind of progress. It is also possible that more favourable conditions will emerge in other regions of the world – and in the United States – at some time in the future.

Rengger bases his pessimism on the twin pillars of tragedy and history. Tragedy and social progress are not necessarily mutually exclusive. If the frequency and scope of tragedy can be reduced through learning, progress is possible even if universal harmony and accurate prediction of the consequences of human behaviour are not. History teaches Rengger that fear-based worlds have always been the default condition of international relations. But the future need not resemble the past. Until the second half of the twentieth century, death by infectious disease was unavoidable – unless one died of some other cause. Enormous progress has been made in reducing the effects of pathogens, and we may be on the cusp of major breakthroughs with respect to mortality itself. If young doctors and scientists did not have faith in the possibility of progress, none of these advances would have been made. Politics is different from science and medicine in the sense that faith in progress can have negative consequences when it is based on incorrect assumptions and leads to naïve and unsuccessful policies. This is, after all, one of the principal insights of tragedy. Policies tempered by the lessons of tragedy and history, and implemented by skilful leaders do hold out the prospect of progress. The so-called lessons of history can be a real impediment to progress if they are uniformly pessimistic. Realism has the unfortunate potential to make our expectations of fear-based world self-fulfilling – just as naïve notions of escaping from them can make them even more fearful.

Is a belief in progress compatible with tragedy? Mayall and Rengger would have us believe not. For classical Greeks, *sophrosunē* (the restraint imposed on desires by reason) was the antidote to hubris. Given the limited ability of ancients to control their environment, *sophrosunē* took the form of accommodation to the vagaries of life and acceptance of its hard realities. The Greek emphasis on *sophrosunē* and the Enlightenment belief in the ability of human beings to harness and tame their environment represent two extreme responses – both based on the exercise of reason. If thoughtful Greeks could observe our world, and rethink their understanding of the human condition in light of modern conditions and possibilities, they might conclude that the golden mean – the *medan agan*, so central to their approach to life – describes a position somewhere between ancient acceptance and modern activism. If so, it would find expression in cautious hopes for progress, tempered by awareness of the dangers of forgetting the inherent limitations of human beings.

Notes

1. M. Frost, 'Tragedy, Ethics, and International Relations', Chapter 2, this volume, pp. 21–43.
2. H. J. Morgenthau (1947) *Scientific Man vs. Power Politics* (Chicago: University of Chicago Press), p. 167.
3. H. J. Morgenthau (1948) *Politics Among Nations* (New York: Alfred Knopf), note 4, p. 11, and (1948) 'The Political Science of E. H. Carr', *World Politics*, 1/127, 127–34.
4. Frost, 'Tragedy, Ethics and International Relations'; Aristotle, *Poetics*, 11.1452 a32 and 24.1460 a27–31.

5. Morgenthau errs in reading into tragedy the Judeo-Christian understandings of sin, a concept that was alien to classical Greek culture.
6. Aristotle, *Rhetoric*, 1378 b28–29.
7. J. Mayall, 'Tragedy, Progress and the International Order', Chapter 3, this volume, pp. 44–52 (p. 45).
8. A. Schutz (1989) *Structures of the Life World*, Vol. 2 (Evanston: Northwestern University Press).
9. Mayall, 'Tragedy, Progress and the International Order', p. 46.
10. N. Rengger, 'Tragedy or Scepticism? Defending the Anti-Pelagian Mind in World Politics', Chapter 4, this volume, pp. 53–62.
11. Rengger, 'Tragedy or Skepticism?'; R. N. Lebow (2003) *The Tragic Vision of Politics: Ethics, Interests, and Orders* (Cambridge: Cambridge University Press), p. 364.
12. Frost, 'Tragedy, Ethics, and International Relations', p. 29.
13. Frost, 'Tragedy, Ethics, and International Relations', pp. 30–31.
14. Frost, 'Tragedy, Ethics, and International Relations', p. 40.
15. Mayall, 'Tragedy, Progress, and the International Order', p. 45.
16. Mayall, 'Tragedy, Progress, and the International Order', p. 51.
17. Rengger, 'Tragedy or Skepticism?', this volume.
18. Morgenthau, *Scientific Man vs. Power Politics*.
19. Morgenthau, *Scientific Man vs. Power Politics*.
20. Lebow, *The Tragic Vision of Politics*, Chapter 5.
21. Rengger, 'Tragedy or Skepticism?', quoting Oakeshott.
22. Hans J. Morgenthau, letter to Michael Oakeshott, 22 May 1948, Morgenthau Papers, B44, quoted in Rengger, 'Tragedy or Skepticism?', p. 59.
23. A. de Tocqueville (2000) *Democracy in America*, trans. and ed. by H. C. Mansfield and D. Winthrop (Chicago: University of Chicago Press), II, pt. 2, Chapter 8, p. 501.
24. Lebow, *Tragic Vision of Politics*, Chapters 4 and 7 for elaboration of this argument.

Part II
Tragedy and International
Relations as Political Theory

6

Tragedy, 'Tragic Choices' and Contemporary International Political Theory

Chris Brown

In popular discourse, 'tragedy' is a term commonly used to describe something almost unbearably sad, such as the death of a child in a road accident, the onset of dementia in a famous novelist, or, rather more absurdly, the loss of an important football match.[1] No one has the authority to say that such a usage is simply wrong, but what we can say is that it is somewhat impoverished and impoverishing; a better under-standing of the history of the term adds to our capacity to make moral judgements. In origin, tragedy was a politico-aesthetic term to refer to a bad situation that grew out of a moral dilemma, rather than developing from something as meaningless, say, as a traffic accident or a disease – but here there are important distinctions to be made. Shakespearean tragedy involves the (essentially Christian) proposition that potentially good people are brought low by character faults – Othello is jealous, Macbeth ambitious – but while some Greek tragedies involve the same notion, others do not.[2] In one of the greatest of Greek tragedies, Antigone has done nothing to deserve her fate, she is simply caught between the familial duty to give a decent burial to her brother, and the edict of her uncle, Creon, who has forbidden such an act in the interest of the city.[3] In the Greek moral universe, as in ours (or at least mine) but (mostly) not in Shakespeare's, bad things do happen to good people, and with no possibility of redemption beyond the grave.

Antigone faces a choice between two duties; she chooses to neglect her duty to the city in favour of her duty to her brother, and we (most of us) – presumably along with Sophocles and his audience – applaud her action, but there can be no denying that she does have a duty to Thebes, her city, which she has ignored. It is this sense that human action sometimes, perhaps often, involves a choice between two radically incompatible but equally undesirable outcomes, that whatever we do in a given situation we will be, from one perspective, acting wrongly, which constitutes for many contemporary writers the essence of a tragic vision of the world.

It is easy to see why this conception of tragedy should have such an appeal to classical realist theorists of international relations. The notion that the search for security can actually lead to insecurity can be expressed as a sort of tragic dilemma. John Mearsheimer does exactly this in his book *The Tragedy of Great Power Politics*.[4] Mearsheimer is a so-called offensive realist who argues that states are obliged to expand and seek hegemony; this is (potentially) a 'tragedy' because it can lead to conflicts which no-one actually sought. Other realists have taken recently to looking to the Classical World for inspiration, and in particular to the Peloponnesian War – see, for example, Richard Ned Lebow's *The Tragic Vision of Politics* – and it is easy to understand how this orientation would feed an interest in 'tragic visions'.[5] Several of the other contributions to this volume so far also revolve around realist themes. Whether James Mayall, Mervyn Frost and Nicholas Rengger would appreciate being described as realists is somewhat doubtful. Nevertheless, at a minimum, their take on the world is largely state-centric and gives due importance to the role of power in international relations, and, as a result, they are sensitive to the tragic dilemmas that the world throws up – even if they differ as to whether such dilemmas are actually resolvable (Frost vs. Mayall) or harbour Oakeshottian doubts as to whether the aesthetic notion of tragedy has any political referent (Rengger).[6]

My focus in this essay is somewhat different. Contra Rengger/Oakeshott, I wish to suggest that the notion of tragedy is one that has political purchase, but rather than make this case in a context where the term is quite widely used – that is, in debates over classical realism – I wish to establish the point in a context where it is rarely, if ever, used – that is, in the work of international political theorists who have addressed notions such as intervention, human rights and international or global justice. Most of these writers, and especially cosmopolitans in the analytical tradition, can find no place for the notion of tragedy in their work, and this, I believe, works to their disadvantage at a number of levels.[7] The same is also true of many of those theorists who emerge from a legal background and of a great deal of popular commentary on these topics, but for my purposes the analytical tradition is particularly interesting because of its antecedents.[8] I want to take a step back, look at these antecedents, and say a few words about the way in which the tradition handles the notion of tragedy. This will involve briefly exploring the notion of 'tragic choices' and setting out why this notion is such a long way away from any idea of tragedy that might be recognized by the Greeks.

Tragic choices?

There is a particular style to analytical political theory which involves an extraordinary, at times painfully detailed, attention to the importance of constructing unbreakable chains of close theoretical reasoning, with the intention of providing an absolutely airtight account of the problem in question. Most such theorists would regard this as a statement of the blindingly obvious; the fact that most, if not all, of the major political philosophers produced work that contained contradictions, and left loose ends untied, is regarded as a strike against those classics, rather than as a reflection of their inevitably inadequate attempts to cope with the untheorizable complexities of human existence. When a writer such as Michael Walzer emulates the past by employing under-specified concepts ('supreme emergency' for example) or leaving certain key questions unresolved, he is described as a 'phenomenologist of the moral life' (Jon Elster's phrase) who stays on the surface of events, unlike proper political philosophers who are intolerant of ambiguity and unresolved dilemmas.[9] Problems are there to be solved, and if we have not solved them it is because we have not thought hard enough about them, or are awaiting a Darwin or a Newton to provide us with a paradigm. Alternatively, when stupidity seems implausible, it might be because we are not motivated to solve them, that is, there is something wrong with our values, or we are dominated by self-interest.

This attitude can be traced back to the hard-line utilitarian belief that all actions are either mandated or forbidden as positive or negative contributions to the greatest happiness, which, of course, is a position that precludes the possibility of a clash between two, effectively morally equal, courses of action. From a Benthamite perspective, one is almost certain to be better than the other and thus can be adopted without regret. There is also, perhaps counter-intuitively, a Kantian dimension to the analytical frame of mind. Although – or perhaps because – Kant stresses intentions rather than consequences, his framework is equally inimical to a tragic view of the world; do the right thing and you will be vindicated, whatever actually happens – and 'the right thing' to do is something that the moral law hard-wired into us all will identify. Action cannot be tragic if it reflects a good will; this is apparently the exact opposite of the utilitarian view that action cannot be tragic if it maximizes utility, but the two leading branches of 'modern moral philosophy' agree in denying the possibility of genuine tragedy.[10]

Ironically, the most prominent work of analytical political theory that investigates so-called tragic choices actually illustrates the absence of a genuine concept of tragedy here, and does so in two distinct ways. First, the kind of tragic choices that Guido Calabresi and Philip Bobbitt analyse concern, for example, a situation in which there is one kidney dialysis machine and two people who need to use it – the choice as to which individual should live is, on their definition, a tragic choice.[11] Actually, such a situation is hardly a conflict between two demanding duties where to act is to act wrongly whatever is done. Wrong-doing is not an issue here; assuming that the physicians use a fair procedure to decide who should have access to the scarce resource they cannot be said to have wronged the patient who dies in the absence of treatment. Her death is unfortunate and sad, but not tragic. But, second, what is actually further away from the notion of tragedy is the approach these writers employ to resolve the dilemmas they have identified. Although they do not deny that in many instances some kind of sacrifice of value will have to be made, most of their effort is devoted to working round the problem, either by attempting to find new ways to get out of the dilemma they find themselves in or by inventing a more sensitive decision procedure which will allow cases to be differentiated, and allow a choice to be made which is not 'tragic'. For the kind of choices with which these writers are concerned, this strategy makes sense – but if these choices were genuinely tragic it would be an inadequate response.

Consider the example offered by Agamemnon, as set out in the first part of the *Oresteia*.[12] As leader of the Greeks he is obliged to do what is necessary to achieve success in the war with Troy, but in order to allow a favourable wind for the Greek fleet, Artemis demands the sacrifice of Agamemnon's daughter Iphigenia, which, obviously, violates his duty as a father. Agamemnon carries out the sacrifice, setting the scene for Clytemnestra's revenge and Aeschylus' trilogy.[13] Has Agamemnon acted wrongly? Of course he has, but had he acted differently he would also have acted wrongly, violating his duty to the Greeks by dooming their common enterprise. Still, interestingly, the thrust of the play is unsympathetic to this dilemma, leaving a clear sense that Agamemnon is unambiguously in the wrong and thus has brought a dishonourable death upon himself. The reason for this attitude appears to be that Agamemnon is at fault for refusing to accept the tragic nature of his decision, and because he does not see the tragedy, we are not obliged to either. The Chorus tells us that, when carrying out the sacrifice, he gags his daughter with a leather strap to prevent her from crying out and uttering a curse;[14] this demeans and trivializes something that is majestic and awful, denying Iphigenia the dignity to which she is entitled.[15] Later, when he returns to Argos he makes no mention of what he has done, offering neither explanation nor any kind of plea for forgiveness to his daughter's mother. Clytemnestra raises the subject herself, in a coded way, referring to her misery at the loss of a child, but then saying she was referring to her son Orestes.[16] Still, Agamemnon refuses to respond. He refuses to accept the implications of what he has done, but this denial does not make the tragedy less real; indeed, this refusal actually ensures that he takes full responsibility for Iphigenia's death. His death, which follows immediately, is equally squalid and unheroic. The Chorus are horrified and at first turn on Clytemnestra, but her invocation of her dead daughter gives them pause for thought – '[Each] charge meets counter-charge. None can judge between them'. Clytemnestra must pay for what she has done, but they acknowledge that hers was not a gratuitous act. '[The] one who acts must suffer – that is law' – and this applies retrospectively to Agamemnon as much as prospectively to Clytemnestra.[17]

The point I wish to make here is that, from the perspective of modern moral philosophy as exemplified by the work of the theorists cited above, Agamemnon has handled the tragic choice posed by the request of Artemis in exactly the right way. He has assessed the situation, decided that one of the two apparently unacceptable alternatives is, in fact, superior to the other, and acted on the basis of this assessment. Then, having done so, he puts the whole affair out of his mind, like a good chief executive who has just made a difficult, but ultimately clear-cut decision. The problem is that this simply does not correspond to our powerful moral intuitions. We cannot accept that the sacrifice of a daughter be treated as an uncontroversial decision, after which we can simply get on with our lives.

Tragedy and international political theory

To summarize the argument so far: tragedy involves a situation where duties are in radical conflict, such that whatever is done will involve wrong-doing; by definition, this conflict cannot be wished away – the only way to preserve integrity and honour is to accept the tragic nature of one's choice, that is, to acknowledge that to act is to do wrong. My contention is that much modern political theory refuses to accept the existence of tragedy or make this acknowledgement. Now, how does this play out with respect to international political theory (IPT)?

First, we must establish that there are genuine tragedies involved in the subject matter of IPT. This, I think, is not too difficult. Consider two notions central to IPT's agenda: humanitarian intervention and global poverty relief. Forceful humanitarian interventions involve a clear clash of duties and values. On the one hand, it is widely agreed (and endorsed by the UN General Assembly) that there is a 'responsibility to protect' populations from extreme oppression and that this responsibility shifts from the domestic to the international level if states themselves are the oppressor.[18] On the other hand, the use of force internationally in circumstances other than self-defence or in the absence of a specific UN Security Council mandate (almost always unobtainable) is contrary to international law, involves violating our duty to respect the choices made by local communities, and will, inevitably, lead to the deaths of innocent third parties.[19] Thus, to act is to do wrong – and 'action' here includes consciously chosen inaction, as in Rwanda in 1994. Global poverty relief poses less dramatic issues (although poverty actually kills far more people than physical oppression), but there are still radical clashes of duty involved. Charitable donations from one country to another involve no tragic choices, but the common assertion that 'we' (individuals, peoples, states, international institutions) have extensive duties to humanity that potentially contradict our duties to our fellow-citizens (and to our own personal projects) does pose potentially tragic choices.[20] This is particularly the case when it comes to trade policy; genuinely free trade clearly involves rich countries sacrificing the interests of domestic workers in the medium term while protectionism clearly damages the interests of workers in low-wage countries. Again, to act is to do wrong to someone to whom one has obligations.

The key question, in both cases, is whether the genuinely tragic nature of these situations is recognized in the discourse. The answer, I think, is generally, no. On the matter of intervention, there is one writer who, although without usually employing the term, clearly understands the tragic nature of the choices that have to be made. Walzer's oeuvre from the early 1970s onwards, including major works such as *Just and Unjust Wars* and *Arguing about War*, has been suffused with just such an understanding.[21] In an early paper, he cast the problem of political action in terms of 'dirty hands' rather than tragedy; the two notions are obviously not the same, but, 'dirty hands' shares with the tragic the central ethical understanding that sometimes to act is to do wrong and, crucially, that this is a fact about the world that must not be denied or glossed over.[22] Setting Walzer's work to one side, it is difficult to find other international political theorists who are sensitive to the dilemmas of intervention. Analytical theorists of justice on the whole do not try to theorize intervention, but when they do, as in Part II of Charles Beitz's *Political Theory and International Relations*, the tendency is to see things in purely pragmatic terms. Beitz sees no principled reason to abstain from intervening when local conditions do not meet universal standards; the only issue is whether or not action will make things worse, with no sense that there might be incompatible values involved.

The absence of a sense of the tragic is illustrated in a recent debate on the 2003 Iraq War between Fernando Tesón and Terry Nardin.[23] Tesón's defence of the war focuses exclusively on Saddam's tyranny; Nardin's rejection of Tesón's position focuses exclusively on US imperialism and the human cost of the war. Nardin cannot see Saddam's mass graves; Tesón cannot see anything else. Like most critics of the war, Nardin cannot see that inaction in the face of tyranny is, in fact, a form of action which brings its own responsibilities and duties.[24] Tesón sees this point, but is less willing to acknowledge that by acting the Coalition took upon itself the responsibility for the subsequent carnage. Neither writer seems willing to accept that a genuinely moral dilemma is involved here. I should add that I have chosen the debate between these two scholars because they are both thoughtful, morally sensitive analysts – other supporters and opponents of the war are so clearly partisan that it is inevitable they would miss the tragic nature of the choice that had to be made in 2003. See, for example, Michael Moore's portrayal of pre-2003 Iraq as a kind of utopia with children happily playing in the streets until overshadowed by US bombers, or Donald Rumsfeld's 'stuff happens' as a response to the chaos caused by the US military's unpreparedness for the occupation of Iraq. The inability of Tesón and Nardin to see the tragic nature of the situation they are discussing is striking precisely because they are not crude propagandists.

When it comes to questions of global distributive justice, the influence of analytical political theory's disdain for tragedy is readily apparent. The first major statement of the case for wholesale redistribution came from Peter Singer, whose utilitarian take on 'Famine, Affluence and Morality' presents the problem in starkly (over) simple terms.[25] Money spent on the Sydney Opera House could be going towards famine relief in Bangladesh; all aspects of human behaviour are reducible to each other, and the felicific calculus will tell us what to do – specifically, reduce our own welfare to the point where transfers to others would equalize marginal utility. Poverty and death from malnutrition are 'bad' and we must do whatever is necessary to abolish them – and if this involves other 'bad' things (e.g., by violating self-determination and personal autonomy), so be it because these bads are not as important as the overriding need to deal with the most pressing source of disutility. Singer, of course, is a professional extremist, someone who cannot resist taking a position and running with it until it makes no sense. Later cosmopolitan writers such as Brian Barry, Beitz and Thomas Pogge accept the case for redistribution without buying into Singer's extreme utilitarianism – indeed the attempt to establish the requirements of global *justice* is precisely intended to provide an alternative to utilitarianism.

Where, however, Singer is typical, is in the way in which he backs away from the implications of his extreme position. First, he allows us to reject his own personal standard and simply transfer wealth to the point at which to continue would involve us in the loss of something of moral significance, rather than of *comparable* moral significance to the death of a child. But then he argues that, actually, world poverty could be ended by a relatively small transfer from the rich to the poor – so the level of sacrifice that is being demanded of us is not such as to destroy our capacity to develop our own projects, and rich countries will not be expected to impoverish their citizens. This sense that, in point of fact, the world's problems can be solved at no great cost to anyone is a common theme of a great deal of cosmopolitan writing – one of the few exceptions to this rule is Barry, who actually acknowledges that people in the West will have to accept radical cuts in their living standards in order to meet the requirements of global justice.[26]

There is a kind of conjuring trick here that is common to much academic writing and popular commentary on the problem of world poverty. The anti-globalization (better, anti-global capitalism) movement, and sympathetic political theorists such as Pogge and Beitz, will argue strongly for global transfers of wealth, for radical change to protect the environment and for changes in the World Trade Organization (WTO) and the International Monetary Fund (IMF) in order to allow 'Southern' producers to compete in Northern markets. But then, when it comes to the implications of these policies for people in the North, something strange happens. 'Fair Trade' is suddenly about protecting jobs in both North *and* South. With no sense of irony, a French farmer, José Bové, becomes an iconic figure in the movement on the principle, apparently, that defending the Common Agricultural Policy and subsidized French farms is a way of showing that 'the world is not for sale'.[27] Meanwhile, Northern trade unions get in on the act, and, at the famous Battle of Seattle in 1999, US steelworkers demonstrated their commitment to global fair trade by throwing imported Brazilian steel into Seattle harbour. These are, of course, popular and not academic positions, but, I would argue, the work of writers such as Pogge and Beitz displays the same contradiction, albeit expressed in more sophisticated terms. Apart from honourable exceptions such as Barry, the relatively few writers who are prepared to acknowledge that genuinely free trade would, in the medium term at least, hurt the interests of Western workers but should, nonetheless, be adopted, are unapologetic supporters of the WTO such as Jagdish Bhagwati, or old style Marxists such as Meghnad Desai.[28] That a Marxist should be so up-front about this need occasion no surprise; Marx himself was originally a classicist, and his work is infused with a very real sense of the tragic. He would have little sympathy for the romanticism of so much modern writing on the failings of global capitalism.

What, then, must we do when confronted with oppression or extreme poverty? My intention here is not to advocate passivity in the face of the world's problems. It may well be the case – I think it is – that some problems have no answer that does not involve genuinely tragic choices, but it is equally true that sometimes we must act even though we know the result will be, one way or another, morally unsatisfactory. What, to me, is important, is that we do not adopt Agamemnon's solution to this dilemma and turn our backs on the tragic element of human existence. Instead, an awareness of tragedy ought to cause us to act modestly, to be aware of our limitations and to be suspicious of grand narratives of salvation which pretend that there are no tragic choices to be made.

Conclusion

IPT is a discourse that is largely devoid of a sense of the tragic dimension to human existence and this absence is intellectually and politically debilitating. It is striking how readily the rhetoric of 'Something must be Done' appeals when people are faced with evidence of oppression and grinding poverty, but it is equally striking how this support usually evaporates when something actually *is* done. The reason for this is not, I suggest, fickleness, or even uncomplicated self-interest, but rather the fact that the original appeal, by failing to acknowledge the moral complexities of the situation, wins a cheap, but transient, victory.

It is, of course, easy to direct such a charge at figures such as Bob Geldof or Bono, but it applies equally, I think, to the more intellectually substantial writers who have been pressing the case for global social justice for a quarter century at least, with very little, if any, impact. These theorists have approached the problem with little sense that there are genuinely tragic choices to be made; instead they have tried to refine away the clashes of duty of which any sensitive observer or citizen will be all too conscious. They try to draw us into a line of reasoning which will take us to a place where we have no alternative but to acknowledge the force of their conclusions. But we (and I speak here for myself, and also for the several generations of students with whom I have read this literature) know that there is something missing, that analytical clarity has been bought at a price, that part of the story is being suppressed. The missing dimension here is, I suggest, a sense of the tragic nature of the dilemmas we face – and perhaps of human existence itself.

Notes

1. I am grateful to Kirsten Ainley, Toni Erskine and Peter Wilson for comments on an earlier version of this paper; the usual disclaimers apply.
2. A. C. Bradley (2005) *Shakespearean Tragedy* ed. John Bayley (London: Penguin Books) was first published in 1904, but is still a core reference point. My thinking on Greek tragedy relies very heavily on M. Nussbaum (1986/2001) *The Fragility of Goodness* (Cambridge: Cambridge University Press) and P. Euben (1990) *The Tragedy of Political Theory* (Princeton: Princeton University Press).
3. Sophocles (1984) *The Three Theban Plays: Antigone*, tr. Robert Fagles (New York: Penguin Books).
4. J. Mearsheimer (2001) *The Tragedy of Great Power Politics* (New York: W. W. Norton).
5. R. N. Lebow (2003) *The Tragic Vision of Politics: Ethics, Interests and Orders* (Cambridge: Cambridge University Press).
6. See M. Frost, 'Tragedy, Ethics and International Relations', Chapter 2; J. Mayall, 'Tragedy, Progress and the International Order', Chapter 3 and N. Rengger, 'Tragedy or Scepticism? Defending the Anti-Pelagian Mind in World Politics', Chapter 4, all in this volume.
7. Representative analytical international/cosmopolitan pieces might include: B. Barry (1998) 'International Society from a Cosmopolitan Perspective', in D. Mapel and T. Nardin (eds) *International Society* (Princeton NJ: Princeton University Press); C. R. Beitz (2000) *Political Theory and International Relations*, 2nd edn (Princeton: Princeton University Press); T. Pogge (2002) *World Poverty and Human Rights* (Cambridge: Polity Press); and their non-cosmopolitan mentor, J. Rawls (1999) *The Law of Peoples* (Cambridge, MA: Harvard University Press).
8. For lawyers working within international political theory see, for example, F. Tesón (1998) *A Philosophy of International Law* (Boulder, CO: Westview Press); T. M. Franck (1992) 'The Emerging Right to Democratic Governance', 86 *American Journal of International Law*, 46.
9. M. Walzer (2000) *Just and Unjust Wars*, 3rd edn (New York: Perseus Books), p. 251 ff. J. Elster (1992) *Local Justice* (New York: Russell Sage Foundation), p. 14.
10. G. E. M. Anscombe (1958) 'Modern Moral Philosophy', *Philosophy*, 33, 1–9.
11. G. Calabresi and P. Bobbitt (1978) *Tragic Choices* (New York: W. W. Norton & Co.). Bobbitt's later work is more sensitive to the tragic dimension of human existence; see, for example, P. Bobbitt (2008) *Terror and Consent* (London: Allen Lane).
12. Aeschylus (1979) *The Oresteia: Agamemnon*, tr. Robert Fagles (London & New York: Penguin Books). Line and page numbers below are taken from

this edition. The influence of Martha Nussbaum and, especially, Peter Euben on the next paragraphs will be immediately apparent.

13. I oversimplify, of course. The house of Atreus is already cursed.

14. Her father called his henchmen on '"[but] slip this strap in her gentle curving lips ... here, gag her hard. A sound will curse the house" – and the bridle choked her voice', line 230 ff. p. 111.

15. A fascinating parallel occurred in a recent English National Opera production of Richard Wagner's Ring Cycle. In the Third Act of *The Valkyre*, in what should be one of the most moving scenes in opera, Wotan takes away the Godhead of his errant but beloved daughter Brunhilde and puts her into a deep sleep by kissing her eyes. ENO's director decided to destroy this scene by having Brunhilde strapped to a gurney and injected with a sedative by white-coated assistants, thereby, presumably deliberately, counteracting what the music is telling us, and making Wotan's action merely sordid.

16. '[Our] child is gone, not standing by our side, the bond of our dearest pledge, mine and yours; by all rights our child should be here ... Orestes. You seem startled.' Line 865 ff., p. 136.

17. Line 1588 ff., p. 167.

18. See International Commission on Intervention and State Sovereignty (2001) *The Responsibility to Protect* (Ottawa: International Development Research Centre); UN General Assembly, World Summit Outcome Document, September 2005, paragraphs 138 and 139.

19. UN Charter, Article 2 (4).

20. The assertion of such as duty – as opposed to simple benevolence – is a feature of all the writers listed in footnote 7 above.

21. See footnote 9 and M. Walzer (2004) *Arguing about War* (New Haven: Yale University Press).

22. M. Walzer (1973) 'Political Action: The Problem of Dirty Hands', *Philosophy and Public Affairs*, 2, 160–80. Collected in M. Walzer (2007) *Thinking Politically: Essays in Political Theory*, ed. David Miller (New Haven: Yale University Press).

23. F. Tesón (2005) 'Ending Tyranny in Iraq'; T. Nardin (2005) 'Humanitarian Imperialism: Response to "Ending Tyranny in Iraq"'; and F. Tesón (2005) 'Of Tyrants and Empires: Response to Terry Nardin', *Ethics & International Affairs*, 19/2.

24. A common failing: virtually all of the academic commentators or 'public intellectuals' who identify themselves as part of the 'Anti-War' movement adopt the same tack. To be against 'war' without any sense of context, of what the alternatives to war in any given situation are, is morally vacuous.

25. P. Singer (1972) 'Famine, Affluence and Morality', *Philosophy and Public Affairs*, 1/1, 229–43.

26. Barry (1998) 'International Society from a Cosmopolitan Perspective'.

27. J. Bové and F. Dufour (2001) *The World is Not for Sale: Farmers against Junk Food* (London: Verso).

28. See J. Baghwati (2004) *In Defence of Globalisation* (Oxford: Oxford University Press) and M. Desai (2002) *Marx's Revenge* (London: Verso).

7
The Tragedy of Tragedy

J. Peter Euben

I am so sympathetic with the enterprise of invigorating classical realism with the study of Greek tragedy and exploring what a tragic sensibility can contribute to international politics generally that my criticisms of the previous chapters may seem perverse. Perverse because I intend to make the appropriation of tragedy for the study of international politics which I endorse *more* rather than less problematic. But I do so in the name of Greek tragedy and ultimately a more challenging appropriation of it.

Mervyn Frost, James Mayall and Nicholas Rengger recognize that you cannot simply use Greek tragedy as if it were a controlled substance or an ingredient in a recipe: adding one part tragedy to one part enlightenment to one part progressivist narrative to one part policy analysis, stir and serve will not do. But though Richard Ned Lebow is right to warn us against the self-fulfilling aspect of pessimism and the convenient political uses to which it has been put, I wonder if he is not too quick to reintegrate tragedy into analysis and faith in progress. For tragedy to 'work' it must master you before you master it. Let me offer three examples from tragedies to dramatize my point.

In Euripides' *Bacchae*, the young King Pentheus refuses to honour the god Dionysus though they are both born in Thebes and are cousins. Indeed, Pentheus tries to imprison the god and what he embodies: the ecstatic, non-rational, boundless, unpredictable pleasures of wine, and forgetfulness, the potentially lethal combination of innocence and violence, play and bloody sacrifice. But the King's attempt to capture the god in the name of security and order not only fails, something like the reverse occurs. It turns out that Pentheus is (or is made to become) attracted to what he so loudly excoriates. Thus the more insistent and frantic his efforts to snare Dionysus, the more he is seduced by him and the more he becomes what he initially dismisses as alien and other.

One of the most chilling scenes in Greek tragedy is where the strutting hyper-masculinist young king, now under the god's sway, dresses as a woman, and preens himself in preparation for spying on what he believes to be women (including his mother), engaging in wanton promiscuity. What he is in fact being prepared for is a sacrifice where he will be beheaded by his own mother.

On my own terms I must be careful how and what sort of 'lessons' I draw from the play. But there are, I think, at least two things one can say about it. The first is that a single-minded devotion to security and order is likely to increase the intensity of the disorder it will eventually bring about, whether it is the return of the repressed or blowback. Secondly, human communities must find a place for the passional foundations of politics even though they are potentially volatile. Reason and reasonableness are as much a part of the problem as they are part of the solution.

That is a conclusion one could draw from my second more famous example: Oedipus in *Oedipus Tyrannos*. As you recall, Oedipus is, or at least starts out being, a consummate problem solver and proto policy analyst. He is quick to see the significance of a problem, analyse its ramifications and possible solutions, and decisive when he thinks he has sufficient information. He is, after all, the man who solved the Sphinx's riddle and saved Thebes and so it is reasonable for him to believe that he is primed to solve the second riddle, 'Who is Laius' killer?', and save Thebes once again. And he does, but at enormous cost and only with the reluctant help of others. The problem is that he is both hunter and hunted, the one who searches and the object of the search, and so when he calls down terrible imprecations against the killer of Laius he is condemning himself.

In fact, it turns out that he has not solved every part of the Sphinx's riddle – 'What creature walks on four legs, two legs, and three legs in a single day' – since *his* feet were bound at birth and he has always walked with a cane.[1] Thus the answer to the riddle, 'man', does not include him, and this exclusion is not only a sign of his 'unnaturalness', but of his ignorance, whether real, feigned, or something in between. For Oedipus's very name points to his feet and the problem of knowledge. If your name were Abandoned Smith you might be curious why.[2]

So this is a man who does not know where he came from nor where he is going. And because he does not (consciously) know who he is, he does not know the meaning of his life and actions. When the meaning becomes clear, and his surface and so far obscured worlds collapse into each other, he puts out his eyes.

What can we say about this man and this play? First of all, this is one enormous case of 'limited information'. But it is a limit that seems endemic to human action. As Frost suggests, seeing or reading *Oedipus Tyrannos* is not a prophylactic. We seem bound to repeat Oedipus's 'mistakes', not in the sense of killing our fathers and marrying our mothers, but in the sense pointed to by Lebow, of becoming subject to what subjected him: confidence that one can see the origins and consequences of one's actions, supposing one has a monopoly of intelligence and foresight, being convinced that prior success guarantees future ones.

Tragedy, Jean-Pierre Vernant wrote, 'has a double character.'

On the one side, it consists in taking counsel with oneself, weighing the for and against and doing the best one can to foresee the order of means and ends. On the other hand, it is to make a bet on the unknown and the incomprehensible and to take a risk on a terrain that remains impenetrable to you. It involves entering the play of supernatural forces ... where one does not know whether they bring success or disaster.[3]

Losing the bet does not excuse the doer because, as Frost and Mayall suggest, tragedy is consequentialist: we are responsible not only for what we have done intentionally but what we have done, period. And what we have done constitutes our character which in turn establishes the kinds of action we will and can do. In these terms it is misleading to concentrate on the moment of decision as a number of contributors do, because that decision is an instance of character and of the aggregate of words and deeds that constitute it.[4]

But what about the audience? Surely they know what Oedipus does not – a situation that establishes what is known as Sophoclean irony. But even this certainty is uncertain. We have been led to believe that the killer of Laius – Oedipus – will be exiled. But he is not (at least in this play). Instead, he is sent back into the house where it all began. In other words, Sophoclean irony is a double irony; we know more but there remains an element of mystery and unpredictability about the course of the play and the course of events. As Rengger puts it in Chapter 4 of this volume, 'the connection between understanding and action' is highly problematic.

It seems that despite our hope, tragedy portrays a world that is not made for us and that we are not made for the world. Human history tells no purposive story and even if it did there is no position outside of ourselves or history from which we could authenticate our activities.[5] As Frost and

Mayall suggest, we have no reason to believe that our lives will come out well in the end, which is why Vernant does *not* talk about good people finding themselves in circumstances where they must choose against something or someone they value. What makes me uneasy about saying (as Frost does) that tragedians were concerned with ethical dilemmas and portray a world full of actors with clashing ethical perspectives and strong unyielding commitments to them is that the language of good and bad seems too much the product of Aristotelian and Christian moralizing.

As an example let me take what Hans Morgenthau (as quoted by Lebow) calls 'the sin of pride'. Leaving aside the problematic use of 'sin', glory, not humility, were important values in Greek culture. More than that, the 'prideful' man made the world come alive, whatever else he might do. In this context it is worth remembering that Oedipus did save Thebes. His knowledge – let us anachronistically call it theoretical – led him to see more comprehensively than others and so allowed him to answer 'man'.[6] But it was precisely that general knowledge that left him blind to the local knowledge about his own particular existence. Is he a victim of pride? The answer is yes and no.

But once again, how can we reconcile such persistent pessimism with the daring of word and deed that characterized Athenian politics? Is it a case of cognitive dissonance? Did the Athenians ignore tragedy on their way to empire? How could they, given that tragedy was part of a religious ritual and form of political education that helped consti- tute democratic culture? How could they if Bernard Knox is right that Oedipus embodied the characteristics of the Athenian audience which means that what they saw on stage as they watched the play was a version of themselves and their current predicaments?[7]

But what exactly did the audience in the theatre take from it to their deliberation in the assembly Council and law courts? It is not easy to say, but I think the speculations of the contributors to this debate over tragedy and international politics are right. Athenians were prob- ably encouraged to rethink their cultural accommodations (such as the status of women and slaves), driven to second thoughts about the relationship of democracy and empire, made a bit less confident about the capacity of human power to shape the practices and ends of collec- tive life, and made even more alert to the dangers of civil war. All these themes are prominent in tragedy.

But how do we reconcile what Lebow calls the pessimism of Greek tragedy with the proverbial daring and extraordinary power of the Athenians? One way is to concentrate not on the content of tragedy but on the writing of it as a thought–deed. Then the 'writing' of tragedy displays the daring the Corinthians (in Thucydides)[8] attribute to the Athenians. Tragedy exemplified an intelligence and insight often absent in the characters on stage. Remember that Sophocles chose his version of the Oedipus story from several possibilities and then added his own inno-vations to that choice. In the play the chorus asks the now blind Oedipus who it was that made him put out his eyes, to which he replies:

It was Apollo, friends, Apollo,
that brought this bitter bitterness, my sorrow to completion.
But the hand that struck me was none but my own.
(1329–33, Grene trans.)

I am suggesting something similar in regard to the creation of the play: there was a tradition that broadly defined who and what Oedipus had to be, but it was Sophocles' hand that shaped the story into the brilliant drama we now have.

My third example is Sophocles' *Antigone* which is referred to by vir-tually every contributor to this debate over tragedy and international politics so far. Here I would make only two points. The first is that the opposition between Antigone (who 'stands for' the family, private life and Chthonic gods) and Creon (who 'stands for' the city, politics and the younger gods) is, at best, overdrawn. Indeed, seeing the world oppositionally is 'Creonic', by which I mean it is part of his strategy of ordering the world into 'with me or against me', impugning the motives of anyone who disagrees with him and insisting on his sanity as opposed to the insanity of Antigone. Even at the outset, his long speech (179–229) defining the attributes of a good leader turns into a loyalty oath from which the old men of the chorus quickly distance themselves. If he 'stands' for anything it is a corrupt political leader who, like Pentheus, takes order as the highest political value. One could say that this is the only rational thing to do, given the preceding civil war. But the question is whether he is not *continuing* the sentiments that underlay that war in the name of preventing a future one. It is worth remembering that Antigone's burying her brother would have saved the *city* of Thebes from destruction; that her last speech honours her fellow citizens, and that despite the family resemblance between the two, the intransigence of a marginal woman does not carry the same ethical weight as the intransigence of the most powerful male.

My second point has to do with the misnamed 'Choral ode in praise of man'.[9] It is an ode all right, but it is not in praise of man. Instead it suggests, as Rengger implies, that every human achievement, including one's capacity for reflection and reason, is shadowed by loss. Such losses are as easily overlooked as Oedipus's feet. In this light one might be sceptical of Lebow's claim that we have made significant improvements in human rights and conflict management by pointing to the presence of child slavery, the sex traffic in young women, and the prevalence of child soldiers.

Drama and the rhythms of politics

Lebow, Frost and Chris Brown emphasize that tragic dramas are particularly memorable ways of telling a story. Paradoxically, stories provide a sense of completion even though each retelling reshapes the story and so reconfigures the completeness. 'The story teller', Walter Benjamin once wrote, 'borrows his authority from death'. Borrowed from the person or people who have died and whose mortality makes a special claim on a shared human condition. Borrowed because speaking of the dead gives them a second voice. That is why tragedy is able to transform suffering that can never be fully spoken or heard into a shared gift of culture. Consider how the beauty of the prose/poetry of Toni Morrison's *Beloved* makes bearable, if it does not partly redeem, the horror of slavery.

But there is a more radical point here and it is made by Brown in his critique of the analytical style's fetish for constructing unbreakable chains of closely-reasoned argument in order to solve political and moral problems. The assumption is that ambiguity and unresolved dilemmas (let us call them riddles) are somehow pathological. But as Brown implies, poetry and drama may better capture the rhythms of action and so of politics than analysis given the latter's epistemological assumptions and methodological endorsements. His point is elaborated by Hannah Arendt who, not coincidentally, is the contemporary theorist who makes the most substantial claims for politics. She is also the thinker who has drawn out the parallels of shared language and resonance between drama and politics. Thus she talks about politics in the language of theatre, of performances and audiences, of those who play a part and those spectators who see the entire play, and of public arenas and spaces of appearance. She even argues that the revelatory quality of action and speech which manifests the agent and speaker, is so tied to the flux of acting and speaking 'that it can be represented only through a kind of repetition, the imitation of mimesis ... which is appropriate only in the drama, whose very name (from the Greek *dran*, to act) indicates that playacting actually is an imitation of acting'.[10]

The contemporary relevance of tragedy

Earlier I warned against any attempt to domesticate Greek tragedy by circumscribing its meaning with familiar categories that allow what is most disturbing about it to be safely assimilated. Part of tragedy's point, I suggested, was the breaking of conventional boundaries as symbolized by Dionysus in Euripides' *Bacchae*. But I have also claimed that Greek drama constituted a form of political education. Here I want to qualify the first claim and elaborate the second as a way of asking what, in the end, is the contemporary relevance of an institution – Greek drama – specific to a time and to a place.

Greek tragedy itself was carefully bounded. It took place at a specific site, a theatre, and at a specified time according to the calendar. Proposed plays competed for the opportunity to be produced and the quality of that production was awarded prizes (or not) by a randomly chosen group of citizens. Unsurprisingly, the meanings of the plays were dependent on the context of performance. It is a context which is, in so many ways, radically different from our own (just consider how significantly Plato, Aristotle and Christianity have influenced our reading of tragedy).

But the theatre was not a wholly enclosed structure. It was open to the sky and the surrounding hills with their monuments and sites for various public functions. I take this combination of enclosure and exposure as a metaphor for reading Greek tragedy. We need to be as attentive to the particular context of performance as we can, so we can translate – literally and metaphorically – the particular into the general. But we must also be attentive to our own context so we can be more attentive to theirs. This means letting the alienness of tragedy work on us even to the extent of letting 'it' interrogate the interpretative apparatus we bring to it.

Indeed, Greek tragedy itself provides a paradigm for us. With few exceptions the action of tragedy was displaced onto other cities (Thebes and Argos) and other times (ancient Athens). This combination of distance and proximity meant that contemporary political and cultural issues were played upon a stage whose historical ground was different from its dramatic ground. The double placement meant that issues were both immediately recognizable and generalized beyond the specific. Whatever else it did and does, Greek tragedy provided and provides paradoxes, dilemmas, riddles, provocations and pathologies about the relationship between violence and ethics; old and young; politics and power; empire and democracy; mortality and divinity; leadership and citizenship; luck and glory; hope and fear; passion and sanity; men and women; rich and poor; the free and enslaved; sight, insight and foresight; and madness and blindness.

Something similar can be said about tragedy as a form of democratic education. What we mean by democracy and culture are importantly different from what the Athenians meant. It would seem peculiar, to say the least, for someone to suggest that people bring the experience of watching television to the sharing of power in the central institutions of our society. Yet there are times when popular culture, including theatre, film and music, play something analogous to a role in challenging the cultural accommodations and political hierarchies that define what the Greeks, looking at us, would probably call a plutocracy.[11]

Thucydides through the lens of tragedy

It seems quite a stretch to claim that Greek tragedy can teach us important things about how to study international politics. But it seems no stretch at all to say that Thucydides can. Indeed, Thucydides has provided a template for analysing two World Wars, the Cold War, the Vietnam War, the Iraq War and even the 'War on Terror'.[12] With this legacy and the authority it conveys, Thucydides helps to define what we mean by politics and political thought. Given this, it is far easier to distil policy implications from the *History* than from the *Bacchae* or *Antigone*, or so it seems.

I believe there are substantial continuities of substance and form between Greek tragedy and Thucydides' *History*, continuities that are significant enough to establish the former as a preface to, and necessary condition for, understanding the latter. If so, then the distance between Greek tragedy and the study of contemporary international politics is not quite the stretch it appeared to be.

I do not want to overstate my case. Greek tragedy was, as I suggested, a cultural, religious and political institution; history was not. There were no history festivals performed before the assembled citizenry in the theatre. Moreover, Thucydides partly defines his project *against* the poets whom he condemns for their rhetorical indulgences and desire for popularity at the expense of truth. While they write to garner applause of the moment before an audience located in specified times and places, he seeks the applause of those future statesmen and citizens who seek to understand the nature of politics.

Yet when we look at what those truths are and how they are presented, both the truths and their presentation are dependent upon the themes and form of tragedy. Let me give two very different examples of the continuity of content and then turn to the way Thucydides' 'arguments' are embedded in the architecture of the *History* in a way that parallels tragedy.

Thucydides uses the word 'possession' (*ktema*) twice. The first is when he claims that the *History* is a 'possession' for all time; the second is when he is describing the suffering of the Athenians after the second Peloponnesian invasion. They were, he says, deprived of their 'beautiful possessions' (*kala ktemata*). The 'tragic' implication is that whatever human beings possess, from their goods to their lives and reputations, remain hostages to fortune and subject to loss. The title of Daniel Mendelsohn's book captures this well (though it is actually drawn from a Tennessee Williams stage direction): 'How Beautiful It Is and How Easily It Can Be Broken'.

My second example has to do with the absence of the gods in Thucydides and their omnipresence in tragedy. It is precisely this difference that makes Thucydides seem so modern and tragedy so archaic. Yet the relative absence of the gods should not blind us to how much of the moral structure of the *History* embodies a theological scaffolding crucial to such plays as the *Oresteia*.

What does it mean to say that Thucydides' argument resides in the architecture of the *History*? One thing it means is that one cannot unproblematically treat one voice in the text as if it were Thucydides' own. To abstract a speech or event from its echoes and anticipations in the rest of the *History* is to lose much of its meaning. For example, to treat what the Athenians say at Melos as what Thucydides says appropriates his authority for a position he almost surely did not share. Consider in this regard the similarities between what Thucydides says in his own voice at the conclusion of the Corcyrean Revolution and what the *Melians* say in the Melian Dialogue. Or compare what the Athenians say there with what they said at Sparta, or the way they have become enslavers of Greeks rather than liberators as they had been at Salamis. Or ask why the Melian Dialogue (which is not much of a dialogue) is followed by the invasion of Sicily. It follows not historically but dramatically. Take the Funeral Oration as another example (my guess is that it and the Melian Dialogue are the most frequently excerpted parts of Thucydides). To understand it means reading it with and against the plague, the other speeches of Pericles, competing visions of democracy, the changes in the nature of leadership over time and in the *History* and the expansion of empire.

It is true that Thucydides makes authorial interventions: judgements about political leaders, clear sympathies as with the Plataeans as against the Thebans, and with the victims of the Thracian massacre of school-boys, 'a calamity inferior to none that had ever fallen upon a whole city ...' (7.29), and of course his masterful editorializing in the description of the civil war at Corcyrea. But even these interventions, as privileged as they deserve to be, must be read in terms of the contrapuntal movement of the work as a whole. It is a movement built on silences as well as speeches, on the dramatic juxtaposition of speeches to each other, and to events, deeds and circumstances and on a complex pattern of allusion and reference. The *History* is nothing less than a textual agora.

In many respects this way of reading the *History* is how we read tragedy. The 'literary' sensibility necessary for enabling the reading prepares interpreters, including policy analysts, to recognize the tragic content of Thucydides' work. Of course this means that drawing policy implications from the *History* is not much easier than drawing them from, say, *Antigone* or *Oedipus Tyrannos*.

In the end, we are left with the question: 'what is the appropriate way (if there is one or only one) of appropriating Thucydides?' How are we to reconcile his practical claim that his work is intended to help future statesmen and citizens and the literary complexity of the text? It is a complexity, I have argued, that is emphasized by reading him through the lens of tragedy. Doing so means the *History* does not yield a set of prescriptions to be applied with certainty and without remainder. There is no way to short-circuit or dispose of the literary qualities of the work. Indeed, these qualities, rather than being impractical, anti-political or obstructive to policy making, enrich our capacity to listen to the voices and intonations that abound in the *History* and in public life. A tragic Thucydides is harder to read (in several senses of that word) but will, I think, lead to 'better' policy. Evidence for this lies in the contributions to this volume.

Notes

1. See the commentary by Thomas Gould in his translation of *Oedipus the King* (Englewood Cliffs, NJ: Prentice Hall (1970)), p. 21. I have abbreviated the riddle which in full runs as follows:

   There exists on land a thing with two feet and four feet, with a single voice, that has three feet as well. It changes shape, alone among the things that move on land or in the air or down through the sea. Yet during the periods when it walks supported by the largest number of feet, then is the speed in its limbs the feeblest of all.

   The answer is 'man', who moves on all four limbs as an infant, on two feet as an adult, and with the aid of a cane in old age. See Gould, p. 19.
2. J. Lear (1999) *Open Minded: Working Out the Logic of the Soul* (Cambridge, MA: Harvard University Press).
3. J. -P. Vernant and P. Vidal-Naquet (1981) *Tragedy and Myth in Ancient Greece*, quoted in B. Williams (1993) *Shame and Necessity* (Berkeley and Los Angeles: University of California Press), p. 19.

4. Heracleitus famously said that 'a man's character is his fate'. I am suggesting (as have others) that we can read the line both ways.

5. Williams (1993) *Shame and Necessity*, p. 166.

6. See note 2, above.

7. B. Knox (1970) *Oedipus at Thebes* (New York: W. W. Norton). But see Froma Zeitlin's critique in F. Zeitlin (1986) 'Thebes: Theater of Self and Society in Athenian Drama', in J. P. Euben (ed.) *Greek Tragedy and Political Theory* (Berkeley and Los Angeles: University of California Press), pp. 101–41.

8. See Thucydides I, 70–1.

9. The recurrent word for wondrous (*deinos*) suggests both wondrous achievement and awful destruction. Given the placement of the ode and the imagery it summarizes and anticipates, it seems that what is distinctively human is our 'existential' homelessness; that, as Rousseau might have put it, it is our nature to be unnatural. I have discussed the ode at length in 'Antigone and the Languages of Politics', in J. P. Euben (1997) *Corrupting Youth: Political Education, Democratic Culture and Political Theory* (Princeton, NJ: Princeton University Press), pp. 139–78.

10. See H. Arendt (1998) *The Human Condition* (Chicago and London: University of Chicago Press), Section V.

11. The self-critique found in drama helped establish a tradition of self-expiation Socrates built upon even as he criticized it. See my *Corrupting Youth*, Chapters 2 and 4.

12. I have discussed the significance of this in 'Thucydides in Baghdad', in K. Bassi and J. P. Euben (eds) (2010) *When Worlds Elide: Classics, Politics, Culture* (Rowman and Littlefield).

8
Tragedy, World Politics and Ethical Community

Richard Beardsworth

In the preceding chapters of this book, an engaging debate has been conducted that concerns the place of tragedy and the tragic in world politics and its theorization. The question has been whether tragedy brings specific insight to our understanding of the relation between international politics and ethics. Since much of the discipline of International Relations (IR) hinges on how this relation is theoretically and empirically conceived, the debate is important. Does tragedy have something to say to international relations, its future conceptualization and practice? To provide the theoretical context for my own thoughts on this issue, I wish to first summarize the three fundamental positions underpinning the preceding arguments made by Richard Ned Lebow, Mervyn Frost, James Mayall, Nicholas Rengger, Chris Brown and Peter Euben. I will then argue that the tragic reveals the immanence of the ethical to the political in a specific, but irreducible, manner. This immanence undermines any theoretical distinction between the normative and the positive in social scientific thinking of international political reality.

The first position concerns Lebow, Euben and Frost: the tragic dimension of international political life involves the internal development of *hubris* among international actors, which cuts them off from international society and leads to tragic consequences (Lebow), and/or the hard ethical dilemmas within such life that are negotiated for better or worse (Euben, Frost). For all three, this tragic dimension is transformative. They maintain that deepening our sensibility to this tragic dimension leads to greater recognition of the aporias of world politics and to a more searching and wise political practice of them, with Euben stressing more than the other two how problematic tragedy shows this practice to be. The second position is shared to greater or lesser degree by all six authors, but is privileged by Mayall, Rengger, and Brown in their criticisms of idealism (and the 'idealist' side to Frost and Lebow's very apology of tragedy). Tragic fate and tragic insight lie in the discrepancy between moral understanding and volition on the one hand, and political practice on the other. The discrepancy comes to the fore in the unintended consequences that necessarily arise in this gap between ethics and politics. Tragedy is, therefore, most useful as a *realist* category of thought that moderates wishful thinking in the political domain. The third position is held by Rengger alone: tragedy and the tragic are not useful categories for world politics since they organize political life in terms that are no longer pertinent to the non-normative structure of modern and contemporary life. Tragedy is an art-form, predicated on a normative notion of humanity; it is not a form of life as such.

This delineation does scant justice to the range of thought within, and between, the previous arguments. It does, however, catch the problem which interests me, one that comes to the fore in the specific differences between Lebow, on the one hand, and Rengger, on the other. Does the Western tragic condition enable us to perceive political life, at an international or global level, from a tragic perspective? This perspective reconfigures given relations between individual and community through the tragic agent's patterns of emotion and reason and of excess and recognition. And, can this perspective, in turn, say something about the immanence of ethics to politics? Or has tragedy, as Rengger argues *contra* Lebow, become an obsolete category of thought that depends on pre-existing structures of substantive community and consensual norms that political modernity and world politics leave behind? In the following pages I will argue a position close to that of Lebow. I wish, however, to make the notion of community with which tragedy is concerned more theoretically precise so as to eschew both the realist-informed responses of Mayall, Rengger and, in part, Brown (second position: 'this is idealist pie in the sky'), and the final Rengger-type stricture (third position: 'this is art, not life'). Indebted to the methodology of post-Kantian German thought, my take on tragedy, like Lebow's, shows how ethics is always already immanent to politics, but needs to be recognized as such. Tragic fate reveals this ethical immanence and explores its recognition. My question is: What kind of immanence and what kind of community does tragic fate connote and what is the specificity of this community in modern life?

To answer this question, I will first rehearse Lebow's argument in his important book, *The Tragic Vision of Politics: Ethics, Interests and Orders*, with the hope of teasing out the notions of immanence and recognition and suggesting why a more theoretically precise concept of 'community' is needed to underpin the one that he takes from Greek tragedy.[1] I will then turn to the early Hegel's conception of the 'causality of fate' to suggest a concept of community, immanent to politics, that lies beyond that of Greek tragedy. As a further step in my argument, I will generalize the early Hegelian concept of community for international political theory. Finally, I will briefly consider the second Iraq war as a way of illustrating how the immanence of ethical community to international politics works in contemporary terms.

The tragic bond and international politics

Lebow affirms that the 'core insight of tragedy' lies in the recognition of one's limits.[2] The example of Oedipus in *Oedipus the King* has privileged status here. Having answered the riddle of the Sphinx and recklessly assured Thebes that he will discover and punish the harbinger of the plague with which the *polis* is infested, Oedipus comes to recognize that he is the very author whom he has condemned. In an attempt to escape his fate – of killing his father and going to bed with his mother – he precisely fulfils it by leaving Corinth. This process of recognition and the overall irony of his fate redraw the relation between Oedipus and the divine, exposing his initial affirmation of human knowledge (solving the riddle) and disregard of oracular prediction (the Delphic oracle, the intervention of Tiresias) to traditional Greek humility and piety before the gods.

Now, Lebow is not concerned with the religious framework, but with the communal bond that underpins it. *Oedipus the King* presents an ironic 'eternal cycle' of *hamartia* (the determining error of the tragic hero), *hubris* (his excessive individuation) and *nemesis* (his downfall) in which Oedipus' very attempt to distinguish himself from the laws of his community (*nomos*) reveals the irreducible relation between himself and those laws: his de-limitation from them confirms all the more forcefully his belonging to them. The tragic dynamic to the irony unfolds in the suffering and loss entailed to bring about the recognition, although the affective nature of the irony fosters the intellectual recognition of his limits in the first place. The passion of suffering engenders, in other words, a re-structuring of Oedipus' reason. Tragic wisdom is thus predicated on the revelation of the *disavowed bond* between individual and community through the individual's fate and on the interaction of emotion and reason through which this revelation is made.

For Lebow, this notion of community is not particular to the ancient Greek *polis*. *Nomos* refers to a broad spectrum of law, value and custom that can be generalized both spatially and temporally.[3] *The Tragic Vision of Politics* constitutes at one and the same time a profound reading of tragic vision within Thucydides (Athens and Sparta), Clausewitz (France and Prussia), and Morgenthau (Cold-War America) and an implicit critique of post-Cold War American foreign policy. My question is this: Is this generalization justified given the structural distinctions between (a) the *nomos* of the Athenian polity in which citizen and *polis* are structured as one identity; (b) the modern *legalism* of liberal democracy in which citizen and polity are distinct, but share the common space of nation-state territoriality and law; and (c) the society of world politics in which nation-states are separate legal entities, but enmeshed in international rule and transnational force that are presently re-organizing the terms of national sovereignty and citizenship? Placing all three notions of rule together, Lebow addresses different units of analysis that may ride the distinction between the domestic and the international too easily. He also addresses different levels of community, civic duty and loyalty, all conflated under the blanket term *nomos*. Lebow's conflation serves well the purpose of his overall argument: the norms and values of international society, conceived of as community at the international level, precede order. The realist assumption that justice is a second-order consideration loses the object of this 'community'. It is important, it said, to be theoretically precise about the structure of community that is presently revealed in contemporary world politics through the individual unit's very disavowal of it. For, the bond revealed between individual unit and international community is much thinner than that in Greek tragedy and, for many thinkers and international actors today, is precisely what is *not* presupposed by international society.[4]

That said, there are obviously several ways in which one can argue for international community despite this type of conflict. The framework of the human rights regime, of international law and its structural constraints, of human development and sustainability, notions of just war, and so on – all form part of this community.[5] Lebow is indeed referring to these increasingly important dimensions to political life when he assumes the idea of international *nomos*. Are they strong enough, however, to allow one to think of world ethical community, its disavowal, and recognition *in tragic terms*? Oedipus' recognition is based on such a strong substantive bond between citizen and polis that the breaking of it *forces* recognition. The possibility of the latter ensues, that is, from the depth of the former. Given the radically different order of political bond in Sophocles' dramatization of the ancient *polis* and in contemporary world politics, to argue *already* for the immanence of ethical community to world politics must, I would argue, be done in less determinate, less substantive terms. Otherwise, Lebow's international *nomos*, underpinning international community and its tragic disavowal, is too formal to trigger the intensity of bond and affect necessary for tragic fate and tragic recognition. In this context Rengger's strictures on tragic textualism begin to sound convincing. I will argue, here, that the early Hegel's reflections on ethical life and the causality of fate are helpful in order to theorize the immanence of ethical community to different orders of political organization.

The causality of fate and world politics

In the discipline of IR, G. W. F. Hegel tends to be considered a 'hard realist'. His *Philosophy of Right* critiques Kantian cosmopolitanism, for example, in terms of the ethical nature of the state-community and the ethical dimension of inter-state violence. There is, however, another reading of Hegel that is foregrounded by his early work. *Contra* Kantian individualism and moralism, he emphasizes the immanence of ethics to politics: the impossibility, that is, of separating the communal bond of social humanity from political organization. For Hegel, the recognition of this bond constitutes the dynamic of both Greek and modern tragedy; it is also at the basis of all religion. In his early writings, he pitches the tragic logic of recognition against modern legal proceduralism. The following attempts to bring this Hegel further into the debate on tragedy and IR.

In 'The Spirit of Christianity' Hegel makes a distinction between two kinds of law: one criminal, the other experiential or phenomenological.[6] In criminal law, there is no meeting between the universality of law (its legal status and necessary application by force) and the particularity of a transgression of it. The particular act of the criminal is annulled by/under the law to allow the law its validity and force. The formalism of modern law is exemplified by criminal law. Against legal formalism, Hegel opposes an understanding of law that he takes from his reading of Greek and Shakespearean tragedy and that he radicalizes, through an ethical interpretation of Christianity, in terms of life: he calls it the law of the 'causality of fate'. He describes how any individual moves within the plurality of life, increasing it, maintaining it or diminishing it. In breaking with life (e.g., killing it), the tragic hero thinks that he has increased his (or her) own power, but in fact he has broken his own life. But he only comes to understand this essential continuity of life between self and other over time, through the consequences of his action and his own suffering. Through the unintended consequences of his act (the end of life, not its expansion), the hero thereby recognizes that in killing the other, he has actually killed himself since he has destroyed what is common to them both: life. Hegel uses the *Oresteia* and *Macbeth* to describe this law of experience:

> The trespass of the man regarded as in the 'toils of fate' is ... not a rebellion, of the subject against the ruler, liberation from subservience ... before he acts there is no opposition [between law and self] ... Only through a departure from that unity of life which is neither regulated by law nor at variance with law, only through the killing of life, is something strange, alien produced. Destruction of life is not the nullification of life but its diremption, its rupture in two (*Entzweiung*), and the destruction consists in its transformation into an enemy. It is immortal, and, if slain, it appears as its terrifying ghost which vindicates every branch of life and lets loose its Eumenides. The illusion of trespass, its belief that it destroys the other's life and thinks itself enlarged thereby, is dissipated by the fact that the disembodied spirit of the injured life comes on the scene against the trespass, just as Banquo who came as a friend to Macbeth was not extinguished but immediately thereafter took his seat, no longer as a guest at the feast, but as evil spirit. The trespasser, Macbeth, intended to have done with another's life, but he has only destroyed his own, for life is not different from life, but dwells in the single Godhead. In his pride, he has destroyed indeed, but only the friendliness of life; he has perverted life into an enemy. It is the deed itself, the killing of life, which has created a law whose domination now comes on the scene. This law is the equality between the injured, alien life and the trespasser's own life ... Hence punishment as fate is the equal reaction of the trespasser's own deed, of a power which he has himself armed, of an enemy made an enemy by himself.[7]

For Hegel, tragic fate reveals the distance the hero has taken from life and the inverse return of life upon him in his own self-destruction. The punishment of fate is not, as in criminal law, the enforcement of the law over the particular, but the enfolding of the individual back into the community of life (although this return will be his very death). Hegel adds:

> Fate has a more extended domain than punishment. It is aroused even by guilt without crime and is therefore more strict than

punishment ... For fate is ... incorruptible and unbounded like life itself. It knows no given ties, no differences of standpoint or position, no domain of virtue. Where life is injured, be it ever so rightly, i.e. even if no dissatisfaction is felt, there fate appears, and one may therefore say [with Antigone] 'never has innocence suffered; every suffering is guilt'.[8]

The ubiquity of fate matches both the ubiquity of life and the human need to delimit life to live within it. Tragic fate exists because humans cannot avoid injuring life in order to live. Delimitations that are tragic *disavow* the equality of life in such a way as to provoke an explicit boomerang effect. Now, this experiential 'law' of fate, together with the community of 'equality of life' that it connotes, are helpful for understanding world politics for the following reasons.

First, although the logic of the causality of fate seems basically concerned with the experience of 'sinning' individuals, the Hegelian understanding of the tragic is valid for any individual unit of life, whatever the level of analysis. For, it concerns how individual units delimit themselves from the manifold web of interdependence that we call life in such a way as to deny the existence or validity of this web. A community of individuals is one such organization of life if those individuals who depart from it recognize that in departing from it they have lost their sense of identity. A system of independent states is another such organization of life *if* those states which depart from it come to recognize that, in so doing, they have lost their ability to maintain themselves, their basic identity. In other words, it is the dynamic of recognition that confirms that the system constitutes a *community* and not only, as the structural realism of Kenneth Waltz argues, a functional set of interacting parts. The law of the community of life underpins relations between individual units within complex organizations of life; its purchase on these relations is to reveal, over time, the constitutive relation between them through the very act of individuation and delimitation from them (*hubris*). Structural functionalism and/or balance of power theories radically underestimate this relation between recognition and community within any system.

Second, while Hegel's manner of thinking the community of life between self and other is essentially Christian, it is possible to generalize the set of relations between self and other in non-specific cultural terms. The tragic development of individuation in terms of the misrecognition and recognition of the continuity of life is general enough to be understood beyond the religious/secular divide and beyond the differences between religions. The European Enlightenment and post-Enlightenment separated ethical life from religion and placed it in relation to the political. But this is a historical contingency. As a logic of law and community that pertains to life *as such*, whatever the community, the tragic constitutes a universal experience. The community of life revealed by the causality of fate transcends, in this regard, both the 'clash of civilizations' and post-modern politico-cultural relativism.

Third, since the above two points may suggest such generality that little is conveyed, it is important to stress that while life is independent of rule, it always underpins informal and formal rules of association. Thought in material rather than in religious terms (life as Hegel's 'one Godhead' above), this tragic interpretation of life indicates, consequently, a community of life the terms of which change according to the time and place under analysis. Lebow argues the same for the concept of *nomos*: hence his generalization of the term across different time periods. Hegel's concept of 'causality of fate' concerns a fundamental pattern of human experience and human organization. It can therefore be more easily generalized across history and across units of political analysis than can the concept of *nomos*. It does not designate a *given* community (specific values, laws and rules) although it is always accompanied by one since individuals or polities are necessarily rooted in a social environment larger than themselves. While humanity's notions of life evolve from one epoch to another, differ from one region to another, the essential continuity of life remains, emerging through these changes in different forms. A couple of examples might be useful here. That I, an atheist child of the European Enlightenment, look to an ethical notion of life – its equality, reversal into death, and recognition – in all religions and cultures in order to transcend revenge-politics, testifies to the historical and geographical universality of the tragic. That Middle East resentment against the West is fuelled, in part, by a desire for reciprocity and symmetry in economic, social and political matters suggests that the equality of life underpins resistance to democratization and the recent, hypocritical moralization of politics.[9] In other words, the community of the equality of life underpins any given community and is revealed through delimitation from it. In philosophical terms, the relation between the community of life and a given community (pre-modern, modern, international) is one of 'identity and difference'. The community of life subtends all political organizations (hierarchical or non-hierarchical), and all political organizations reduce it.

Fourth, in a highly interdependent world, this logic of the equality of life is all the more pertinent to individual agents and their behaviour.

Since nation-states are increasingly enmeshed in international rules and transnational forces, these agents must be more and more attentive to the relations that enfold them. Modern delimitation from them in the form of pure national sovereignty, unilateralism or economic protectionism is more likely to trigger a causality of fate than 50 years ago. Let me be clear here. As contemporary neo-realism demonstrates through game theory, increasing interdependence is not necessarily accompanied by increasing cooperation. Rather, such interdependence may well imply greater acts of delimitation and conflict. The tightening of international law does not imply increasing obligation on the part of states. Rather, it may well lead to increasing defection or opt-out clauses. Growing interdependence does not mean increasing convergence and cooperation. It does mean, however, that any act of delimitation will have unintended consequences that will re-relate the delimited agent back to the 'whole'. Only with recognition of the common equality of life is this systemic 'whole' revealed as a 'community'; but, without this 'whole', there would be no possibility of community in the first place.

Fifth, this community of the equality of life appears through the fateful consequences of individuation and delimitation. The community of relations between self and other does not comprise a substantive community in the Greek sense of *polis* or a formal community in either the modern sense of liberal democracy or in the contemporary international sense of the human-rights regime. It embodies a set of often unrecognized or loose dispositions that embody life in any given historical epoch relative to the surrounding environment: for example, the gradual construction of national loyalty in the modern period or the progressive complication of belonging and responsibility in our own era. Preceding determination, it is, again, not a given community of law, rule or value in itself; the community only emerges *through* the process of misrecognition and recognition. For me, the contribution that the category of tragedy can make to international political theory lies here. It traces a community of the equality of life that is not given in any specific institutional form, but that appears, negatively, through the excessive delimitation of individuality from its epoch's *general disposition towards life*. The Israeli bombardment of Southern Lebanon in July 2006 was condemned by the majority of the international community, with the exception of the US and the UK, not because Israel does not have the right to self-defence according to many of that same majority. Rather, the loss of material life exceeded what is now considered internationally tolerable in state military engagement. Military self-restraint is, of course, determined by international convention and law. But, in the context of this argument, the international outcry indicated that these conventions translate a basic understanding of life particular to our epoch as much as they suggest the constraint that these conventions exercise upon power. War crimes and crimes against humanity suggest something similar. They are not only constraints upon individual behaviour; these constraints signal a general threshold of life defined in terms of the conventions of the epoch. For the moment, this still remains the regime of rights.[10] Amidst crucial concerns for order, the pentagon's present rethinking of security in the context of the enormous threats in Afghanistan indicates, I would argue, similar negotiation with this threshold.

Sixth, this community of life is ethical; it is not political. The individual unit always already presupposes relations with other units given the 'equality' of life. These relations only come through the tragic fate of the individual, through the ironic inversions of life into death, creation into destruction. The community of the equality of life between aggressor and victim informs these inversions and recognitions but does not assume a particular form. It emerges, negatively, through the fate of the tragic agent, through the consequences of its initial act. This ethical community is therefore *neither* empirical *nor* normative. Almost all IR theory considers the ethical in normative terms, not in terms of immanence. The specificity of the Hegelian point and the interest of tragedy in IR thought lie here. The community of life is immanent to political acts of power, but it is only revealed through the individual units' fate. Empirically non-verifiable, it has ethical status only; but immanent to political power, it is *within* the movement of the real. Presupposed by all acts of individuation, it appears through the forms of misrecognition and recognition of these acts. Tragic disavowal of community blurs and rearranges, therefore, hard distinctions between the normative and the positive and the idealist and the realist within social science. For Lebow, power is restrained by a culture of norms, and tragedy shows this through the *hamartia, hubris* and *nemesis* of pure power. In my terms, tragic fate points to the transgression of an epoch's general *sense of life*. The revealed equality of life between aggressor and aggressed confirms *and* anticipates the terms of legitimacy under which any unit can work.

Finally, therefore, while the community of life is ethical, not political, it anticipates political construction and institutional concretization of what is legitimate and illegitimate in life. An individual act of delimitation from life awaits the precise terms in which such delimitation is annulled. These terms are to be found and practiced by creative violence (in the Machiavellian sense of leadership that releases more life than less). Injuring the unbounded plurality of life, new political institutions must engender their own fate. The tragic dimension to politics within life is recurrent. Given the immanent relation and distinction between the ethical and the political, the tragic is therefore a historically specific, but repetitive experience of ethical life. And emphasis on the politically transformative nature of tragedy is important precisely because such political recognition remains contingent. Recognition may not happen or it may be too weak, with regard to other forces within a given system of relations, to engender reconstruction.

To summarize the above points: agreeing with Lebow's reinterpretation of classical realism in *The Tragic Vision of Politics*, I have argued that justice is an immanent constraint upon power, and tragic fate reveals this immanence. Rather than consider this constraint in terms of *nomos*, however, I have used Hegel's understanding of the law of the 'causality of fate' in tragedy to show the immanence of ethical life to power in terms of the common equality of life. This community of life underpins all variations of normative rule, and it is what triggers the inversions of misrecognition and recognition. Immanent to power, this community is neither empirical nor normative. Confirming retrospectively disavowed rules of life, its immanence to power at the same time anticipates further construction. The tragic purchase on political life is inevitable and recurrent. It equally provides the affective framework in which legitimate political transformation is possible. Tragedy is, in this sense, rightly understood as beyond pessimism or optimism. With regard to the domain of contemporary international politics, it moves the terms of destruction and creation in contemporary political life towards a *cosmopolitan realism of the lesser violence*. The ethical community of life subtending the relations between states and between states and international organization, when theorized normatively, is increasingly considered in cosmopolitan terms. Principles of symmetry, reciprocity, autonomy and subsidiarity are foregrounded in holistic approaches to world political issues. As the present global financial crisis underscores, states remain, however, the major political decision-makers. But to maintain their interests they must act more and more in concert, a form of cooperation that anticipates a new order of interest and decision-making. Between ethical community and specific political organization, the question of what order of action and decision is legitimate within a web of interdependence becomes important. Since all decisions are particular and delimiting, tragic delimitation today reveals the increasing need to make decisions within a global web of life. For the moment, such decisions of the lesser violence will focus, through exemplary state leadership in concert with international institution, on immediate planetary problems.[11]

The second Iraq war as tragic error and tragic recognition

A great deal has now been written on 9/11 and the second Iraq war. The fate of the latter illustrates my argument well, so I will end the above points with a few comments on it. The Bush regime's stepping aside from the international community set off its own causality of fate because no such act, *perpetrated in the terms that it was*, could survive the interdependent web of life within which the US regime first struck. American forces on the border of Saudi Arabia were crucial to convince the Iraqi regime that the UN was serious. Universal law, to be law, depends on force, as Hegel reminds us in his description of criminal law above. But, the political instrumentalization of lies to justify the invasion, the belief in a rapid military victory and in top-down democratization, the subsequent revelations around torture, and so on – all speak of a disavowal of the community of 'international' life at the beginning of the twenty-first century that can be traced, empirically, to the American regime's flouting of international rules and law. What underlies the increasing complexity of these rules, however, is the increasing complexity of life at the global level. It is this equality of life that comes through the misrecognition and recognitions of present American power.

Rengger remarks at one point in his essay that 'at the beginning of the twenty-first century ... conflict and war seem to be everywhere in the ascendant' and 'the optimistic assumptions of the early 1990s have been revealed as facile and deluded'.[12] This is in part true, and a realist analysis of the irreducible distribution of power in international relations remains critical. That said, that recent American use and abuse of power in the Middle East is today described as 'tragic' both for Americans and international politics at large, that unilateralism in the twenty-first century has produced such resentment and depression both inside America and outside, that after *only* five years of war (compare Vietnam), America opted for a radical change of government and a staggered withdrawal from Iraq, that the majority of players in world politics now accept the end of American hegemony – all point, in my terms, to the persistent, immanent nature of ethical community in the very delimitation of such power. Global life is *too* complex and intricate today – economically, socially, communicationally and politically – for any act of individuation and delimitation *not to harm or destroy its own standing at a world level*. This does not mean that such acts will not continue. A world of interdependence is dangerous, and a realist analysis of the disequilibria involved is necessary for good statesman-ship and diplomacy. But the equality of life signalled in the fate of such acts, within the context of increasing complexity of international rule and norm, points to a community of life that is also irreducible. It is the nature of the bond of life at whatever level of social and political organization. This bond is ethical. It cannot be instantiated or instituted as such; but it is always immanent to political force and will both be misrecognized by excessive power politics and can lead, following the fate of misrecognition, to the further empirical invention of rules of association. The 'tragic' nature of recent American foreign policy reveals this equality of life and its suspension. It thereby points, at one and the same time, to contemporary frustration at the empirical absence of ethical community and to the radical promise of such a community (often re-articulated in religio-social terms). This frustration considers neo-conservative and political Islamist uses of force as two symmetrical dimensions of the same tragic irony: disavowal of life. The proposed equation is correct in the sense that the American regime's response to political Islam excessively strayed from life, but wrong in the sense that there remains a qualitative difference between disavowing the community of life and seeking a community of death. Terrorism can-not be tragic; American foreign policy can be. One must hope that present American leadership is both powerful and creative enough to help reshape the above frustration. Its political challenge is nevertheless clear: the invention of legitimate rule within the web of global life.[13]

The community immanent to tragic de-limitation in international politics will be increasingly felt affectively in terms of illegitimacy and legitimacy. The mechanism of legitimacy at the level of world governance remains very unclear. The sensible affect tending towards such legitimacy is disclosed, however, each time, today and in the future, life is considered to be annulled 'tragically'. Within the continuum of the necessary self-delimitation of life, such destruction of life triggers a process of recog-nition, but this process can always be left undone. *There is no necessary deduction of the political from the ethical.* World politics may remain tragic for decades to come. It is therefore incumbent upon those theorizing world politics to press the case upon those who wield power that they translate in concrete political terms the very notion of legitimacy that illegitimate behaviour betokens. As Lebow argues, tragic insight into world politics reinforces the *immanent* claim of justice upon power. It does not indicate, however, what political community should come. The international community upon which the category of the tragic has purchase is, I have argued, to be situated in this immanence of the ethical to the political and in the concomitant tension and work between them.

Notes

1. R. N. Lebow (2003) *The Tragic Vision of Politics: Ethics, Interests and Orders* (Cambridge: Cambridge University Press).
2. R. N. Lebow 'Tragedy, Politics and Political Science', Chapter 5, in this volume, pp. 63–71; Lebow (2003) *The Tragic Vision*, pp. 25, 59, 116, and 258.
3. Lebow (2003) *The Tragic Vision*, Chapter 7, especially p. 268 on the 'normative values of international society'; p. 275 on the necessary implication of justice and interest for power to work long-term; and pp. 328–9 on the everyday practice of state compliance to international norms that imply a community of cooperation. These conceptions are all considered in terms of the notion of *nomos*.
4. For the classic argument concerning the aporia between community and society at an international level, see H. Bull (2002) *The Anarchical Society: A Study of Order in World Politics* (London: Palgrave Macmillan). International institution presupposes international community to be legitimate but international community presupposes international institution to emerge as such. This aporia affects all political will-formation. The idea of an ethical community immanent to the non-communal forms of political practice attempts to negotiate this aporia in tragic terms: by increasing recognition of the need for new political practice through the widening of sensibility.
5. See S. Caney (2005) *Justice beyond Borders: A Global Political Theory* (Cambridge: Cambridge University Press).
6. G. W. F. Hegel 'Spirit of Christianity and Its Fate', in *Early Theological Writings*, trans. T. M. Knox (Philadelphia: University of Pennsylvania Press (1971)), pp. 182–301.
7. Hegel 'Spirit of Christianity', pp. 229–30.
8. Hegel 'Spirit of Christianity', p. 233.
9. These comments were written in the context of the American intervention in Iraq. While the examples here might be updated in the light of more recent events, the theoretical argument remains, I believe, valid.
10. Mervyn Frost's contribution (see Chapter 2) considers the relevance of the tragic to IR in terms of the irreconcilable conflict between two ethical codes or forms that have claim on the tragic agent. The tragic is revealed in the negative consequences that emerge from endorsing one form to the detriment of the other. This 'lose/lose' situation is intractable with divine transcendence, but signals the need for institutional reform in modern societies. From this perspective, Frost argues that the contemporary conundrum of 'intervention/non-intervention' in states that do intolerable violence to their own citizens is to be considered as a *tragic* dilemma for agents of

intervention *qua* 'rights-holders of global civil society', on the one hand, and, bearers of citizenships rights on the other, for whom the sovereignty of the state is the condition of their citizenship. This same tragic dilemma persists in the tension between human rights and national/regional migration policy and human rights and national/regional protectionist trade policy. We could say, following Frost then, that tragic choice emerges in modern life each time the sovereignty of human rights is opposed to the sovereignty of the nation-state/EU and to its own possibility of providing public goods. Frost sees no easy solutions to these dilemmas, but considers an awareness of their tragic nature as a pre-condition of their future eradication. My own perspective does not foreground the problem of tragic choice between ethical constants, but emphasizes the irreducibility of the equality of life upon which any choice falls. That life is configured today between two mutually incompatible forms of human sovereignty suggests that the principle of subsidiarity will gradually replace that of sovereignty. I therefore agree with Frost that tragic choice and its consequences anticipate institutional reform, but would stress the non-normative immanence of ethical life to the political as a result.

11. For further elaboration of this argument, see R. Beardsworth (2008) 'Cosmopolitanism and Realism: Towards a Theoretical Convergence' *Millennium: Journal of International Relations* (2008) 37 (1), 69–96 and R. Beardsworth *Cosmopolitanism and International Relations Theory* (Cambridge: Polity, 2011), pp. 96–8, pp. 210–23.
12. Rengger 'Tragedy or Scepticism?', Chapter 4, this volume, 53–62 (p. 55).
13. President Obama's 'A New Beginning' speech at Cairo University on 4 June 2009, addressed to the Islamic World, showed how aware he was of the stakes of his American presidency. To pitch his call for cooperation between the US and the Islamic World in terms of the unity of life, as given by the three monotheisms, was a sophisticated move, both diplomatic and sincere (given his own faith), that could have found the form of affective resonance needed to begin to overcome non-Western hatred of, and frustration with, Western power. Given the continuing priority of Israel for all American administrations, this opportunity has been squandered. Religion constitutes, nevertheless, an important tool of intra-state cultural diplomacy because ethical life sits within it.

9
Tragic Vision and Vigilant Realism: Progressivism without an Ideal

Kamila Stullerova

Introduction

This chapter examines the relationship between tragedy and international political theory from the perspective of what I will follow others in calling the 'tragic vision'.[1] The tragic vision, I claim, is a specific kind of inspiration by tragedy, which shapes the very nature of a theory's ethical and analytical makeup. Two paramount examples of such 'tragic vision theorizing' are Hans J. Morgenthau's *Scientific Man versus Power Politics*[2] and Richard Ned Lebow's *The Tragic Vision of Politics: Ethics, Interests and Orders*[3] – the two works this chapter explores in order to identify which aspects of theory are affected by tragedy, in what way, and to what effects. I put forth an argument that the tragic vision brings about particular theoretical outcomes and characterize the resulting theory as 'vigilant realism'. This kind of realism gives expression to what is shared between the respective variations on (classical) realism of Morgenthau and Lebow.

My use of the concept 'tragic vision' is, obviously, closely inspired by Ned Lebow's formulation, as it is by Sheldon Wolin's broader concept of vision as 'the imaginative element in political ·thought'.[4] But my emphasis is different because I distinguish the tragic vision from a larger array of appreciations of tragedy in (international) political theory. The tragic vision involves only one kind of stimulation by tragedy, described here with the help of Peter Euben's process of 'nurturing',[5] which influences a theorist's philosophical reasoning. It stands out as a framework of political imagination, on par with concepts like the 'state of nature' or 'utopia'. This distinguishes the tragic vision from what I call 'tragic inspiration', which includes any stimulation by tragedy that does not affect the theory's very philosophical reasoning. Various kinds of

theories – radically differ   inspired by
tragedy and lead to varie

This chapter is divided   section one, I will look at
the framework of the tra   sophical reasoning and trace
the process of nurturing. In section two, I will demonstrate how the
tragic vision imposes fundamental theoretical requirements that rule out
some analytical possibilities and ethical propositions while ascertaining
others. Importantly, these specific analytical and ethical requirements are
not separable from each other. This will be shown through Morgenthau's
work, which is – due to limited space as well as the instructiveness of
his argument, including an argumentative impasse – the main focus of
this section. Lebow is brought in as Morgenthau's interpreter and as a
theorist who succeeds in developing vigilant realism from Morgenthau's
impasse. Vigilant realism's theoretical implications, especially in relation
to the notion of progress, will be outlined in the conclusion.

By differentiating the tragic vision from the tragic inspiration, the
chapter addresses a larger question of whether a theorist's appreciation
for tragedy can have an impact on her theory's political and ethical
categorization, at least within the broad dichotomy of conservatism and
progressivism. 'What are you? Are you a conservative? Are you a liberal?
Where is your position within the contemporary possibilities?'[6] These
are questions Morgenthau asked another theorist who acknowledged
the centrality of tragedy for political theory, and whose work he greatly
admired: Hannah Arendt.[7] Not only because these were Morgenthau's
questions (to which Arendt replied that she did not know and did not
care to know the answers)[8] should we now ask the following: what is
the position of vigilant realism within the contemporary possibilities?
And, more specifically, how does it address the questions of progress
and progressive social change, so central to contemporary international
ethics?

When thinking about the merits of tragedy, the question of progress,
or of ethics as a vehicle of progress, has been central to the present
discussion from its very onset. Mervyn Frost sees James Mayall challenge his theory as 'too progressive' and as 'fail[ing] to take account
of the tragic dimensions of international relations'.[9] In his response,
Mayall reiterates his point about 'unduly optimistic' progressivism that
characterizes almost the whole field of International Relations (IR).[10]
However, he also stresses that his 'emphasis on the tragic dimension' is
in no opposition to 'the ideas of progress or efforts to improve the quality of international life'.[11] Frost, in turn, is ready to admit that tragedy
can make a scholar more sensitive towards the complexities of life, to

people's diversity of commitments and identities, but not much more. At stake here is the question of whether tragedy can inform ethics at all, and several other contributors to this discussion doubt or qualify such a proposition. Tragedy, the argument goes, is primarily a dramatic genre and one closely tied to a particular tradition; classical tragic dramas do not aim at providing ethical solutions.[12] At best, the sceptics admit, tragedy may support, but not independently generate, pluralist accounts of international ethics.

But such a view of tragedy's link to progressive ethics may easily be turned around. Tragedy seems to have equal potential to prop up ethical and political conservatism. Reflection on tragic dramas may effectively discourage any intervention into the inherited world. Since any change could bring about outcomes worse than in the known world, the status quo is the best choice. Internationally, tragedy might inspire arguments for crude, self-centered power politics, isolationism or denial of normative concerns of any kind. Michael Oakeshott's suggestion, voiced in this volume by Nicholas Rengger, to keep tragedy in the world of art and not mingle it with social and political thought, might thus belong to more perceptive propositions on the relationship of tragedy and politics.[13]

That both Morgenthau and Lebow, two probing theorists interested in ethics and its relationship to politics, claim that tragedy is central to their respective theories is therefore remarkable. By examining how tragedy shapes their theoretical choices, this chapter advances an argument that political theory grounded in the tragic vision is progressive in the sense that it is responsive to, and constitutive of, moral and political change. Yet, the tragic vision makes theory critical of any transcendent ideal of progress by undermining the possibility of such an ideal's knowledge-base and moral force. Intrinsic to this critique is a worry that overarching political ideals – by definition not grounded in social experience but in the vision of better societies to which we should advance – open the door to strife rather than the enhancement of social life. As a consequence, the chapter joins those voices in this volume that reinforce tragedy's relevance to ethical questions of contemporary international relations, but it fundamentally qualifies the mode of such relevance.

The tragic vision

To appreciate how the tragic vision differs from the less overbearing tragic inspiration, one must do what Peter Euben proposes in *Greek*

Tragedy and Political Theory: ask what tragedy does *for* and *with* the theorist as a political philosopher. In his theoretical introduction to the book, Euben challenges claims that 'tragedy and theory (or philosophy) are radically opposite activities' and sees them as nurturing each other.[14]

To explicate the nurturing process, Euben draws on Margaret Leslie's 'In Defence of Anachronism'.[15] Leslie's claim, expressed as a polemics with Quentin Skinner,[16] is that political theory benefits from the canon of past texts even when, and especially when, it disregards methodological constraints of 'historical asceticism', which addresses past works exclusively as objects of scholarly study.[17] What matters is 'how and why the thought of our ancestors becomes relevant to our thinking'. Leslie uses here the example of Antonio Gramsci reading *The Prince*. In Euben's succinct summary, 'Gramsci did not work out a political position and then apply it to understanding Machiavelli; nor did he study Machiavelli and then extract lessons relevant to his own situation and time'. It was 'a single dialectical process'. Thus, it is impossible to sequence the two processes: doing interpretation and doing philosophy becomes a single activity. But it is the interpreted text (in the broad sense, which includes reading social practices as texts) that sets limits on the process of doing philosophy more notably than the other way round.

Admittedly, in IR theory, philosophical reasoning is often hidden, assumed rather than pronounced. Morgenthau and Lebow pay varied attention to the underpinning political philosophy in their theories. While not speaking about philosophical reasoning, Lebow is clearly interested in what tragedy does to and for his theory and major figures in the tradition of classical realism; namely, Thucydides, Clausewitz, and Morgenthau. Morgenthau himself seems less interested in this issue. In *Scientific Man* it is as if he were fully engrossed in 'reading' the world as tragedy, presenting it as the only option. Yet, it makes little difference that Morgenthau was not interested in a meta-theory of tragedy and IR as long as his theorizing was precise and perceptive.

Euben characterizes philosophies nourished by tragedy as critical of 'anti-traditional, ahistorical, conceptually self-conscious, intellectually privileged and foundational' philosophies.[18] Critiques of each of these can be found also in Morgenthau and Lebow. They amalgamate into epistemological and moral scepticism that is mostly expressed through 'historicism', a view that while all knowledge must be doubted, history, including the history of human self-reflection, is the best source of knowledge. Writing about the use of history for IR and analysing Lebow's book from this perspective, Hidemi Suganami points out that tragedy is one possible 'emplotment' of history, others being comedy, romance and satire.[19] While agreeing with Suganami that narratives about the social world need to be made into plausible, plotted segments, I disagree that 'emplotments', including tragedy, 'embody different modes of explanation and political ideologies'.[20] 'Emplotments' do not store ready-made modes of explanation or ideological preferences. The link between tragedy and social science/ethics – like 'learning from history' in general – is less direct and requires the creative process of nurturing.

For a sceptical historicist, neither general laws of behaviour nor fundamental moral principles can be abstracted from history. As Lebow also stresses, knowledge is always limited to the time and place of its origin.[21] History gives us accounts of completed stories of what happened to people who were physically and psychologically similar to us. From these completed stories we can develop a perceptiveness to similar, yet unfinished stories and to their potentially critical moments in our own social lives. Such perceptiveness increases with one's readiness to acknowledge psychological likeness with previous generations, to the point that specific lessons about what kinds of situations and states of mind are critical can be drawn.

Crucial here is one's identification with a story as a plausible account of people *like* me, not the story's factual correctness or even its actual occurrence. Therefore, the best stories, most poignantly capturing (aspects of) human sameness across time and space, are pieces of art rather than works of academic history.[22] Cultures have developed multiple modes of framing stories and engaging audiences' imagination/ identification. The history of political ideas knows several such modes of framing. In addition to those mentioned by Suganami, and even more prominently, they include stories of creation, utopias, dystopias, genealogies, or varieties of state-of-nature and social-contract stories.

Writing on the role of imagination in political theory, Wolin ties it to the recognition of the 'impossibility of direct observation', as a 'means for understanding a world [one] can never know in an intimate way'.[23] Indeed, each of these frames makes use of the distance between the social world we live in, but cannot fully grasp, and the world(s) that we can imagine, make sense of, and plausibly relate to, but which we do not expect to represent our actual past or future.[24] The two worlds are not separable but they never meet. Philosophical reasoning that makes use of such frames is a reflection on these two worlds by the means of narrowing, widening, and questioning the distance between them. As a caveat, it needs to be mentioned that creative work with the distance between the two worlds is not the only philosophical option. Another approach fully separates the two worlds and ways of knowing each. That the tragic vision theorists prefer the former approach demonstrates their rejection of separating knowing into ahistorical, normative foundationalism and positivist social science.

Tragedy is particularly well-suited to international relations, making the tragic vision more useful to IR theorists than, for example, a social-contract story, which stresses individuals' moral autonomy more than anything else. Firstly, tragedy is distinctive in its emphasis on negative emotions. Tragic dramas often depict tensions between heroes' two or more moral commitments, demonstrating their fatal incompatibility. This is emotionally demanding on the hero(ine) as well as the spectator. The tragedian's focus is on situations of suffering, and often death, which can be explained as neither meaningful nor just, nor, often, unequivocally unjust. International relations are flagged by points of interest such as war, existential conflict, or severely limited knowledge of the other. Being fundamentally interested in unbridgeable discrepancies between rational, moral and emotional reactions to suffering and death, tragedy brings to the fore incompatibilities between our emotional, moral and rational aspirations and needs. It presents this incompatibility as a property of the human condition, a point Morgenthau repeatedly emphasizes and Lebow similarly employs.[25]

Secondly, by the virtue of depicting incompatible moral commitments pursued to fatal ends, tragedy presents every agent – be it a ruler or a child – as equally significant. It is one of the few narrative frames which focuses on heroes' different social positioning (e.g., one belonging to the domestics sphere, another to the public sphere) to then show that they are equally determined to make judgments and act on them, usually with consequences that defy the boundaries of one's respective social position. In this way, tragedy brings attention to, and makes sense of situations when unexpected actors pursue externally inconceivable ends at unpredictable times – a trait particularly useful for students of IR.

Tragedy carries a particular insight about those who do not listen to its message that (in the long run) everyone's actions matter. Ignoring the existence of other actors, usually in situations of unlimited power or following a military victory, makes one replicate this state of mind (hubris).[26] This is to such effect that others are accounted for only when encountered in an existential conflict (*hamartia, nemesis*),[27] rather than through ordinary social contact (politics), which might have prevented the very conflict. Limiting hubris is the single invitation for ethical intervention Morgenthau and Lebow consider inherent to tragedy.

The notion of limits on power and moral satisfaction permeates the whole ethical arguments of Morgenthau and Lebow. Besides advocating limits on actual international power-players, they call for limits on theory. Even a generally adequate theory eventually fails when it does not incorporate limits – mechanisms of critical self-reflection – on its one-time successful explanatory and normative propositions. Morgenthau sees liberalism as being in a state of hubris; nevertheless, his harsh criticism of contemporary 'decadent' liberalism[28] does not obliterate his quest to preserve the liberal political order.[29] Lebow wants to salvage realism from the hubris of Waltzian neorealism by reinvigorating the self-imposed limits on knowing, certainty, and predictability of classical realism. Morgenthau's and Lebow's respective theoretical positions are undoubtedly also motivated by factors other than engagement with tragedy. But, through the Leslie-Euben process of nurturing, the tragic vision inspires and authenticates their ontological, epistemological, and ethical choices by providing plausible stories of a social world, in which such choices are made or are fatally lacking.

Vigilant realism

Two key aspects of Morgenthau's theory are products of tragic vision nurturing. The first product is his view of knowledge. *Scientific Man* presents a critique of rationalist approaches to social science, using methods of natural science and seeking to formulate laws of social behaviour. Morgenthau does not rule out generalization about the social world. While rationalists claim harmony of purposes, Morgenthau argues that human actions are fundamentally incompatible. But his generalizations do not have predictive power. Some human actions are incompatible and some are not – but we cannot say once and for all which are which. It is the purpose of politics to generate knowledge of which are which at a given time and place. This claim amounts to a procedural account of politics and political analysis, in which knowledge is historically specific, provisional and in need of ongoing reconsideration of its 'validity or utility' (p. 55).

The second aspect of Morgenthau's theory that is a product of tragic vision nurturing is his view of a human being, his main unit of analysis. Individuals are endowed with an *animus dominandi*, 'lust for power', which exposes them to endless conflicts with others (p. 192). This is the same type of claim as that on incompatibility of actions; we cannot make a general argument about the occurrence and objects of such social conflicts, they change over time. *Animus dominandi* is also a source of moral subjectivity, or freedom, giving expression to a 'desire to maintain the range of one's own person with regards to others, to increase it, or to demonstrate it' (p. 192). These two features of the lust for power correspond to two central types of human experience, the active and the contemplative (p. 206).

Such conceptualization of social knowledge and human nature, however, means that Morgenthau is confronted with a problem of ethics. While the lust for power is essential in creating human subjectivity, power's hegemonic tendency drives people to social conflicts with fatal consequences. Moral rules to curb power, avoid hubris and stream action into life-preserving practices are needed as an essential element of social life. But if knowledge is provisional, what provides for the knowledge-base for such rules? Morality requires a precisely opposite view of knowledge. By judging what is good and bad, morality conserves knowledge from its past moment of creation (the historical, worldly occurrence of which is often suppressed by stories of divine origin) to its present application. Once developed, it arrests processes of knowledge-formation and brings about certainty and guidance.

Morgenthau's *Scientific Man* may well be read as an attempt to grapple with this issue. He rejects the dominant, deontological theory of ethics which focuses on the morality of agents' intentions. Like the tragic drama, he points out a discrepancy between actors' intentions and the consequences of their actions, the former being generally good while the latter generally not (p. 188). But he also stops short of favoring the opposite ethical approach, ethical consequentialism – which he equates with utilitarianism – because he has an issue with utilitarianism's reliance on the collectivist calculation of utility and the prior judgment of the future consequences of actions (p. 189). Again, like in tragic dramas, knowledge of consequences is rarely fully available before actions occur.

While challenging both deontology and consequentialism as insufficient for political life, Morgenthau appreciates elements of each ethical theory. He uses the idea of the 'good' as moral measure, which, as he also admits, is deontological by origin, whether expressed as Kant's 'taking others as ends in themselves' or as the Decalogue (p. 209). However, the notion of the good is useless in social life, as no action can be deemed good. Each intervention into the status quo benefits some and injures others. There are only evil and less evil actions. Whether an action is evil or less so is decided by its future consequences, which must be in some way assessed *a priori*, if morality is to guide action and not only judge it *ex post*. Hence Morgenthau's concession to consequentialism.

Decision-making, or social action, in the situation of provisional knowledge elucidates how Morgenthau unravels the maze he creates when thinking about ethics and knowledge. An informed decision *can* be made and one can pick the least evil choice out of a range of possibilities. The validity of this choice is limited. It is a 'provisional solution' because – with some dramatic exaggeration – the circumstances will change tomorrow and the social problem must be 'solved every day anew' (p. 216). But it is the sheer possibility to discriminate between choices of future actions that interest us here.

A decision-maker has to judge every potential decision according to 'the contingencies of the social world' and 'the concretizations of eternal laws' (p. 220). By eternal laws, as already suggested, Morgenthau means the unchanging human psychological makeup demonstrated in the quest for power. Judgment requires assessment of present contingencies in respect to past situations, the outcomes of which are known to us (either by experience or by historical learning as addressed above), and consideration of the ways in which *animus dominandi* of all those affected by the decision might be injured or satiated. While decision-making resembles more gambling than (natural) science (p. 221), it is the most satisfying option. Non-action is not an alternative, since in Morgenthau's interdependent world even non-action brings about social consequences (p. 202).

This point helps Morgenthau to foster rudiments of issue-oriented moral consequentialism and to elucidate the strain on personal character such an approach to ethics makes compared to utilitarian versions of consequentialism. The quality of judgment in the social world is dependent on the depth of insight into *animus dominandi* and into multiple ways in which power demonstrates itself in social intercourse. A deep insight into the lust for power cannot be made without awareness of one's own power aspirations. But the more people are to be affected by one's decision, the more one's *animus dominandi* and its short-term, instinctive satiation must be moderated and others be taken into account – or, in Michael Williams's language, the more one must seek wilful self-limitation.[30] In Morgenthau's words, an individual experiences 'the contrast between the longings of his mind and his actual condition' (p. 221).

Like other key components of Morgenthau's theory, self-limitation is a provisional quality. It does not mean development of a submissive, selfless character. On the contrary, it refers to a character that knows her passions, does not suppress them, and consciously decides to limit them in exchange for the best judgment she can make about her impending action. Morgenthau calls this 'eternal vigilance', a term that captures well the most distinct quality of his judgment and decision-making. 'Eternal vigilance', he writes, 'is the price of freedom, so is the provisional solution of all social problems paid for with never ending effort' (p. 216). Taking for granted here that his social theory is realist, I propose to recognize its distinctive trait and call it 'vigilant realism'.

A disadvantage of such a conceptualization of judgment- and decision-making is that its rightness can be assessed only *ex post*. Moreover, the more people and social relationships a decision (in itself not easily separable from other social action) affects, the more difficult is its assessment. In fact, evaluation of Morgenthau's own intellectual and ethical conduct suffered from this difficulty. Various commentators at various times of his life and afterwards saw him as liberal and others as conservative.[31] As Lebow usefully explains, for Morgenthau, as a scholar, vigilance also encompassed one's professional life as a specific mode of social agency and he painstakingly embodied the following dictum: 'When the reality of power is being lost sight of over its moral and legal limitations, [IR scholarship] must point to that reality. When law and morality are judged as nothing, it must assign them their rightful place'.[32] To say, then, that Morgenthau was a wilfully self-limiting progressive[33] corresponds to his own view of progress:

> There is no progress toward the good, noticeable from year to year, but undecided conflict which sees today good, tomorrow evil, prevail; and only at the end of time, immeasurably removed from the here and now of our earthly life, the ultimate triumph of the forces of goodness and light will be assured.
>
> (pp. 205–6)

Morgenthau's (otherwise undeveloped) comment that social action necessitates 'a moral climate which allows men to expect at least an approximation to justice here and now and thus offers a substitute for strife as a means to achieve justice' (p. 217) can be read in several ways. One possible reading emphasizes morality as a replacement of strife, which resonates with Morgenthau's overall role – though not description – of morality vis-à-vis social life. Morality transmits ossified knowledge about past, repeated, critical encounters of human quests to actualize power in particular social configurations. It decisively aids vigilant decision-making by conveying knowledge, which otherwise every new generation would have to attain through experience, including mortal strife.

When it comes to ethical vocabulary, Morgenthau nonetheless refers to deontological, strictly 'nonutilitarian' conceptions of the good and virtuous (p. 209), even though he finds the very idea of 'the good' wholly inapplicable to social action and, in effect, psychologically strenuous (p. 202). His ethical language with an unattainable transcendent good and discrimination between worse and lesser evil is inappropriate to his worldly, vigilant 'ethics of consequences'.[34] This is an argumentative impasse in Morgenthau's theory, which does not entail any means to justify deontological ethics while using its language to support an essentially consequentialist argument. The one-time meticulous student of Nietzsche seems to worry that anything other than deontological language – essentially rooted in religious codices – would not be respected as indeed ethical, carrying timeless insights. Morgenthau appears concerned that the social practice of ongoing knowledge revision would discredit this particular realm of ossified knowledge and submit human beings (to the need) to experience all social situations all the time anew, including those endangering life.

It is Lebow who succeeds in articulating (rudiments of) an appropriate moral language for vigilant realism and who does not shy away from justifying ethics by the virtue of its 'instrumental merit'[35] for politics and a peaceful social life. By theorizing its link to justice, Lebow develops normative aspects of Morgenthau's concept of interest.[36] Interest joins self-awareness with recognition of others as agents endowed with equal lust for power, and hence ethical subjectivity. This is Morgenthau's 'lesser evil' seen from actors' subjective perspectives. Like interest, justice is a concept exclusive to social life. Conceptions of justice change over time, but each 'viable community'[37] develops a notion that gives expression to legitimate (and hence inter-subjectively, intra-communally defined) merit, which we call justice. It serves as a 'source of self-restraint'[38] for those who seek ethical conduct in the social world.

Lebow's theoretical advancement is paid for at the price of making a teleological argument. Inspired by Greek thought, especially Thucydides, Lebow fully embraces such teleology. Ethics is grounded in 'observable empirical regularities',[39] for instance that *hamartia* follows hubris, while the aim of ethics is to avert hubris. What then differentiates particular moral codes from other forms of knowledge-formation is not transcendent origin but the length of time and complexity of processes to formulate and conventionally accept an insight about social experience as a moral rule and, conversely, to demote its moral status. The temporal and procedural distance between the formation of a moral norm and more recent social knowledge applicable to an issue provides for the vantage point for moral judgment and, conversely, for the norm to be challenged.

One essential norm-forming process is reflection on moral psychology, on how particular experiences and moral rules already in use affect human psyche in its manifold situations. Because it may challenge accepted understanding on how power is actualized, such reflection, often emerging through emotions, is more likely in art than in more purposeful reflection on social experience. Thus, Morgenthau cites Goethe for his 'wisdom' and Lebow makes full sense of such inclination. If we want to gain knowledge on how present moral norms and social practices are felt, we need a 'bridg[e] to the humanities and creative arts' and, consequently, 'renegotiate' our political practice in order to put us more 'in touch with ourselves and others'.[40]

Conclusion

Vigilant realism is a theoretical abstraction from the theories of Morgenthau and Lebow, which suppresses some idiosyncrasies and differences between the two. Its main attributes are an analysis that singles out human power-aspiration as an underlying social and psychological force and a consequence-oriented, socially embedded ethic. Both are results of a particular inspiration by tragedy, the tragic vision, which takes place in a specific moment of theory construction, its philosophical reasoning.

Compared to many IR theories endowed with a guiding ideal of progress – most notably various liberal (progress as perfection) and critical theory (progress as emancipation) approaches – vigilant realism's progressivism is slow and its expectations on occurrences of full-fledged social change are modest but resolute. This is because such progressivism depends on summative 'vigilance' of a particular society/culture. It is proportionate to the occurrence of creative expression within the society and to the quality of reflection on such expression translatable into new social knowledge and, eventually, maybe also changed social practices and norms. For the sake of *progressive* social change, it matters that those effects of present norms and practices are expressed which do not get a hearing as expected realizations of power/agency in contemporary political practice. Although against its impulses, it is in the interest of those with greatest power/agency to support such grass-roots expression and concomitant new knowledge-formation, because they give power instruction on where to limit its hubris-prone tendencies, which would otherwise lead to strife and possible annihilation.

Vigilant realism's viability as a theory of politics and political change, therefore, rests on a cognitive and emotional paradox. On the one hand, it is essential that ethics be affirmed as an indispensable, irreplaceable practice of knowledge-transmission across time and place, which instructs us how to navigate political action away from hubris and strife. In order to be accepted as such, ethical knowledge must be perceived as authoritative, timeless, wise, satisfying, meaningful, sufficient, and so on. On the other hand, vigilant realism requires that particular moral norms, including conceptions of justice, be always open to challenge and exposed as limited, changeable, relative, localized, and time-bound. Doubt, insecurity, confusion, or nihilism accompany such vulnerability to challenge.

Theory might succeed in explaining the usefulness of contradictions like this one. However, complicated explanations rarely suffice to take away disappointment over mixed messages and accompanying emotional tension, or attract audiences in the first place. It is – again – art, through which cultures engage with contradictions. By not adjudicating between motives of action and depicting only their critical incompatibility, tragedy has the specific power to uphold ethics and affirm the need of moral life as such, while simultaneously deeming particular moral norms wanting, shortsighted, or partial. Tragedy cultivates ethical scepticism without giving way to nihilism.[41] This is the way vigilant realism reaches to the much broader tragic inspiration even after the tragic vision discriminates its theoretical makeup. It is also a door through which vigilant realism presents a standing invitation to philosophical reasoning similar to that of Morgenthau and Lebow.

Notes

I am very grateful to Toni Erskine, Ned Lebow and Jan Ruzicka for their excellent comments/suggestions on several versions of this chapter. I am also indebted to Ken Booth for comments on an earlier draft, although I failed to address some of his pertinent questions, especially on the sources of moral motivation in vigilant realism. I would also like to thank Catherine Lu and Ben Schupmann for stimulating discussions on the topic of tragedy and theory and for comments on an earlier draft.

1. I consider the divide between international relations theory and political theory one of academic practice, not of substance. See B. C. Schmidt (2002) 'Together Again: Reuniting Political Theory and International Relations Theory', *British Journal of Politics and International Relations*, 4/1, 115–40.
2. Chicago: The University of Chicago Press (1965 [1946]).
3. Cambridge: Cambridge University Press (2003).

Kamila Stullerova 125

4. S. S. Wolin ([1960] 2004) *Politics and Vision: Continuity and Innovation in Western Political Thought* (Princeton: Princeton University Press), p. 19.
5. J. P. Euben (1986) *Greek Tragedy and Political Theory* (Berkeley and Los Angeles: University of California Press), p. 4.
6. Edited transcript of the round table at the conference 'The Work of Hannah Arendt', Toronto, November (1972), in M. A. Hill (ed.) (1979) *Hannah Arendt: The Recovery of the Public World* (New York: St Martin's Press), p. 333.
7. R. C. Pirro (2000) *Hannah Arendt and the Politics of Tragedy* (DeKalb: Northern Illinois University Press); J. P. Euben (2000) 'Arendt's Hellenism', in D. Villa (ed.) *The Cambridge Companion to Hannah Arendt* (Cambridge: Cambridge University Press), pp. 158–62, and E. Young-Bruehl (1982) *Hannah Arendt: For the Love of the World* (New Haven: Yale University Press), pp. 451, 453–4.
8. Hill (ed.) (1979) *Hannah Arendt*, pp. 333–4.
9. M. Frost, 'Tragedy, Ethics and International Relations', this volume, pp. 21–43.
10. J. Mayall, 'Tragedy, Progress and the International Order', this volume, pp. 44–52 (p. 44).
11. Ibid.
12. J. P. Euben, 'The Tragedy of Tragedy', this volume, pp. 86–96.
13. M. Oakeshott (1996) *Religion, Politics and the Moral Life* (New Haven: Yale University Press), p. 107; cited in N. Rengger, 'Tragedy or Scepticism? Defending the Anti-Pelagian Mind in World Politics', this volume, pp. 53–62.
14. Euben (1986) *Greek Tragedy*, p. 13.
15. M. Leslie (1970) 'In Defence of Anachronism', *Political Studies*, 18/4, 433–7; cited in Euben (1986) *Greek Tragedy*, p. 3. Leslie was the maiden name of the political theorist now known as Margaret Canovan.
16. Leslie addresses Quentin Skinner's 1969 article 'Meaning and Understanding in the History of Ideas', *History and Theory*, 8/1, 3–53.
17. Euben (1986) *Greek Tragedy*, p. 4. The following quotations in this paragraph are all from this page.
18. Euben (1986) *Greek Tragedy*, p. 13.
19. H. Suganami (2008) 'Narrative and Explanation in International Relations: Back to Basics', *Millennium*, 37/2, 349–50. (Suganami draws on H. White (1973) *Metahistory* (Baltimore: The Johns Hopkins University Press), pp. 7–11.)
20. Suganami (2008) 'Narrative and Explanation in International Relations: Back to Basics', p. 350.
21. Lebow (2003) *The Tragic Vision*, p. 360.
22. Academic historians tend to create identification through shared group belonging, hence the popularity of national history as opposed to other historical subjects.
23. Wolin ([1960] 2004) *Politics and Vision*, p. 19.
24. See J. N. Shklar ([1965] 1973) 'Political Theory of Utopia: From Melancholy to Nostalgia', in F. E. Manuel (ed.) *Utopias and Utopian Thought* (London: Souvenir Press), pp. 102–5, for an insightful account of esthetic and intellectual tensions accompanying classical utopia.
25. Especially in the opening chapter/story 'Nixon in hell'.
26. Lebow (2003) *The Tragic Vision*, p. 47.
27. Lebow (2003) *The Tragic Vision*, pp. 47, 150, 266.
28. Morgenthau ([1946] 1965) *Scientific Man*, p. 68.

29. M. C. Williams (2005) *The Realist Tradition and the Limits of International Relations* (Cambridge: Cambridge University Press), p. 83.
30. Williams (2005) *The Realist Tradition*, p. 172.
31. See Lebow (2003) *The Tragic Vision*, p. 250, for references.
32. H. J. Morgenthau (1966) 'The Purpose of Political Science', in J. C. Charlesworth (ed.) *A Design for Political Science: Scope, Objectives and Methods* (Philadelphia: American Academy of Political and Social Sciences), p. 77; cited in Lebow (2003) *The Tragic Vision*, p. 239.
33. This view is shared by Lebow and Williams.
34. Williams (2005) *The Realist Tradition*, p. 174.
35. Lebow (2003) *The Tragic Vision*, p. 389.
36. From Morgenthau's later works, where interest is used as a quasi-normative concept but which lack *Scientific Man's* direct engagement with ethical theory.
37. Lebow (2003) *The Tragic Vision*, p. 356.
38. Lebow (2003) *The Tragic Vision*, p. 283.
39. Lebow (2003) *The Tragic Vision*, p. 355.
40. Lebow (2003) *The Tragic Vision*, pp. xiii, 63, 357, 388, and 360–92.
41. On tragedy's capacity to avert nihilism see O. Conolly (1998) 'Pity, Tragedy and the Pathos of Distance', *European Journal of Philosophy*, 6/3, 277–96.

Part III
On the Nature of Tragedy in International Relations

10
A Pessimism of Strength? Tragedy and Political Virtue

Benjamin A. Schupmann

Introduction

This volume includes references to many important texts on tragedy, including works by Sophocles, Aristotle, and Hegel. However, thus far one author who may be able to provide further insight into the relationship between tragedy and politics remains conspicuously absent: Nietzsche. Nietzsche's work on tragedy is particularly compelling because of its original analysis of tragedy and science in terms of political efficacy. Through this analysis, Nietzsche links the concept of tragedy to both politics and epistemology. Besides providing this insight, Nietzsche's account overlaps with the debate in this volume between Richard Ned Lebow and Nicholas Rengger on the question of whether tragedy embodies a category broader than tragic art and makes a positive contribution to understanding politics and international relations.

Walter Kaufmann begins his introduction to Nietzsche's *The Birth of Tragedy* by remarking that 'for all its faults, [it is] one of the most suggestive and influential studies of tragedy ever written. Perhaps only Aristotle's *Poetics* excels it'.[1] Although Nietzsche would later reject substantial portions of the text in his scathing 'Attempt at Self-Criticism', he did retain this important thesis: there is a relationship between tragedy and the ability to affect intentional change in the world and, conversely, societies that lack an appreciation of tragic art will decline.[2] In this context, 'intentional' means willed or realizing one's normative objectives in the world through action, while 'decline' here refers to the inability of a society's constituents to realize its values through action. Although he appeals to Greek society, Nietzsche has in mind its parallel with a Europe faced with a pervasive rationalization arising from the success of modern science. Thus, for Nietzsche, the relationship lies in the fact that as tragic art disappears from a society, its constituents become less and less able to act intentionally, or meaningfully, in the world.

Obviously then, Nietzsche is making a strong claim about the relevance of tragedy to effective political action. But what exactly does Nietzsche say and what are the consequences of his argument? This chapter will answer these questions first by defining what constitutes tragedy. It will maintain that at least six criteria, which will be explained below, are central to tragedy: the presence of genuine moral dilemmas, *peripeteia*, fate, the perspectivism of human nature, hubris, and theodicy. Second, it will explain that the decline of tragedy is a consequence of a kind of rationalism akin to scientific method, which holds that political action can be understood and prescribed with unprecedented accuracy – thus overcoming the problems tragedy presents. However, this chapter will argue, following Nietzsche, that the adoption of such an approach not only fosters misunderstanding of political affairs but also results in the decline of a society's capacity to act intentionally, leading either to immoderate and irresponsible actions or to a retreat away from action altogether, into theory. Finally, and in contrast to scientism, it will present a tragic account of reality as encouraging responsible, moderate action. Thus, the relationship between tragedy and what Nietzsche calls 'strength' – to act intentionally – will be shown to be more than merely correlative; it will be presented as causal.

What constitutes a tragedy?

Like any art form, tragic art is an imitation (*mimesis*) of reality.[3] Art belongs to the field of aesthetics; in its broadest sense, aesthetics means that which is knowable first through the senses (as opposed to known *a priori*, or without any basis in sense perception). According to this definition, then, tragic art is merely an idealization of real phenomena. It seems to be particularly akin to politics because of the aspects of reality that it imitates: the pathologies of normative deliberation and acting intentionally in the world.[4] Tragic art teaches an irrational reality – one that is morally neutral (neither just nor unjust).[5] Although Nietzsche never explicitly presents criteria for what constitutes tragedy, he would accept the following analytic outline of the constituents of tragedy, drawn from examples in other chapters in this volume.

The presence of genuine moral dilemmas

Nietzsche describes Prometheus' tragedy as: 'All that exists is just and unjust and equally justified.'[6] This is to say that conflicting and irresolvable – yet equally legitimate – normative demands are made upon or among actors; dilemmas that demand that the actor choose one moral commitment that may deny the possibility of satisfying another moral commitment, resulting in a moral impasse.[7] A moral dilemma is one in which there is no right course of action among the alternatives, objectively speaking. Consider the illustration of Antigone and Creon (in which one's moral duties to one's family are set against one's moral duties to one's *polis*).[8]

Peripeteia (the divide between intention and outcome)

This characteristic means actors' intentions can be undermined by their own actions or the consequences of those actions.[9] An actor's best attempt to act intentionally results in an outcome that paradoxically undermines that same intent. Oedipus fled Corinth to avoid his fate. He did not know (nor could he have known – which relates to the notion of fate and perspectivism) that only on leaving Corinth could the possibility to murder his father arise, and it was on that road that Oedipus actualized the prophecy.

Inevitability or fate

This illustrates the unavoidability of some actions and consequences, given the duty to abide certain normative restrictions on actions.[10] An actor's fate is pre-determined, to a variable but limited extent; identity constrains one's possibilities and delimits contingent ethical obligations.[11]

Perspectivism

According to this characteristic, the only way to avoid catastrophe with certainty, and realize one's normative intentions, would be if an actor possessed the ability to foresee the causal effects of any act *perfectly*, that is, if that actor were omniscient.[12] Tragically, any actor's inherent perspectivism, and corresponding limited knowledge of reality, limits his or her capacity to analyse and predict the causal effects of actions.[13] In turn, he or she is limited by this imperfect knowledge to affect reality. Ignoring these limits of knowledge, along with the constraints fate imposes, leads to hubris.

Hubris

Described as the error of thinking that we can 'transcend' our status and limitations,[14] hubris can also be explained as an actor's ignorance of their potential for *hamartia* – which is the occurrence of a justifiable (i.e. unpreventable and explainable) error because of the lack of knowledge about reality and self. To return to Oedipus, in killing the stranger who attacked him, his hubristic attempt to transcend fate was struck down; his belief that he was in control of his reality was self-delusional.

Theodicy

This is the problem that there is no correlation between suffering, goodness, and justice: justice is not a property of the world. Although it is often discussed in reference to god, it deals specifically with this problem. To present this, tragic art idealizes its characters by presenting them as the most virtuous agents: they are the wisest, best-intentioned, and strongest individuals, yet even they are subject to tragedy, catastrophe, and downfall.[15] '[In tragedy,] virtuous people are victims of disease, death, and every kind of social misfortune. No amount of knowledge or power can protect against the kind of reversals tragic heroes encounter or the suffering they bring on'.[16]

Although it may not be the case that all are present in a particular tragedy, these six criteria are relevant constituents of what one would call tragic art. Moreover, these criteria all seem to be accurate representations of problems that face real agents in their quotidian lives. It is with this notion of tragedy that Nietzsche's analysis of tragedy's political efficacy will be explored.

The rise of optimism from Socratic rationalism

Tragedy declined for what initially seems to be good reason, however. Its decline came out of a Socratic innovation. Socrates refined a better way of understanding reality, one more akin to modern science than had yet existed: the concept.[17] At the heart of this approach is a pervasive rationalization of phenomena that allows for the logical equation of things and events in the real world by discovering their rational essences as quasi-noumenal 'forms'. This does not seem to have been a novel approach *per se*; rationalization is a normal mental occurrence. Nietzsche puts it well when he says:

> Thus there is in every judgment the avowal of having encountered an 'identical case': it therefore presupposes comparison with the aid of memory. The judgment does not produce the appearance of an identical case. Rather it believes it perceives one: it works under the presupposition that identical cases exist ... There could be no judgments at all if a kind of equalization were not practiced within

sensations ... Before judgment occurs, the process of assimilation must already have taken place.[18]

The appeal of conceptual abstraction, or rationalization, lies in that it fosters good judgement; Socrates' development seems to be a primordial form of scientific method.[19] In contrast, modern scientific method can be defined by three related criteria:[20] formalization (conclusions drawn from a phenomenon are general, not particular); causal formulation (conclusions drawn from a phenomenon are understood by definitive and communicable causal sequences (e.g. if/then formulae)); and repeatability given *ceteris paribus*[21] (the conclusion holds always, given relevantly similar conditions). Intentional human action is predicated upon the reasonable belief that relevantly similar/identical actions in relevantly similar/identical circumstances will definitely produce relevantly similar/identical outcomes. Put differently, to be able to act intentionally, an agent must adopt some derivative of the above inductive, scientific approach. For Nietzsche, Socrates merely refined this natural mental process by appealing to some essential form underlying all phenomena, which makes identity more explicit and accessible in such reasoning.

Nietzsche saw the seeds for modern science and its impressive ability to change the natural world in Socrates' revolution, and he equates Socratic rationalism with scientism. In fact, modern scientific method has shown the success and power of the rationalization of phenomena. This has been the case in particular with natural science, as well as with the application of 'pure' analytical approaches like mathematics. An increasing understanding of 'natural' causal relations and the accumulation of that knowledge have led to countless advances, allowing humanity to better its own condition by affecting the natural world. This success has engendered the reasonable belief that less obviously rationalizable phenomena, 'human' phenomena, are also susceptible to this method.[22] What has grown from the seed of Socratic rationalism promises an unprecedented achievement of agents' intentions to shape the world, and has shown amazing success already in the natural world.

Accordingly, tragedy declines because the problems it presents, in the criteria outlined above, are taught to be surmountable by rationalization and by rationality. Scientific method, when properly applied, can effectively resolve the problems tragedy presents.[23] The imitation of reality that tragedy presents is then seen as unnecessarily pessimistic, or even unreasonable and counterfactual in the sense that it discourages positive normative change in human life through an irrational fear of the unknown and causality.[24] The claim is that, because tragedy is generally perceived as representing reality poorly, as an irrational discouragement, the contemporary response has been to demote it conceptually to the status of mere staged entertainment. Seen in this light, it certainly has nothing to offer to agents empowered with scientific method who would seek to shape the political world intentionally.

Thus, Nietzsche claims that the pervasive rationalization resulting from Socrates' scientific approach, and the corresponding decline of tragedy results in an optimistic 'cheerfulness' about reality:[25] among other things, *peripeteia* loses its force and agents applying scientific method come to believe reality can be directed according to their (presumably good) intentions. Understanding reality according to scientific method allows the essence or nature of any phenomenon to be discovered. Moreover, because what is manipulated is the underlying form of a phenomenon, that is, its nature (which consists of inalienable and determining properties), there is a corresponding certitude that the casual effect intended will come about. Nature is necessary. Phenomena properly understood can be manipulated at will and with causal certainty towards whatever ends an agent sees fit. Thus, scientific manipulation is certain and provides agents with security that actions can be undertaken according to the dictates of abstract rationality, through knowledge of nature and cause and effect. Moreover, should incidentals or mistakes occur because of insufficient knowledge (incidentals being unpredicted side-effects; mistakes being misunderstandings of nature due to insufficient knowledge of a phenomenon), they can be corrected, as long as sufficient study is given to the incidental or mistake to properly understand its cause, its nature and how to rectify it. Presuming the above is correct, there is good reason to be cheerful.

More than a coincidence – the decline of tragedy and intentional political action

Nietzsche's point, however, is not to endorse this cheerful optimism. The rationalization of reality, the understanding of reality provided by scientific method, and the corresponding 'cheerful optimism' they produce, are built upon an unstable foundation. He states clearly that Socrates' work was a positive milestone for humanity:[26] science does have an appropriate place, as evidenced by its success in predicting and affecting aspects of the natural world. Nevertheless, one makes a profound error by attempting to apply scientific method to human nature, as it is an inappropriate device both for understanding and manipulating human affairs. No meaningful rationalizations of human nature can be made: it cannot be relevantly universalized and it cannot be reduced to only a rational core. Causal relations are impossible to establish, given that the intentions of agents are knowable only to that agent (if even to that agent).[27] Finally, the establishment of *ceteris paribus* is a questionable claim for any particular social situation, given the infinitude of social variables and the diverse mentalities of agents and how this undermines formalizing human nature.[28] All three criteria of scientific method are questionable in the context of human nature, thus scientific method may not be the most appropriate epistemological device by which to understand it. With this in mind, Nietzsche responds to Socrates and modern science in saying that tragedy actually may be not only an accurate imitation of human affairs, but a better methodological approach with which to understand social reality.

Despite the impediments, the need for similitude to act intentionally in human affairs makes scientific method psychologically appealing, given its ability to manipulate causally the object's actual nature when properly applied. When this is coupled with both the success of scientific method in intentionally acting in the natural world and the above conclusion about incidentals or mistakes, an overestimation of the power and range of applicability of scientific method naturally occurred. Thus, when scientific method fails accurately to account for human affairs in terms of formality, repeatability and causality, the presumption is not that the epistemological device itself is questionable or inappropriately applied to its object, but that the failure was due to either an insufficient understanding of an empirical causal relationship or an insufficient rationalization of the object itself, that is, the object was imprecisely conceptualized as if it were an error of arithmetic or measurement in the natural sciences. The shortcomings of social reality to conform to scientific rationalizations are altogether ignored and efforts to rationalize it continue because science, when unguided by anything more substantial, is blind to its limits and finds itself in a vicious circle.[29]

Rengger's contribution to this volume points to this phenomenon. Morgenthau and Oakeshott agreed with each other (and Nietzsche) on the problems that this scientism represented for politics: scientific method does have legitimate limits – the phenomena it investigates must be susceptible to scientific method; what phenomena are susceptible has not been accurately determined yet. Social reality, for one, is not the rational construct that a scientific account of it would depend upon. This point is extended further by other important political thinkers, and presented in both Rengger's and Lebow's contributions to this volume. Rengger reports that, 'Oakeshott agreed with Morgenthau about the problems and the errors in rationalism and scientism ... and their baleful consequences for modern thought'.[30] Both maintained that political science, the 'rationalized' enterprise that politics was being reconstructed as, was a mistake, and that the application of scientism to politics was likely to be dangerous to international peace and stability because the prescriptions of a scientistic approach are founded upon a causal certitude that is simply not there.[31]

Scientific approaches to human affairs are dangerous – even hubristic – because they naturally make immoderate prescriptions, grounded upon the certainty of the method itself. No method is truth, however; method is merely a conceptual instrument, an epistemological device. Instruments have realms in which they are applicable and realms in which they are not, of which their user should be aware. In not accounting for the possibility of scientific method's limitations – that reality cannot be rationalized significantly or even made to correspond perfectly to the abstracted concept – human agency cannot conceive of the possibility of the method's inherent inability to correctly determine the nature of social reality (or the impossibility of resolving any failure through further application of scientific method). Therefore, if an action cannot fail, or if the unintended consequences can be repaired by further study of the necessary laws of the natural properties of a phenomenon, then there is no reason *not* to attempt to realize actions that might risk dangerous or even catastrophic consequences from mistakes or incidentals. That is, certainty allows one to undertake any endeavour, regardless of peripheral risk, because, in fact, the knowledge obtained with scientific method logically eliminates any gamble – it is causally certain that an outcome can be accomplished, given *ceteris paribus*. Certitude breeds confidence; false certitude breeds false confidence. Thus, actions guided by only scientific considerations are intrinsically immoderate – 'science, spurred by its powerful illusion, speeds irresistibly towards its limits where its optimism, concealed in the essence of logic, suffers shipwreck'.[32] The immoderation of science, when applied to human affairs, is *hamartia* or the fatal flaw that leads to catastrophe. There is a limit to what is knowable, especially when knowledge is defined as only that which can be obtained by scientific method, and this relevantly constrains the possibility to act in human affairs. Science's cheerful optimism is blind to the limits of its method and thus forces and repeats this error unintentionally.

The tragic recognition

Conversely, Nietzsche recognizes the limits of scientific method. To recap from above, all three criteria of scientific method are undermined by the nature of human affairs: human nature cannot be sufficiently rationalized and thus made formal; causal relationships may be supposed but not established with certitude; and *ceteris paribus* cannot be established, so social phenomena are not repeatable at will. However, this recognition of both the legitimacy of tragedy as imitative of reality and the limits of certainty in realizing one's aims has a corresponding negative effect on intentional social action. Nietzsche believes, perhaps taking the notion too far, that this inherent uncertainty of action grounded in the unscientific character of human affairs/nature, when combined with the real pathologies inherent to intentional human action (those which are imitated by tragedy), overwhelms, or 'nauseates', an agent – rendering the agent incapable of acting because of his or her own perceived impotence in affecting reality.[33]

What Nietzsche points towards,[34] and what other theorists like Max Weber[35] would conclude from this, is an epistemological claim that there is a relevant distinction to be made between reality and mind: the rational structures which the mind is capable of imposing upon reality must be qualified with their actual absence in reality itself. The presence of rationality in a phenomenon is a product of a mind's idealization of that phenomenon, not a quality of the phenomenon itself; for Nietzsche reality precedes its Socratic form. In other words, reality is particular, concrete, qualitative, and contingent – whereas concepts are de facto abstract, general, consistent, and often lend themselves to quantitative analysis. In addition, reality is infinitely complex – both qualitatively and quantitatively – which renders it irreducible to any concept.[36] This means that concepts and science cannot comprehensively account for reality. Social science is not able to surmount this problem because its interest in affecting change in particulars of social reality makes an unqualified scientific method *a priori* inapplicable.[37]

Present in *The Birth of Tragedy* is a primordial form of Nietzsche's Platonic inversion.[38] This holds that the empirical world is primary, and it is an aesthetic phenomenon, in the above-defined sense, before anything else.[39] Concepts are secondary and spring from human representations of what is real: phenomena. The human mind conceives of future actions first on a foundation derived from what has been perceived and second through what rational conceptual formulation of those perceptions is possible; an agent's deliberation about possible actions is derived from particular aesthetic perceptions the agent has accumulated and also the situation as communicated to an agent by external sources of information, which in turn were derived aesthetically by another agent.[40] Concepts are an idealization of these phenomena logically necessary for intentional action, but that does not grant them a reality more real or true than the aesthetic phenomena from which they are derived. What this epistemological argument means for political action in this case is that, because of the inherent uncertainty of actions, agents perceive the futility of intentional action in an irrational world. The pessimism of the tragic recognition then might overwhelm them. This paralytic nausea is exemplified in the character of Hamlet: 'true knowledge ['that action could not change anything in the eternal nature of things in order to set right a world that is out of joint'], an insight into the horrible truth, outweighs any motive for action ...'[41] The realization of the impotence and absurdity of action – granted by the tragic recognition – shatters one's will to affect the world.

Yet Nietzsche calls the tragic recognition 'a pessimism of strength'.[42] Initially this seems a contradiction. However, despite a pessimistic attitude towards the possibilities of intentional actions, tragedy actually works to overcome nihilism and permit intentional action. How it does this can be presented with the following 'syllogism':[43]

(a) → (not-a) → (A),

where (a) means that tragedy has the *positive* epistemological function of revealing a truth of life. This is accomplished through imitating life's inherent moral dilemmas, *peripeteia*, fate, the perspectivism of human nature, hubris, and theodicy. (not-a) is the natural pessimistic conclusion: tragedy and tragic art seem to discourage and even nauseate; if one cannot know with certainty whether one will be able to affect one's intention and acts are consequently 'tragic', then why would one even attempt to act meaningfully at all? In other words, why is the tragic recognition not nihilistic? Oakeshott makes a similar point when he makes his criticism of Morgenthau's adoption of tragedy, saying of Morgenthau that 'only a rationalistic reformer will confuse the imperfections which can be remedied with the so-called imperfections which cannot, and will think of the irremovability of the latter as a tragedy'.[44] That is, labelling the pathologies of action as 'tragic' is unnecessary; doing so mixes an emotionally pejorative sense into a 'fact' of action, which discourages action.

Nietzsche's analysis does not end with this pessimistic conclusion, however. The tragic syllogism concludes with (A): tragedy and tragic art revitalize the will to act by endowing acts with aesthetic significance, and through the virtues that those qualities entail. Despite the failures, sufferings, sadness and eventual death to which every human is condemned, tragedy comforts with the idea that 'it is only as an *aesthetic phenomenon* that existence and the world are eternally *justified*'.[45] Thus, to solve this second dilemma of tragedy's seeming condemnation of intentional social action (the first being that of cheerful, yet dangerously immoderate scientism), Nietzsche proposes the aesthetic ideal of living 'beautifully' in the empirical world ('beautifully' here is in its broad sense, meaning excellently or nobly).[46] In spite of what one has suffered, one can justify oneself and one's actions aesthetically and find some *empirical* redemption in this, as opposed to extra-worldly redemption that would rely on the primacy of a noumenal world. Tragedy achieves this precisely because it gives values to the only world that is unqualifiedly real. Especially important for this notion of noble living is the virtue of courage, which entails facing one's inability to act with certainty and the tragic implications of uncertainty but acting nonetheless in a manner responsible to both justice and one's limits. The relevance of noble living relates back to the notion of fate. Although one may not be able to prevent catastrophe, one is justified in acting in the best-intentioned and most noble ways to avert it.

Politics in light of tragedy

As Lebow rightly argues in the conclusion to his chapter, tragedy instills recognition of the uncertainty of actions and their consequences in agents, and this knowledge extends beyond just the intentions that motivate the actions themselves. This knowledge necessarily moderates an agent's actions; it qualifies the intentions of the agent with a prudent scepticism of the certainty of any outcome – but this prudent scepticism is not discouragement if one can recognize that one acted as responsibly and as well as one could, given that uncertainty and what it entailed. Tragedy is actually the antidote for hubris.[47] It moderates because, without certainty, the gravity of an action – in particular an agent's potential for *hamartia* and double effects – becomes a vital consideration. Every action's outcome becomes an unquantifiable probability, which, if it fails to achieve what one intends, may not be rectifiable and could result in a downfall into catastrophe from which no recovery is possible. The agent is compelled to moderate action to safeguard not only the normative ideals sought in action but also the existence of his or her very self and community (that is, a significant source of his or her identity).[48] Fear that the act may undermine everything, even the intention for acting itself, will cause very careful consideration of things that cannot be undone and cannot be risked. This is ultimately a very different attitude from cheerful scientism, which mitigates this fear and allows unmoderated action with its confidence in knowledge of cause and effect as well as the ability to solve its mistakes and incidentals.

Rengger, Oakeshott, and Lebow all conclude rightly that scientism misunderstands the nature of international relations and even brings about international catastrophe, but this conclusion suggests that one already recognizes as real the above characteristics that tragic art imitates. Oakeshott and Rengger treat the concept of tragedy as unnecessary or even harmful to political deliberation and international relations theory because the notion of tragedy introduces a misleading evaluative element.[49] However, this may miss the point of what tragic art and the criteria constituting tragedy really are. Tragic art is just an imitation of phenomena – real things perceived by the senses. It is not clear that Rengger or Oakeshott would disagree that the phenomena that tragic art imitates are legitimate concerns for a political agent. Moreover, recognizing the insufficiency of scientism for grasping political phenomena should imply that they must be approached as particulars first, which is to say through aesthetic perception rather than through *a priori* assumptions. Thus, tragedy *is* what 'human beings, and human actions, simply are',[50] or at least a relevant part of that, unless one believes that the criteria that constitute what tragedy imitates and idealizes – inherent moral dilemmas, *peripeteia*, fate, the perspectivism of human nature, hubris and theodicy – are not real phenomena that occur. Lebow, in dialogue with Rengger, is right in claiming that politics does have an inherent tragic quality as well as that the aesthetic notion of tragedy cannot be separated from politics because of its educative value.[51] Particularly acute here, for Lebow, is that deliberation on irreconcilable moral dilemmas is something that real political leaders face on a regular basis.

To press this even further, insofar as tragedy is relevant to politics, it seems that the conclusions about tragedy and politics would be especially relevant to theorizing about international relations. International relations are not qualitatively different from other kinds of politics, but it does occur on a significantly grander scale. In particular, the potential for moral dilemmas is significantly greater because of the greater diversity in identity, and its import. Moreover, the complexity of variables, due to the broader scale of international relations, also implies that the chance for *peripeteia* and perspectivism are significantly greater. *Hamartia's* consequences are particularly grave here because of the potentially greater catastrophe *hamartia* would produce, such as international war and even nuclear conflict. All of this makes tragedy's warning against treating politics as a science and its plea for virtues such as self-moderation essential to discussions of international relations. Whatever it contributes to politics, the concept of tragedy seems to have greater value for those who deliberate about international relations because of the greater incidence of these characteristics and the catastrophes that could result from *hamartia*. This is illustrated well by other contributions to this volume, such as Frost and Mayall's meditations on global civil society and Western liberal democratic values, accompanied by particular tragic examples such as Somalia and Iraq.

In sum, the phenomena that tragic art imitates do exist, and this makes the concept of tragedy legitimate for understanding politics. Tragedy is further legitimated by its ability to didactically represent phenomena that may have great value in future political deliberation and action. To dismiss tragedy risks divorcing the value of the imitative idealization of these phenomena, and thus risks obscuring the aspects of reality that tragic art attempts to make more explicit for the understanding of politics.[52] That is, dismissing tragic art or diminishing its role in political deliberation is a misunderstanding of exactly the relational dependence that tragic art has, as an ideal-type, upon real political phenomena. Divorcing tragic art from reality and dismissing it as 'merely art' risks diminishing the significance of what is being imitated. Because of this, there is more than just a coincidence between tragedy and the ability of a society to actualize its intentions. Tragedy is an essential account of what human beings and human actions are – the understanding of which political agents should discard only at their own risk. This is why the pre-Socratic Greeks – who believed the highest mode of life to be political – held tragedy to be the highest art form.

Notes

I am grateful to David Rasmussen, Michael C. Williams, Alessandro Ferrara, Mario De Caro, Aakash Singh, Stefano Guzzini, Jean Cohen, William Bain, Hidemi Suganami, Howard Williams, Luigi Caranti, Kamila Stullerova, the Aberystwyth Critical and Cultural Politics Group, the Luiss Guido Carli Graduate Research Seminar, Christopher Hobson, David Lievens, and the editors, Toni Erskine and Richard Ned Lebow, for their help and comments in developing this article.

1. W. Kaufmann (1967) 'Translator's Introduction', in F. W. Nietzsche, *The Birth of Tragedy and the Case of Wagner*, trans. W. Kaufmann (New York: Random House, Inc.), p. 3.

2. Nietzsche (1967) *Birth of Tragedy*, pp. 17–18, 59–60, 84, 96–8.
3. Aristotle *Poetics*, 1447 a15.
4. Aristotle *Poetics*, 1449 b24–25, 1450 a16–19.
5. Nietzsche (1967) *Birth of Tragedy*, pp. 23, 89, 91.
6. Nietzsche (1967) *Birth of Tragedy*, p. 72; Albert Camus remarks, 'the forces confronting each other in tragedy are equally legitimate, equally justified ... each force is at the same time both good and bad ... the tragic formula would be: 'All can be justified, no one is just'. A. Camus (1970) 'On the Future of Tragedy', in P. Thody (ed.) *Lyrical and Critical Essays*, trans. E. Conroy Kennedy (New York: Vintage Books), p. 301.
7. M. Frost, 'Tragedy, Ethics and International Relations', this volume, pp. 21–43; J. Mayall, 'Tragedy, Progress and the International Order, this volume, pp. 44–52; J. P. Euben (1986) 'Introduction', in J. P. Euben (ed.) *Greek Tragedy and Political Theory* (Berkeley: University of California Press), p. 17; A. Ferrara (1998) *Reflective Authenticity* (New York: Routledge), pp. 52, 55.
8. Cf. Frost, 'Tragedy, Ethics and International Relations, p. 28.
9. Nietzsche (1967) *Birth of Tragedy*, pp. 67; Frost, 'Tragedy, Ethics and International Relations'; Lebow, 'Tragedy, Politics and Political Science', pp. 63–71.
10. Nietzsche (1967) *Birth of Tragedy*, pp. 60, 67; Frost, 'Tragedy, Ethics and International Relations'.
11. Frost, 'Tragedy, Ethics and International Relations'; Lebow, 'Tragedy, Politics and Political Science'.
12. Frost, 'Tragedy, Ethics and International Relations', p. 32.
13. Nietzsche (1967) *Birth of Tragedy*, pp. 23, 67.
14. Lebow, 'Tragedy, Politics and Political Science', p. 64.
15. Nietzsche (1967) *Birth of Tragedy*, p. 67; Cf. Nietzsche (1967) *Birth of Tragedy*, pp. 77–8; Aristotle *Poetics*, 1454 b9.
16. R. N. Lebow (2003) *The Tragic Vision of Politics: Ethics, Interests and Orders* (Cambridge: Cambridge University Press), pp. 364–5. Cf. S. G. Salkever (1986) 'Tragedy and the Education of the *Dêmos*: Aristotle's Response to Plato', in Euben (ed.) *Greek Tragedy and Political Theory*, pp. 290, 297, 300.
17. Nietzsche (1967) *Birth of Tragedy*, pp. 90, 94, 97; Cf. M. Weber (1959) 'Science as a Vocation', in *From Max Weber: Essays in Sociology*, trans. H. H. Gerth and C. Wright Mills (New York City: Oxford University Press), p. 141.
18. F. W. Nietzsche (1968) *The Will to Power*, trans. W. Kaufmann and R. J. Hollingdale (New York: Vintage Books), aphorism 532 (p. 289); Cf. aphorisms 477, 499, 500, 515 (pp. 264, 273, 278).
19. Nietzsche (1967) *Birth of Tragedy*, pp. 95–6, 84.
20. All three criteria are drawn from J. Elster (1990) 'When Rationality Fails', in K. Schweers Cook and M. Levi (eds) *The Limits of Rationality* (London: The University of Chicago Press), p. 24.
21. Cf. J. Dupré (2001) *Human Nature and the Limits of Science* (Oxford: Oxford University Press), p. 10.
22. Nietzsche (1967) *Birth of Tragedy*, p. 95.
23. Nietzsche (1967) *Birth of Tragedy*, pp. 83–4, 91.
24. Nietzsche (1967) *Birth of Tragedy*, p. 89.
25. Cf. Nietzsche (1967) *Birth of Tragedy*, pp. 18, 21, 67, 78, 97.
26. Nietzsche (1967) *Birth of Tragedy*, pp. 93, 97; Cf. Kaufmann (1967) 'Translator's Introduction', pp. 11–12.

27. Cf. F. W. Nietzsche (1982) *Daybreak*, trans. R. J. Hollingdale (Cambridge: Cambridge University Press), Aphorism 116; J. Heil (2004) *Philosophy of Mind: A Contemporary Introduction* (London: Routledge), pp. 17–18, 53, 226–30.

28. M. Weber (1969) *The Methodology of the Social Sciences*, trans. E. A. Shils and H. A. Finch (New York: Free Press), pp. 42, 82, 110–11, 169–70.

29. Nietzsche (1967) *Birth of Tragedy*, pp. 97–8.

30. N. Rengger, 'Tragedy, or Scepticism? Defending the Anti-Pelagian Mind in World Politics', this volume, pp. 53–62 (p. 59).

31. M. Oakeshott (1996) 'Scientific Politics', in T. Fuller (ed.) *Religion, Politics and the Moral Life* (New Haven: Yale University Press), pp. 97–106.

32. Nietzsche (1967) *Birth of Tragedy*, p. 97.

33. Nietzsche (1967) *Birth of Tragedy*, pp. 59–60; Cf. M. Warren (1988) *Nietzsche and Political Thought* (Cambridge, MA: The MIT Press), pp. 127–8, 232.

34. Nietzsche (1967) *Birth of Tragedy*, pp. 21–2, 78, 84.

35. G. Oakes (1988) *Weber and Rickert: Concept Formation in the Cultural Sciences* (Cambridge, MA: The MIT Press), pp. 49–53, 53–6, 64–8.

36. Oakes (1988) *Weber and Rickert*, pp. 22, 54.

37. Weber (1969) *The Methodology of the Social Sciences*, pp. 90–5, 99, 105; Oakes (1988) *Weber and Rickert*, pp. 22–3.

38. F. W. Nietzsche (1982) 'Twilight of the Idols', in W. Kaufmann (ed.) *The Portable Nietzsche*, trans. W. Kaufmann (New York: Viking Penguin Inc.), pp. 485–6.

39. Nietzsche (1967) *Birth of Tragedy*, pp. 22, 52.

40. A. Ferrara (2008) *The Force of the Example* (New York: Columbia University Press), pp. 57–61.

41. Nietzsche (1967) *Birth of Tragedy*, p. 60.

42. Nietzsche (1967) *Birth of Tragedy*, p. 17.

43. This syllogism has been adopted from M. S. Silk and J. P. Stern (1981) *Nietzsche on Tragedy* (Cambridge: Cambridge University Press), pp. 351–2.

44. Oakeshott (1996) 'Scientific Politics', p. 108.

45. Nietzsche (1967) *Birth of Tragedy*, p. 52.

46. Viz. the Greek notion of *arête*; Cf. T. H. Brobjer (2003) 'Nietzsche's Affirmative Morality: An Ethics of Virtue', *Journal of Nietzsche Studies*, 26, pp. 67, 70–4; C. Daigle (2006) 'Nietzsche: Virtue Ethics … Virtue Politics?' *Journal of Nietzsche Studies*, 32, pp. 6–11.

47. Lebow, 'Tragedy, Politics and Political Science', this volume; Cf. Salkever (1986) 'Tragedy and the Education of the *Dêmos*', p. 300.

48. Cf. Frost, 'Tragedy, Ethics and International Relations.'

49. N. Rengger, 'Tragedy, or Scepticism?'.

50. N. Rengger, 'Tragedy, or Scepticism?', p. 59; p. Salkever (1986) 'Tragedy and the Education of the *Dêmos*', p. 290.

51. Lebow, 'Tragedy, Politics and Political Science', this volume.

52. Salkever (1986) 'Tragedy and the Education of the *Dêmos*', p. 276.

11
Nietzsche and Questions of Tragedy, Tyranny and International Relations

Tracy B. Strong

> It is no tragic death to be killed by a failed state.
> See Aristotle, *Poetics*[1]

I want to raise three questions in this chapter. The first has to do with Nietzsche's understanding of tragedy and of its importance politically. The second has to do with what a world *without* tragedy would be like. Finally, I ask what might be the implications of such a world for international relations in our times.

Nietzsche on tragedy and politics

Nietzsche's first book, *The Birth of Tragedy from the Spirit of Music*, is not just about birth. It is also about the *death* of tragedy, about that which makes tragedy unavailable. (Nicholas Rengger picks up on this quizzically and calls attention to the book by George Steiner, *The Death of Tragedy*).[2] 'Greek tragedy', writes Nietzsche, 'met an end different from that of her older sister-arts [the epic and lyric poetry]: she died by suicide, in consequence of an irreconcilable conflict'.[3] That tragedy can 'die' means that tragedy is a particular way of viewing or understanding the world, an understanding that may not always be available.

Here one must proceed carefully. There is a tendency to use the word tragedy and the predicate 'tragic' somewhat promiscuously. There is a tendency, as Richard Ned Lebow points out not unsympathetically, to see tragedy simply as the consequence of what has come to be called 'value pluralism'.[4] You have your ethics and interests, I have mine, and the twain are not commensurable. Mervyn Frost, in particular, tends to read tragedy in this manner.[5] We find elements of this in Hans Morgenthau and it is the *Grundprinzip* of realism in international relations theory.[6]

Surely Isaiah Berlin also had this way of understanding tragedy. It is often forgotten that in his well-known 'Two Concepts of Liberty', the vision of positive and negative liberty overlays a terrorized picture of what Berlin takes to be our world. Our lot, for Berlin is *constantly* to confront diverging paths, choices that we must make in a void.

> The world that we encounter in ordinary experience is one in which we are faced with choices between ends equally ultimate and claims equally absolute, the realization of some of which must inevitably involve the sacrifice of the other.[7]

What strikes one here is that this is 'ordinary experience' for Berlin. For him, we are all Antigones, all the time, and this is because all we have are 'the ordinary resources of empirical observation and ordinary human knowledge'. I am sure that in my Christian mode I leave undone those things which I ought to have done and I do those things that I ought not to have done and even that 'there is no health in me'. But this is *not* tragic: it is sin. The problem with the conflicting demands view is that there is nothing for tragedy to accomplish. As the way of dealing with the conflict of values all that can be done is to establish toleration. John Rawls, for instance, finds a robust or 'thick' conception of the good to be incompatible with liberal politics.[8] The permanent conflict-of-values understanding of the tragic leaves no room for the possibility of political education – the central importance of which Euben reminds us – and there is also no possibility of the tragic ever disappearing from our world, since this situation is, as Berlin says, ubiquitous.

Here the tendency to amalgamate 'tragic' to 'tragedy' leads us astray. A tragedy was first and foremost a *play*, a play that performed and was intended to perform a significant political and cultural education. The word τραγῳδία, *tragōidia,* is a contraction from *tragos* (goat) and *aeidein* ('to sing') – it refers originally to a ritual at which a song was sung before the sacrifice of a goat in a religious ceremony (and, I believe, was also sung to the goat).[9] Before tragedy became a play, it was thus already an activity whereby some issue of importance in the city was addressed and by which the city performed a ritual for a purpose related to the health of the city.

In a tragedy, that which is tragic is *not* the confrontation of two non-commensurable values (*pace* Hegel and to some degree a number of the other contributors to this volume) but is rather that which is *consequent* to the insistence that one's own stance and point of view is the only admissible one.[10] We are not to *choose* between Antigone's understanding and Creon's. Likewise after Athena breaks a tie vote at the end of the

Eumenides, the Furies are neither defeated nor banished. They remain a part of the city.[11]

The tragedy – the play – is for the political education of the audience and is designed to keep them from resting on the need to believe, as it were, that a word has one and only one correct meaning. Thus Euben adduces the double appearance of *ktema* (possession) in Thucydides.[12] In the *Antigone*, both Antigone and Creon explicitly rest their stance on the requirements of *nomos*. It is wrong to say that they mean 'different things' by the word: what is wrong is that they have staked their life and soul on the word meaning only what they use it to mean. The point is that such words (indeed, I believe, potentially all words) are essentially contestable *and* that one is not free to make them mean what one wants (nor is the question who is to be the stronger, as we shall see below).

This gives us some sense of what tragedy was designed to accomplish. *The Birth of Tragedy* summarizes its political themes in the twenty-first chapter. Its matter is the 'most basic foundation of the life of a people' (*den innersten Lebensgrund eines Volkes*).[13] The earliest foundation had been in and from Homer. However, with the gradual development of living in cities focused around an agora rather than a palace, of commerce, of the breakdown of the preeminence of blood relations, and of the development of currency and writing, and with the victory over the Persians and a broader peace in the eastern Mediterranean, the model of society based on the contest found in Homer no longer sufficed.[14] (One can already see premonitions of the resultant tensions in the *Iliad*).[15] That which was Greece was in need of refounding – that is, in need of dealing with the new developments while remaining 'Greek'. It was in tragedy, Nietzsche argues, that the Greeks managed to accomplish this: 'Placed between India and Rome and pressed towards a seductive choice, the Greeks succeeded in inventing a third form, in classical purity' (BT 21). India is the undervaluation of politics and leads, says Nietzsche, to the orgy and then Buddhism; Rome is the overvaluation of politics and leads to secularization and the Roman imperium. Note by the way that tragedy – 'the tragic age' – is in effect the resolution to what one might call a proto-problem of international relations or at least of cultural imperialism.[16]

The greatest danger for Greece was that it would become caught in a single way of thinking and acting. Nietzsche considers this a form of tyranny. In *Beyond Good and Evil* he argues that the limitations of the Stoics came from the fact that they insisted on seeing nature as 'Stoic and that with time this became what nature was for them … But this is an old everlasting story: what happened then with the Stoics still happens today, *as soon as ever a philosophy begins to believe in itself.* It always creates the world in its own image; it cannot do otherwise; *philosophy is this tyrannical impulse itself,* the most spiritual will to power, to the 'creation of the world', to the *causa prima*'.[17] Though it is not only in doing philosophy that one creates the world in one's own image – so much we might say is the lesson that Nietzsche draws from Kant – the philosophical and eventually political difficulty comes when one comes to believe *and* insist that the image that one has created is in fact the way that the world is.[18] Here Nietzsche designates the belief in the naturalness of what one understands the world to be as the essence of the tyrannical impulse and holds it to be a more or less natural consequence of any philosophy. Philosophy is or wants to be a creation of the world, but it also fatally takes the world it creates to be the world *simpliciter.* Philosophy is in effect a form of lawgiving, of saying 'thus it shall be'.[19]

Tyranny thus arises for Nietzsche from *the failure to remember* that we live in worlds that we have made: tyranny is thus a forgetting of human agency, one might say. Much as in the famous passage about 'truth' as a 'worn out metaphor', as an 'illusion of which one has forgotten what it really is',[20] there is thus a kind of built-in amnesia about tyranny, an amnesia that accompanies all acts of volition.

The point here, however, has to do with what tyranny *means*: it is, in essence, taking as accomplished the world that one has defined and forgetting that the world in which one lives is one that one has made. It is for this reason that Nietzsche can write in *Beyond Good and Evil* that the 'will to truth is – *will to power*'.[21] It follows from this, however, that Nietzsche does not, and cannot, simply assume that one can at one's leisure forego this process. Why not? The most noteworthy characteristics of the tyrant are his (her?) belief in his own understanding of the world as simply and finally true and his failure to question that belief. The knowledge that the world in which one lives is one's own world means that that world has no more validity than one has oneself: this can induce modesty or megalomania, but it is not a matter of a mitigating Humean scepticism. Nietzsche does not think that one could simply *not* believe in what one does, adopting, as it were, a kind of benevolent scepticism toward oneself.

What, though, can be done about the impulse to forget? Nietzsche says that one of the cures that the Greeks apparently found for the amnesia inherent in tyranny was murder. Thus, 'the tyrants of the spirit were almost always murdered and had only sparse lasting consequences (*Nachkommenschaft*)'.[22] The solution may appear drastic, but Nietzsche holds it as part of the virtue of Greek politics that those who would fix once and for all the polis in their own terms were soon done away with. Thus in the first volume of *Human, All-Too-Human* Nietzsche writes of ancient philosophers. Each of them, he says,

> was an aggressive violent tyrant. The happiness in the belief that one possessed the truth has perhaps never been greater – so also the hardness, the exuberance, the tyrannical and the evil of such a belief. They were tyrants, that is, that which each Greek wanted to be and which each was when he could be. Perhaps Solon constitutes an exception; in his poems he speaks of how he spurned personal tyranny. But he did this out of love for his work, for his law giving, and the lawgiver is a sublimated form of the tyrannical.[23]

Inherent in philosophizing is a tyrannical element, which is the belief in the possession of the truth. The desire that what one believes in one's heart be true for all is both the essence of that element and a goal fervently sought after by ancient Greeks. It follows from this that the restraint on tyranny will not come from philosophy. This is not only because, as Alexandre Kojève writes, 'the philosopher's every attempt at directly influencing the tyrant is necessarily ineffectual' but because *philosophy is in itself tyrannizing*.[24]

The additional element here is that law is understood as a form of violence, as a sublimation of the tyrannical impulse. In addition, it is clear that the drive to tyranny is a necessary quality of thought. If all will is will to power, as Nietzsche will write later, then all will is the will to make the world in one's own image (whatever that image be). The praise that Nietzsche finds for this arrangement derives from the fact that precisely the competition set up by the desire of each to-be tyrant produces a situation where nothing is lasting.

In this early period, what kept philosophy from tyrannizing? Here Nietzsche's answer is importantly political. The political system required the killing of tyrants. Yet this solution to tyranny – one that was later to be given a central place in Machiavelli's conception of political foundation – cannot be complete. What if a tyrant is not killed? What if he constantly wins, if the populace flocks to him and shares his vision? This matter is not limited to what we would ordinarily name 'philosopher'. The paradigmatic case here is Homer, who is in effect a kind of philosopher-tyrant for Nietzsche. He writes:

> *Homer* – The greatest fact about Greek culture remains the fact that Homer became Panhellenic so soon. All the spiritual and human

freedom the Greeks attained goes back to this fact. But at the same time it was also the actual doom of Greek culture, for, by centralizing, Homer made shallow and dissolved the more serious instincts of independence. From time to time an opposition to Homer arose from the depths of Hellenic feeling; but he always triumphed. All great spiritual powers exercise a suppressing effect in addition to their liberating one.

Homer, Nietzsche concludes, 'tyrannizes'.[25]

Homer had in effect defined what it meant to be Greek; a problem arose when that which was Greek had difficulty in transforming the definition that Homer had achieved. (One must remember here that in *The Birth of Tragedy from the Spirit of Music*, Nietzsche had designated Homer as the prototype of the Apollonian. It is worth noting here also that Nietzsche does not attribute this achievement to a putative person, 'Homer', but thinks that 'Homer' became the name for what was achieved).[26] The point of his analysis both of the 'pre-Socratics' and of tragedy as a political educational activity was to explore how it was possible (for it was necessary) to redefine what it meant to be Greek in light of the developments (that had intervened). This was one of the central concerns of his early book, *Philosophy in the Tragic Age of the Greeks*.[27] This book, which remained unpublished and indeed unfinished, is about philosophy and politics and tragedy, about the possibility of philosophy and about the role of philosophy in making culture possible, about what that might mean in terms of a valuation of the everyday. Philosophy offers the possibility of the production of (one's own) genius. Nietzsche saw tragedy as the locus of collective participation, a common festival, the focus where the culture came together and pursued its understanding of itself.

What, though, was the relation of tragedy to philosophy? Here Nietzsche's analysis is one of a failed opportunity – a political failure. In *Philosophy in the Tragic Age of the Greeks*, Nietzsche argues that the philosophers before Socrates had political reformation in mind. They were, as he says at one point, *lauter Staatsmänner*.[28] But, he is clear also, that the project of reformation failed: the 'dawn remained almost only a ghostly appearance'. Failure came even to the philosopher who came the closest – Empedocles – whose 'soul had more compassions [*Mitleiden*] than any Greek soul [and] perhaps still not enough, for in the end, Greeks are poor at this and the tyrannical element became a hindrance in the blood of even the great philosophers'. This, despite the fact that 'something new was in the air, as proves the simultaneous emergence of tragedy'.[29]

The point here is that *the function of tragedy is to prevent tyranny*, that is to prevent the emergence and dominance of any individual who was so exceptional as to be unchallengeable or of any perspective on the world that was beyond question (likewise the point of ostracism was to prevent the same and ensure the possibility of conflict, of the *agon*). The political realm is, or should be, not about reaching 'rational' agreement, but about conflict. I am here placing central emphasis not on 'tragic' situations but on the ability to grasp a situation as tragic. Playwrights were to make a tragic situation available to an audience without however resolving it for them. The end of *Oedipus Tyrannos* urges the audience not to take anything as defined and definite before one is dead. At the end of *Oedipus at Colonus*, Antigone says that they are in even worse state than at the beginning ('How again to get us home/ I know not'). They are 'still driven by the ocean waves', sings the chorus. At the end of the *Antigone*, the chorus reminds us (as if we had not yet fully assimilated it) that 'Swelling words of high-flown might/Mightily the gods do smite.'

A world without tragedy

Genug: die Zeit kommt, wo man über Politik umlernen wird.	Enough: the time is come for us to transform all our views about politics. (KWG VIII-1, p. 85)

Hence to be a political education, tragedy requires an audience. Being a member of the audience requires a particular mode. This is the gist of Nietzsche's accusation against Socrates: his desire of rational explanation made it impossible for him to be a member of an audience (if you keep asking yourself why Othello just doesn't go have a talk with Desdemona about that handkerchief, you will never experience the play). Thus Socrates, in what Nietzsche sees as his insistence on determining *the* meaning of a word (what *is* justice, piety, etc ... ?), makes tragedy impossible and opens the door to the tyrannical impulse. As Nietzsche writes:

> Whoever wishes to test rigorously to what extent he himself is related to the true aesthetic listener or belongs to the community of the Socratic-critical persons needs only to examine sincerely the feeling with which he accepts *miracles* represented on the stage: whether he feels his historical sense, which insists on strict psychological causality, insulted by them, whether he makes a benevolent concession

and admits the miracle as a phenomenon intelligible to childhood but alien to him, or whether he experiences anything else. For in this way he will be able to determine to what extent he is capable of understanding *myth* as a concentrated image of the world that, as a condensation of phenomena, cannot dispense with miracles. It is probable however, that almost everyone, upon close examination, finds that the critical-historical spirit of our culture has so affected him that he can only make the former existence of myth credible to himself by means of scholarship, through intermediary abstractions. But without myth every culture loses the healthy natural power of its creativity: only a horizon defined by myths completes and unifies a whole cultural movement.[30]

Nietzsche describes here a *test* by which to determine if one is capable of being a (true) audience member. I cannot in this space explore more fully Nietzsche's notion of audience,[31] but it is important to note that Nietzsche wrote *The Birth of Tragedy* in the particular style in which he did with the intention that it too be for the present age the test of one's capacity to be an audience that he thought necessary.[32] I have insisted that what the plays made possible as political education was not a benign pluralism but an agonism that sought only a word and never a final word. This does not mean that Antigone and Creon should work out their differences over a couple of glasses of retsina. It does mean that one took responsibility for what one did and said without, however, requiring that the other acquiesce. It does not mean that neither of them may justify what they do on the grounds of being the final word – for each that leads to an embrace of death.

Thus to experience the tragic requires certain qualities of character that not all have, qualities that can also be lost. What Nietzsche clearly indicates here is that there exists the very real possibility that a world could exist in which some, perhaps most, were incapable of grasping tragedy and of responding to it in the manner set out above. In that case, policies could be pursued without doubt and in the absolute certainty of being correct. In such a world, *la raison du plus fort sera toujours la meilleur*, to paraphrase La Fontaine only slightly.

Nietzsche understood that modernity had changed the nature of politics. Central to modern international or 'great' politics is that the populace will be involved. In section 482 of the first volume of *Human, All-too-Human*, he is at pains to note the financial burden that the mobilization needed for great politics involves. As he notes: 'The demagogic character and intention to appeal to the masses is at present common to all political parties'. He goes on to compare this development to an 'earthquake' that has 'displaced ... former boundaries' and changed the ordering of the world.[33] In a discussion between 'two old 'patriots'' in *Beyond Good and Evil*, paragraph 241, Nietzsche has one of them ask if a statesman that requires his people to go in for 'great politics', even if, and especially if, their tastes lay elsewhere, could ever be called great. The other 'patriot' replies that certainly he would be called great, if only for the ability to get people to do such a thing. Nietzsche continues by having the first patriot reply: 'An abuse of words! ... strong and insane! Not great!'[34] The aphorism ends ambiguously as it leads us to believe that the will of one people comes to dominate over another but only at the cost of a 'spiritual flattening' of one and a concurrent 'deepening' of another.

The unspoken context is almost certainly the immediate aftermath of the Franco-Prussian war and the first speaker is almost certainly Adolphe Thiers, who had served as Prime Minister in the 1830s and then as Head of State after the Commune in 1871; the second speaker would then be Bismarck. Nietzsche is here centrally concerned with the transformation of politics that is resulting in his time (and will continue in the future), a transformation that comes from the mobilization of the populace in the pursuit of a country's aims. In a section of *Daybreak* entitled 'On great [i.e., international] politics', Nietzsche says that when the ruler involves the populace or believes that what he does is what the populace wants, he can then 'let loose a war and cloak his crimes in the good conscience of his people'. He will see what he does as the good: 'Strange madness of moral judgments!'[35] The danger of modern politics – in a world where humans do not understand the tragic – is that not only leaders but whole countries can come to think that what they do is what is good. In effect this makes their actions tyrannical. The claim of moral correctness leads Agamemnon to *justify* the sacrifice of his daughter; it can lead to the invasion of another country. The point is not to not sacrifice: the damage comes from the assurance of justification. Lincoln caught this in a paper found in his personal effects after his death: 'The will of God prevails – In great contests each party claims to act in accordance with the will of God. Both *may* be, and one *must* be wrong. God cannot be *for*, and *against* the same thing at the same time. In the present civil war it is quite possible that God's purpose is somewhat different from the purpose of either party – and yet the human instrumentalities, working just as they do, are of the best adaptation to effect this.'[36] Lincoln's key realization was that it was possible that the 'will of God' has a *completely different purpose* than do either of the parties to the conflict. When Thurlow Weed complimented him on the Second Inaugural Address, he replied: 'I believe it is not immediately popular. Men are not flattered by being shown that there has been a difference of purpose between the Almighty and them.'[37] To claim that what one does is for the good is to abrogate the position of God. Tragedy reminds us that we live without access to that position, however much we may wish to claim it, and Lincoln's greatness as a leader in relation to the Civil War comes from the fact that he experienced it as an authentic tragedy.

Does this not in practice amount to a form of realism? I seem to come close to Lebow's position. In *The Tragic Vision of Politics: Ethics, Interests and Orders* he argues that 'classical realism is an expression of the tragic understanding of politics, and of life more generally'.[38] Overall, his achievement in that book is to have shown the presence of an important moral element in classical realism.

But my position is not quite the same. One can recast the quarrel between Morgenthau and Oakeshott that Rengger gives us in a different manner. Oakeshott had insisted that 'tragedy was art not life'.[39] Morgenthau had insisted that it was a quality of existence. In fact, for there to be tragedy, I have argued with Nietzsche, one has to view existence in a certain manner. The characters in a tragedy are unable to acknowledge each other.[40] This is Morgenthau's existence. The consequences of this constitute the tragedy. The lesson of these consequences can be experienced by the audience – but only if it does not decide for one or another. This is Oakeshott's art.

And this itself is not without consequences.

Contemporary international relations in a world without tragedy

As a personal, but not only personal, note by way of concluding: in a public forum, George Kateb of Princeton University called President Bush a 'tyrant'.[41] In what does tyranny consist? We miss something important if we construe it only on the model of our picture of Stalin or Hitler. For Nietzsche, as we have seen, it is the insistence that the world is and is only as I will it to be. Challenges should be ignored or eliminated. Similarly, in the *Persian Letters*, Montesquieu argued that it consists in requiring that others have no existence for one except that which one allows them.[42] This seems to me exactly right: tyranny consists in speaking for oneself and having the power to impose that speech on others, to hear only one's own words.

On 14 and 23 September 2001, President Bush invoked the National Emergencies Act[43] and subsequently justified his actions (such as spying on individuals without court orders) on the grounds that 'it is a necessary part of my job'.[44] Jay Bybee, head of the Legal Council of the Justice Department, said in August 2002 that 'The President enjoys complete discretion in the exercise of his Commander-in-Chief authority and in conducting operations against hostile forces'[45] and in a memo from February of that year had argued that 'detainees have no inherent protection under the Geneva Convention – the condition of their imprisonment, good, bad and otherwise, is solely at the discretion of the President'.[46] The actions of the Bush administration in the context of the so-called war on terror are thus entirely consonant with tyranny and of the kind of justification that the tyrant can offer himself for his acts in such cases.

It is *not* my claim here that the Bush administration (or important members of it) has unusual evil qualities, except perhaps in the Arendtian sense of banality. We saw in Nietzsche's analysis of tragedy that the problem with Socrates was that he *lacked* certain qualities. Take the following case, admittedly extreme. In the late 1930s the psychologist Bruno Bettelheim was imprisoned for about a year in Dachau and Buchenwald. He details the various techniques of domination that were used to disrupt the ordinary world of the inmates and replace it with a world determined by the administration of the camps. What he found was that prisoners were unable over a long period of time (about five years) to resist moulding themselves to camp structures unless they consciously and with forethought drew some mental line over which they would not allow themselves to be moved. Their humanity, says, Bettelheim, was in their own hands and its loss could be prevented only by the insistence that one retain some human acts as one's own. André Malraux, in his *Antimemoirs*, writes of those in the camps:

> Humanness, that is what they wanted to rip out of them. The human condition is the condition of creature hood, the condition that imposes destiny on the human the way that a mortal illness imposes it on human beings. The destruction of this condition is the destruction of life; to kill. But the extermination camps, by trying to transform the human into a beast, have made us feel that one is not human simply by living.[47]

The point here is that it is the *institution* of the camp – admittedly an extreme situation – that makes it easy and possible for those with absolute power, to allow to those in their power only that existence that they wish to allow. And in this they deny something about themselves, that is, what I might call their 'internal relation' with these people.[48] Once someone is an 'enemy of humanity', nothing will do except extermination.[49] This is what Creon does and it is what Rudolf Höss did at Auschwitz. Whether or not, as Theodor Adorno once remarked, 'there can be no poetry after Auschwitz', it is clear that Auschwitz can make tragedy unavailable.

And here there is a lesson for our only slightly less-extreme situation. One can only note in this day and age, as William Scheuerman reminds us,[50] that the United States today has on its books a sufficient number of emergency powers, established *sine die*, to allow the executive free hand at the rule of all aspects of this country. The Bush administration ruled that certain prisoners in the 'war against terrorism' had in effect no status at all, not even that of a person charged with a crime.[51] As such their existence was entirely determined by the power that be. The occasional conflict between the determination of the executive and the resistance of the judiciary was testimony to the tyrannical intentions of the executive.

This brings us back to tragedy, or rather to its absence. Indeed, it would seem to follow that the nature of modernity is to increasingly make all situations exceptional and thus to legitimize the tyrannical. Ours is a world in which the availability of the tragic is rapidly fading.

Notes

1. This is my parody of Aristotle, where he suggests in book IX of the *Poetics* that it is not a tragic death to be killed by a falling statue. See Aristotle, *Poetics* in J. Barnes (ed.) (1984) *Complete Works of Aristotle, Volume 2: The Revised Oxford Translation* (Princeton: Princeton University Press) 1452a lines 3–11.
2. N. Rengger, 'Tragedy or Scepticism? Defending the Anti-Pelagian Mind in World Politics', Chapter 4, this volume, pp. 53–62 (p. 60).
3. *Birth of Tragedy* 11 WKG III-1, p. 71. Citations to Nietzsche are given by the book in which they appear (abbreviated by initials thereafter) and internal division, then with reference to the *Werke Kritische Gesamtausgabe* (Gruyter, Berlin, 1966 ff.) division and volume in the division, and the page number. As such one should be able to find them in an English edition. Thus BT 1 WKG III-1, 6 is *Birth of Tragedy*, section one, on page 6 of the German edition. *Nachlass* material is cited only from the WKG.
4. R. N. Lebow, 'Tragedy, Politics and Political Science', Chapter 5, this volume, pp. 63–71.
5. M. Frost, 'Tragedy, Ethics and International Relations', Chapter 2, this volume pp. 21–43; see J. P. Euben, 'The Tragedy of Tragedy', Chapter 7, this volume, pp. 86–96. See Lebow, op cit.
6. Here Rengger's (op. cit.) interesting reading of Morgenthau is apposite.
7. I. Berlin (1969) *Four Essays on Liberty* (Oxford: Oxford University Press), p. 168. See the discussion in my 1990 monograph *The Idea of Political Theory* (Notre Dame: Notre Dame University Press), Chapter 4.

8. See J. Rawls (1971) *A Theory of Justice* (Cambridge, MA: Harvard University Press), pp. 395–9.
9. The goat is thus a kind of *pharmakon*—the objective correlative of a crime and the cure for that crime. See Jacques Derrida's classic essay, 'Plato's Pharmacy', in Derrida, *Dissemination*, trans. by Barbara Johnson (Chicago: University of Chicago Press (1981)).
10. I am drawing here, obviously, on M. Nussbaum (1989) *The Fragility of Goodness: Luck and Ethics in Greek Tragedy and Philosophy* (Cambridge: Cambridge University Press), but also, and perhaps more so, on J. P. Euben (1990) *The Tragedy of Political Theory: The Road Not Taken* (Princeton: Princeton University Press).
11. *Eumenides*, lines 998 ff.
12. Euben, 'The Tragedy of Tragedy'.
13. *BT* 21 WKG III-1, p. 128.
14. It is often overlooked that Nietzsche discusses all these matters in both *Birth of Tragedy* and *On the Genealogy of Morals*, as well as elsewhere.
15. Compare the quarrel between Agamemnon and Achilles over Briseus in book 2 with that between Menelaus and Antilochus over the relation between the order of victory and reward in the chariot race, as mediated by Achilles in book 23.
16. See my 2001 book *Friedrich Nietzsche and the Politics of Transfiguration*, 3rd edn (University of Illinois Press (2001)), Chapter 6. See also G. Gambino (1996) 'Nietzsche and the Greeks: Identity, Politics, and Tragedy', *Polity*, 28/4, 415–44.
17. *Beyond Good and Evil* 9 WKG VI-2, p. 15, emphasis added; see also WKG VI-2, p. 215.
18. I have explored this in the context of an analysis of the will to power in Chapter 8 of my *Friedrich Nietzsche and the Politics of Transfiguration*.
19. See the important discussion of the affinities between philosophy and tyranny in Euben (1990) *The Tragedy of Political Theory*, pp. 36–8, 248–50.
20. 'On Truth and Lies in an Extra-Moral Sense', WKG III-2, p. 369.
21. BGE 211 WKG VI-2, p. 148.
22. WKG IV-1, p. 118; cf. *WKG* IV-1, p. 190: *Nachkommenschaft* translates usually as 'descendants' or 'offspring'.
23. *Human, All-Too-Human* 261 WKG IV-2, p. 219.
24. The quote is from an exchange between Leo Strauss and Alexandre Kojève in L. Strauss (1991) *On Tyranny: Including the Strauss-Kojève Debate*, ed. Victor Gourevitch and Michael Roth (New York: Free Press), pp. 165–6. See also my 'Dimensions of the New Debate around Carl Schmitt' in C. Schmitt (1996) *The Concept of the Political* (Chicago: University of Chicago Press), pp. ix–xxvii; and my 'The Sovereign and the Exception', introduction to C. Schmitt (2004) *Political Theology* (Chicago: University of Chicago Press), pp. vi–xxv.
25. HATH 262 WKG IV-2, p. 222.
26. This was the subject of his inaugural lecture at Basel, 'Homer and Classical Philology': 'We believe in a great poet as the author of the *Iliad* and the *Odyssey*—but not that Homer was this poet' (WKG II-1, p. 266).
27. See especially WKG IV-1, pp. 180–1.
28. 'Wisdom and Science in Conflict', WKG IV-1, pp. 178–9.
29. WKG III-4, p. 131.

30. BT 23 WKG III-1.
31. See my *Friedrich Nietzsche and the Politics of Transfiguration*, Chapter 6.
32. See my 'Philosophy and the Project of Cultural Revolution', *Philosophical Topics*, 33 (2) (2008).
33. HATH 8 WKG IV-2, p. 293. The entry is ambiguously titled 'To ask to speak' (*Um das Wort bitten*). See also 'Last consideration: If we can forego wars, so much the better. I know of a better use for the twelve billions that the armed peace in Europe costs each year; there are other means to bring physiology to honor than military hospitals ...' (WKG VIII-3, p. 460).
34. BGE 241 WKG VI-2, p. 188; See also HATH 453 WKG IV-2, p. 403.
35. Daybreak 189 WKG V-1, p. 161.
36. *The Collected Works of Abraham Lincoln* (New Brunswick: Rutgers University Press (1953)), Vol. V, pp. 403–4.
37. *Op. cit.*, volume VIII, p. 356.
38. R. N. Lebow (2003) *The Tragic Vision of Politics: Ethics, Interests and Orders* (Cambridge: Cambridge University Press), p. 63.
39. See the account of this debate in Rengger, 'Tragedy or Scepticism?'.
40. This is true of just one character also: Oedipus is unable to acknowledge that he is the son of Laius and insists on holding that his *tekne* can solve all problems.
41. At a conference at Yale University, in October 2006. See also G. Kateb (2006) *Patriotism and Other Mistakes* (New Haven and London: Yale University Press), Chapter 4 'A Life of Fear', especially pp. 61–2.
42. Uzbek, the Persian visiting France, is astonished to find that his wives, who he has left behind in Persia, have any life (including love affairs) other than that which he has first assumed and then ordered them to have. The more he suspects that they do have their own life, the more tyrannical he becomes, leading eventually to the death of the wives. See for instance, letter 166 from Roxanne to Uzbek.
43. See H. Relyea (2005) 'Terrorist Attacks and National Emergencies Act Declarations', for the *Congressional Research Service*, Library of Congress (RS21017), January 7, 2005.
44. News conference as per Associated Press, 19 December 2005.
45. Available at http://www.washingtonpost.com/wp-srv/nation/documents/dojinterrogation memo20020801.pdf. See also M. Tushnet (2007) *Weak Courts, Strong Rights: Judicial Review and Social Welfare Rights in Comparative Constitutional Law* (Princeton: Princeton University Press), Chapter 5.
46. Cited in S. Hersch (2005) *Chain of Command: The Road from 9/11 to Abu Ghraib* (New York: Harper Collins), p. 5. See W. Scheuerman (2006) 'Carl Schmitt and the Road to Abu Ghraib', *Constellations*, 13/1, 108–24.
47. A. Malraux (1967) *Antimémoires* (Paris: Gallimard), p. 587 (my translation).
48. See S. Cavell (1979) *The Claim of Reason* (New York: Oxford University Press), p. 376.
49. See the remarks by Carl Schmitt (2007) *The Concept of the Political* (Chicago: University of Chicago Press), expanded edition, pp. 54–5.
50. See W. Scheuerman (2001) 'Down on Law. The Complicated Legacy of the Authoritarian Jurist Carl Schmitt', *Boston Review* April–May (2001) (review of Balakrishnan, *The Enemy: An Intellectual Portrait of Carl Schmitt*).
51. G. Agamben (2005) *State of Exception* (Chicago: University of Chicago Press), p. 4, compares their situation to those of Jews in Nazi concentration camps.

12
Tragedies and International Relations

Catherine Lu

In what ways would our ability to understand, analyse and resolve problems in world politics benefit from a study of tragedy or from adopting 'the tragic vision'?[1] Although disagreements on this basic question abound between contributors to this volume, many of them surprisingly agree on the constitutive features of tragedy. According to Mervyn Frost, who eloquently launched this discussion, at 'the heart of all tragedy is an ethical *agon*',[2] which he characterizes as a conflict between equally compelling but incompatible ethical principles or duties. From this perspective, ancient Greek tragedy presents human characters who must choose a course of action in the face of conflicting legitimate ethical commitments; their 'tragic choices', however, typically yield some negative consequence that thwarts basic human strivings. Chris Brown gives a similar account of tragedy as constituted by clashes of duties that produce lose-lose choices – 'human action sometimes, perhaps often, involves a choice between two radically incompatible but equally undesirable outcomes, that whatever we do in a given situation we will be, from one perspective, acting wrongly'. Tragic conflict is 'a conflict between two demanding duties where to act is to act wrongly whatever is done'.[3] While Frost and Brown disagree on how to respond to such tragic conflict, they are united in their interpretation of tragedy as an ethical dilemma between equally legitimate and compelling values, principles or duties that produces moral loss or inescapable moral wrongdoing.

This narrow account of tragedy as ethical dilemma, I argue, deprives the genre of its stimulating and provocative role in political and theoretical analysis. Thus, while I agree with Frost that tragedy 'does not solve ethical problems, but poses them to us',[4] I will argue that the genre of tragedy produces a greater plurality of questions than Frost's restrictive interpretation envisions.

This is because there are different types of tragedies, and a tragic analysis of any given problem in international relations, such as global severe poverty or humanitarian intervention, involves argument, not mainly about whether or not such problems are tragic, but what kinds of tragedy they are. All tragedies are stories of moral incoherence in which important human strivings are thwarted, but there are typically different and multiple sources of that incoherence. To illuminate the provocative nature of tragedy, I forward a typology of tragedies that exposes different ways to describe or account for the actual or prospective derailment of basic human ethical strivings: (1) tragedies of virtuous or innocent suffering, or situations in which 'bad things happen to good people'; (2) tragedies of character, where fallible persons bring about their own ruin and the ruin of others; (3) tragedies of hard choices, involving practical moral conflicts that entail significant losses of value; and (4) tragedies of moral dilemmas, for which there is either no moral answer or no way to escape wrongdoing. This typology of tragedies is useful for clarifying and assessing the ethical challenges and debates that problems such as global severe poverty and other political humanitarian disasters raise. A pluralistic account of tragedies rather than a singular 'tragic vision' reveals the ways in which the genre of tragedy ought to open up rather than settle ethical debate and reflection about human agency and responsibility in world politics.

The tragedian's universe

All tragedies involve some form of moral incoherence. In the tragedian's universe, human beings are vulnerable to having their important strivings, often of an ethical nature, thwarted in various ways. If there is one persistent theme of classical tragedy, it is this: to be human is to be vulnerable. Neither knowledge nor power nor virtue can make human beings and human endeavours invulnerable to suffering tragic instability.[5] Tragedy thus brings home a keen sense of the fragility and instability of human things. In what ways could tragedy's attention to human vulnerabilities contribute to the study and practice of international relations? How might tragedy's insistence on the fragility of being human improve the way that International Relations (IR) scholars study their subject, or the way that various political actors engage in politics within and beyond borders?

One unhelpful way that the concept of tragedy has been used in theorizing about international relations can be found in the work of some contemporary realists. John Mearsheimer, for example, has argued that due to 'the structure of the international system' which 'no one consciously designed or intended', great powers cannot help but adopt a strategy of offensive realism.[6] The 'tragedy school of realism'[7] has interpreted the tragic vision as one that explains and justifies closing the door on ethical reasoning, judgement and agency in the realm of international politics. Realists who tend to emphasize the permanence of conflict in human life interpret tragedy as depicting a world that is not only 'not made for us',[8] but actually made against us. Their response to a world that 'is only partially intelligible to human agency and in itself is not necessarily well adjusted to ethical aspirations'[9] is to disparage ethical strivings altogether. Such conclusions reflect dogmatic pessimism, a view that the universe is inherently and permanently structured against human ethical strivings or to produce perverted outcomes. In breeding moral cynicism, despair and resignation, such strands of realism have been truly 'intellectually and politically debilitating'.[10]

The dogmatic pessimist, however, misunderstands the tragedian's universe, which is more accurately characterized by the *indeterminacy* of human (ethical) agency, rather than its futility or irrelevance. Tragedy supports the Machiavellian admonition that no state should 'ever believe that it can always adopt safe courses; on the contrary, it should think it has to take them all as doubtful', but does not support the anti-Machiavellian claim that all human political and ethical action is futile.[11] As Raymond Geuss has noted in a discussion of Thucydides, 'To think either that … [rationality, individual happiness, natural human development, socially desirable action] are set up so as to cohere, or that they are 'by nature' ineluctably fated to conflict in an unresolvable way – to be either an old-style philosophical optimist or a dogmatic pessimist – is still to be prey to notions that are theological in their origins and implications.'[12] Tragedies expose various human vulnerabilities to do with the limits and defects of human character, agency and the human condition, but they do not support a dogmatic pessimist's belief in the intrinsic or inevitable moral perversion of the universe. The tragedian's universe is far more complicated and indeterminate than that.

Consider Shakespeare's well-known tale of star-crossed lovers, *Romeo and Juliet*.[13] The background of powerful feuding families, coupled with a weak public authority, form the structural conditions of conflict that make ordinary love between two adolescents personally and politically dangerous. Romeo's youthful immaturity also contributes to the tragedy's unfolding, as he impulsively kills Tybalt to avenge his friend Mercutio's death. The well-meaning Friar's good intentions to help the young lovers lead to disastrous outcomes, partly because of contingent factors beyond his or anyone else's control. The story of *Romeo and Juliet* is tragic because it is a morally incoherent story in which important (and ordinary) human strivings are thwarted. As this brief account reveals, however, no tragic story is simple. To capture the provocative nature of tragedy, and the rich ethical debates that tragic analysis should foster, I endorse thinking about problems in world politics from the perspective, not of tragedy, but of *tragedies*.

Tragedies

Tragedies of unmerited suffering (typically of the innocent or virtuous and powerless)

Many tragic stories involve unmerited suffering and ill fortune, captured by observations such as 'bad things happen to good people'. Human ethical strivings are thwarted and moral incoherence is introduced when we see innocent or virtuous people suffer hardships or ill fortune. Ancient Greek and other tragic narratives are full of innocents who suffer incurable catastrophe, such as Agamemnon's daughter, Iphigenia, the beauty of his house and a 'stainless maiden',[14] sacrificed like a goat by her own father for a dubious political imperative. Euripides's *Trojan Women* recounts the anguish of Andromache, and the other women of the Trojan royal household, who 'can do nothing'[15] to stop her young son (possibly a baby) from being thrown from the towers of Troy by the conquering Athenians (who fear that he would seek vengeance as a grown man).

Tragedies of unmerited suffering also include the destruction of the virtuous. Thucydides provides an example of virtuous suffering in his account of the Athenian general, Nicias, 'a man who, of all the Hellenes in my time, least deserved to come to so miserable an end, since the whole of his life had been devoted to the study and the practice of virtue'.[16] Nicias' virtue and practical wisdom are clear in his attempts to turn his fellow citizens against the invasion of Sicily. At one point, he urges the president of the Athenian assembly to call another vote on the Sicilian expedition, making a Socratic argument about political duty: 'you will be acting as the physician for your misguided city, and that the duty of those who hold office is simply this, to do all the good they can to their country, or in any case never to do any harm that can be avoided.'[17] The problem for Nicias, as it was for Socrates, is that when virtue and power conflict, the virtuous often suffer from political marginalization, if not destruction. In the corrupted imperialistic Athens, good intentions and right actions are perverted; thus Nicias' second speech to the Athenians, intended to curb their appetite for invading Sicily, instead makes them feel invincible and certain of victory. It is not the case that Nicias lacked prudence or wisdom – the problem is that in severely corrupted political conditions, wisdom and virtue have no efficacy. The suffering of the innocent and the virtuous point to the 'capriciousness of Dionysos';[18] even when one has not acted wrongly, one may be destroyed.

Our contemporary world is full of moral incoherence arising from political and structural injustices that produce the suffering of inno-cents.[19] For example, the World Health Organization (WHO) estimates that at any given time in our world, 20 million young children suffer from acute malnutrition, a condition that typically leads to severe wast-ing, where a child's body starts to consume its own tissues in an effort to compensate for nutritional deficiencies. Whoever or whatever the causes of this state of affairs, few would deny that such consequences of severe poverty are tragic. In this situation we recognize an important human striving thwarted on a massive scale, for human beings univer-sally wish for their children to grow up and lead fulfilling lives. Moral incoherence is introduced into our world when young children are deprived of the ability to develop to their adult potential.

Tragedies of virtuous and innocent suffering are tragedies of the pow-erless. Paying attention to such tragedies should lead us to question the political and structural conditions that produce such powerlessness, as well as scrutinize arguments about the exercise of power that attempt to resolve the moral incoherence of such situations through the language of political or economic necessity. Global humanitarian activists as well as international political theorists have been at the forefront of recog-nizing tragedies of innocent suffering from various contexts of politi-cally induced humanitarian disaster; such recognition has been vital to stimulating political analysis and ethical reflection and debates about human agency and responsibility for such tragedies in world politics.

Tragedies of character (arising from ignorance, hubris, corruption and other character deficiencies)

Tragedy does not only afflict the powerless; ancient Greek tragedy also exposes the hazards of possessing and exercising power. Humans can suffer catastrophic reversals of fortune, despite acting on good inten-tions or despite pursuing worthy goals. Typically in a tragedy, 'what was most expected/has not been accomplished', and that which transpires is what no human has expected or wanted.[20] Tragedies of character high-light aspects of human ignorance, character defects, or other types of human fallibility that produce disproportionate catastrophe. Oedipus, for example, has good intentions, but his lack of self-knowledge contributes to his own calamity. Richard Ned Lebow refutes structural realists' claim that the Peloponnesian war was inevitable for structural reasons; his account of Athens as a tragic character embroiled in a tragic cycle of success, hubris, miscalculation and nemesis, focuses on human character and judgement as sources of tragic actions and outcomes.[21]

Ancient Greek tragedy is full of characters whose vices, defective judgements or limited virtues contribute to disaster. Clytemnestra is surely aggrieved about her daughter's death at the hands of Agamemnon, but she is a complicated character who also has political ambitions and other grievances that motivate her to kill her husband. In Aeschylus's *Eumenides*, the vengeful Furies and the god Apollo court prospective catastrophe in asserting irreconcilable claims. Peter Euben has argued that the *Oresteia* trilogy provides a moral education about justice for democratic Athens; it suggests that 'injustice in the broadest sense is pushing one's claims too far, seeking mastery and domination instead of recognizing the legitimacy of what is other ... Claiming too much for themselves and recognizing too little in their adversaries, both [Apollo and the Furies] dishonour justice and destroy the balance of nature'.[22] The idea of justice forwarded 'involves the reconciliation of diversities', and 'a continuous though imprecisely defined sharing of authority and mutuality of decision; although it does not posit equality of power, it does preclude domination'.[23] In this light, the intractable conflict between the Furies and Apollo was not an inevitable outcome of practical conflict between equally valid principles. Rather, the deterioration of the conflict into an intractable one exhibited a lack of democratic virtues in both parties that bred a politics of mutual disrespect, bitterness and enmity.

Since all political action involves human judgement and agency, it is fitting that tragic situations in which important human strivings are thwarted generate discussion and debate about the virtues, judgements, reasons and actions of the human agents involved. Brown complains that when faced with oppression or poverty, people appeal to the rhetoric that 'Something must be done,' but 'this support usually evaporates when something actually *is* done'.[24] Just because 'something must be done', however, does not mean that we cannot judge or evaluate or disapprove of what is done or how agents make or carry out their decisions. In the context of ancient Greek tragedy, 'necessity' and 'agency' are not mutually exclusive, and tragedies of character focus our attention precisely on examining and evaluating how well agents exercise their power, as well as the different kinds and degrees of responsibility they bear for the political outcomes.[25]

Tragedies as hard choices (involving losses of significant value)

Practical conflict is endemic to human life. There is a thriving debate in modern moral philosophy about the nature of the ethical challenges posed by practical conflicts arising from divergent 'desires, preferences, emotions, interests, goals, plans, commitments, values, virtues, obligations and moral norms'.[26] One of the most important insights of these philosophical investigations is that not all practical conflicts are tragic. For example, Ann may be very ambitious in her academic career and want to spend all her weekends writing articles and papers. At the same time, her stepdaughter may need help on her homework, or Ann may also want to spend time enjoying a relationship. The fact that Ann faces time constraints presents a conflict, but hardly a tragic one. If the fact of needing to make choices among goods or values constitutes tragedy, then the concept becomes analytically meaningless, as we would all lead tragic lives. One might say that Ann faces luxurious conflicting choices; she has reason to value all these goods, and she faces no losses of significant value in balancing a rewarding career with a fulfilling family life and/or personal relationship. A human life is finite and has some fixed limits, and competing values and goods often have to be traded off against one another – these facts of life do not in themselves constitute tragedy.

Hard choices can be characterized as tragic when they involve losses of significant value that constitute a subversion of basic human strivings. The agents of humanitarian action in conflict zones and global poverty or emergency relief typically face many hard choices of the tragic kind. Consider the question of how to distribute the limited funds for health care in sub-Saharan Africa. William Easterly has argued that, despite the focus on Africa's HIV/AIDS epidemic, it is 'inefficient to supply antiviral HIV treatment as opposed to treating other diseases that are much cheaper to cure'. Furthermore, he argues that the small budget for AIDS would save more people if it were spent on prevention rather than treatment: 'For the same money spent giving one more year of life to an AIDS patient, you could give 75 to 1500 years of additional life ... to the rest of the population through AIDS prevention'.[27] Scarce resources mean that not everyone can be saved. Those involved in global health care and poverty relief must determine the best principles, policies and strategies for helping the global poor fairly, effectively and efficiently.

Brown is right to distinguish between hard choices involving losses of significant value, and moral dilemmas characterized by inescapable moral wrongdoing. Most moral philosophers agree with him: 'Where the lives of identical twins are in jeopardy and I can save one but only one, every serious rationalist moral system lays down that, whatever I do, I must save one of them'.[28] Hard choices are not dilemmas of inescapable wrongdoing because in a situation of hard choices, there are better and worse things to do, all things considered. Hard choices, then, involve moral reasoning and judgement, and decision-makers may be praised or blamed for making better or worse choices. Brown unnecessarily limits the concept of tragedy to 'tragic choices', by which he means only moral dilemmas involving inescapable wrongdoing. In doing so, he ignores tragedies of hard choices involving losses of significant value; yet, such choices are also tragic when their costs constitute a subversion of fundamental human strivings.

Tragedies as moral dilemmas (involving inescapable moral wrongdoing)

According to Martha Nussbaum, a 'tragedy of ethical dilemma' consists in 'a contingent conflict of two important obligations, in such a way that no innocent course is available'.[29] While this form of tragedy is distinct from the tragedy of hard choices, it is an open question whether the majority of policy problems produced by political oppression or global poverty should be characterized as tragedies of moral dilemmas or tragedies of hard choices. For example, a highly effective remedy for severely malnourished children has been developed in the past decade, in the form of nutrition-packed ready-to-use food (RUF). According to Médecins Sans Frontières (MSF), currently, this therapeutic RUF only reaches about three per cent of severely malnourished children; malnutrition continues to contribute to the deaths of five million young children every year.[30] Prioritizing the widespread adoption of RUF might seem warranted, and even though such policies may have costs to certain food producers, as long as the costs are not comparable to the terrible costs of malnutrition, it is implausible to argue that a decision to produce an adequate supply of RUF to address the malnutrition problem would be to do wrong, or that pursuing such policies wrongs food producers in any morally significant way. Such a case might involve hard choices of a tragic kind at the policy level, but is not likely to qualify as a moral dilemma consisting of inescapable moral wrongdoing.

Tragedies as moral dilemmas may abound in our world, but not primarily among those in positions of power and privilege in the international system. Genuine moral dilemmas are more likely to afflict the bottom billion of the world's population in more immediate ways. Consider the dilemma of a mother in Malawi whose son is ill with malaria. She has gone to the hospital and been told to give her son a certain medication, but its cost is too prohibitive. If she buys the medication, her other young children who are dependent on her will not get enough to eat. If she does not buy the medication, her son will likely die. There are many parents in such situations among the global poor. Often they resort to buying medicine from 'schmocters', who offer a consoling visit but fake and ineffective medicines. Such scenarios qualify as ethical dilemmas as they involve conflicts of important obligations.

Brown faults cosmopolitan theorists in the analytical tradition for finding 'no place for the notion of tragedy in their work', for being 'intolerant of ambiguity and unresolved dilemmas', and for 'denying the possibility of genuine tragedy'.[31] Yet it is not clear that acknowledging the reality of ethical dilemmas dispels the need for rigorous ethical analysis, reasoning and judgement. For one thing, admitting the possibility of genuine moral dilemmas or irresolvable moral conflicts does not say anything about their frequency, permanence or pervasiveness in human life. Humanitarian activist James Orbinski, for example, recounts the struggles of MSF and other organizations to make antiretroviral (ARV) drugs more accessible to populations in sub-Saharan Africa ravaged by the AIDS epidemic. Orbinski notes that ten years ago, although such drugs were proven to be effective in reducing the mortality rate by 70 per cent, they were so costly that only *one* per cent of all ARV drugs was sold in sub-Saharan Africa, where 11 million children have been orphaned due to the AIDS epidemic. The tireless efforts of MSF and Orbinski's new organization, Dignitas, to make essential medicines more accessible to the global poor, including cutting the cost of ARV drugs from US $15,000 to $200 a year, demonstrated 'that it was possible to treat AIDS, even in what had earlier been considered by others to be impossible conditions'.[32] If ethical dilemmas force impossible moral choices on human beings, recognizing such dilemmas in contexts of pervasive injustice should open up questions about political responsibility for states of affairs in which only dilemmas remain.[33]

Conclusion: Learning from tragedies

Tragedies expose us to experiences of moral incoherence, but raise questions about the various sources of incoherence, to do with human character, agency and the human condition. Tragic stories thus provoke moral analysis and evaluation of the kind of people we are, the kind of practices we engage in, the kind of world we live in. The value of recognizing different types of tragedy is not that any given case or situation can fit neatly into one type or another; rather, such recognition enables us to engage in a lively and constructive analysis and debate about human judgement, agency and responsibility for acts, structures or conditions that thwart basic and important human strivings. For example, both Brown and Frost (in their contributions to this volume) interpret the tragic conflict between Creon and Antigone as an ethical dilemma or a case of clashing ethical duties, but Danielle Allen challenges that interpretation by focusing on the defective characters and judgements of both actors. According to Allen, the royal house of Thebes is ruined not because its members faced an intractable moral dilemma, but because 'both Antigone and Creon want to act on the basis of laws that they have written for themselves in violation of community norms'.[34] Far from cultivating moral resignation and cynicism, tragic drama continues to live beyond its time because of its enduring ability to provoke profound ethical reflection and debate. In stimulating the search for ethical understanding and reconciliation, some might even argue that tragedy gave birth to political theory.[35]

Is it the case, however, that a pluralistic account of tragedies makes the genre incapable of generating any action-guiding claims? What, if anything, can we learn from tragedies? The various contributors to this volume offer divergent interpretations of the ethical lessons that tragedy purports to teach us. Frost argues that 'tragic texts challenge us (the audience) to consider whether the ethical arrangements that gave rise to the tragedies ought to be reformed or whether they ought to be changed ... [T]ragic stories raise the possibility of changing, reforming or transforming the social institutions under consideration'.[36] Similarly, Nussbaum argues that tragedies as ethical dilemmas pose an implicit challenge – 'how might this tragic conflict have been avoided?' – and 'far from encouraging resignation and pessimism, frequently challenge their audience to constructive political action'.[37] Brown, however, argues that 'an awareness of tragedy' understood as ethical dilemmas 'ought to cause us to act modestly, to be aware of our limitations and to be suspicious of grand narratives of salvation which pretend that there are no tragic choices to be made'.[38] Where contributors such as Frost and Lebow see tragedy as illuminating the potential for ethical reconciliation, transformation and improvement, Mayall, Brown and Nicholas Rengger emphasize the intractability and persistence of practical conflict and moral loss. Rengger comments that these divergent prescriptions require proponents of the tragic vision to 'square an almost impossible circle by arguing on the one hand that recognizing the reality of "tragedy" in human life should make us more aware of the precariousness of our situation and should discourage us from hubris, and on the other that we can learn from this – somehow – ways of making the world a better and safer place'.[39] Put in this way, the genre of tragedy seems to be embarrassingly incoherent and incapable of providing any tangible guidance on how to live or act in this world.

These divergent lessons, however, can be traced to tragedy's pluralism, its insistence on the vulnerability of all to tragic instability and its recognition of the indeterminacy of human agency. Different types of tragedies translate into different lessons for the powerful and the powerless, weak or oppressed. To the powerful, tragedy warns against *hubris*, an excessive confidence in human rationality and power – material, intellectual or moral – to insulate us from the vulnerabilities that attend the human condition. Neither power nor rationality can make us invulnerable; recognition of this tragic truth should lead to humility about all forms of human knowledge or know-how, and moderation in the quest for as well as the exercise of power. The powerful should not expect that accumulating more power or maintaining a position of domination over others can guarantee total invulnerability. Tragedies that expose the hazards of power thus militate against the desire to dominate others, since they deprive domination of one of its driving motivations – security from vulnerability.

To the powerless and the oppressed, however, tragedy counsels against despair – things are indeterminate, and the seeming invulnerability of the tyrant or the oppressor is not something that can be expected to endure. Whereas a dogmatic pessimist would assert the futility of ethical action, breeding cynicism, rage and despair, the tragedian's recognition of the indeterminacy of human agency supports a sober commitment to ethical action. The tragedian does not claim that human ethical strivings (to do good, to seek justice, or to resist injustice) are irrelevant, futile or unimportant, only that the human condition – marked by various kinds of internal and external vulnerabilities – make the pursuit of worthy human strivings uncertain, and the outcomes of our ethical and political struggles indeterminate.[40]

In my view, it is not international political theorists writing on humanitarian intervention and global poverty who have exhibited a lack of tragic insight. Rather, that defect has been more apparent in American neoconservatives who believe that there can be an 'end to evil' and who have pursued destructive international policies without any sense of the costs. Prominent 'neocons' David Frum and Richard Perle thus wrote, 'For us, terrorism remains the greatest evil of our time, and the war against this evil, our generation's great cause. We do not believe that Americans are fighting this evil to minimize it or to manage it. We believe they are fighting to win – to end this evil before it kills again and on a genocidal scale. There is no middle way for Americans: It is victory or holocaust'. The authors then explicitly offer their book as 'a manual for victory'.[41] Today, we see more clearly where this anti-tragic quest for invulnerability has taken America and the world.

In the tragedian's universe, the quest for total security is an illusory and de-humanizing project; to be human is to live with varieties of vulnerability. The tragedian thus denies that there can be any manual for victory, given the vulnerability of the powerful and the powerless alike to tragic instability. Yet in focusing our attention on experiences of moral incoherence that are generated when basic human ethical strivings are thwarted, the tragedian, like the philosopher, also challenges us to engage in ethical and political reflection, debate and action in the world.

Notes

The author wishes to thank Peter Schaber, Susanne Boshammer and other participants of a seminar in April 2008 at the Ethics Research Institute in Zürich, participants at a workshop in December 2008 at McGill University, and Kurt Spillmann, Nancy Kokaz, David Welch, Mervyn Frost, Doug Hanes, and the editors of this volume for their comments and conversations on the chapter's theme or previous drafts of this chapter.

1. R. N. Lebow (2003) *The Tragic Vision of Politics: Ethics, Interests and Orders* (Cambridge: Cambridge University Press).
2. M. Frost, 'Tragedy, Ethics and International Relations', Chapter 2, this volume, pp. 21–43 (p. 27).
3. C. Brown, Chapter 6, this volume, pp. 75–85.
4. Frost, 'Tragedy, Ethics and International Relations', this volume, p. 42.
5. S. Halliwell (1998) *Aristotle's Poetics* (Chicago: University of Chicago Press).
6. J. J. Mearsheimer (2001) *The Tragedy of Great Power Politics* (New York: W.W. Norton), p. 3.
7. M. Spirtas (1996) 'A House Divided: Tragedy and Evil in Realist Theory' in B. Frankel (ed.) *Realism: Restatements and Renewal* (Portland, Oregon: Frank Cass), pp. 385–423. For a fuller critique, see C. Lu (2004) 'Agents, Structures and Evil in World Politics', *International Relations*, 18/4, 498–509.
8. B. Williams (1993) *Shame and Necessity* (Berkeley: University of California Press), p. 166. See also P. Euben, 'The Tragedy of Tragedy', Chapter 7, this volume, pp. 86–96 (p. 88).
9. Williams (1993) *Shame and Necessity*, p. 164.

10. Brown, 'Tragedy, "Tragic Choices" and Contemporary International Political Theory', Chapter 6, this volume, pp. 75–85 (p. 83).
11. N. Machiavelli, *The Prince*, Harvey Mansfield trans. (Chicago: University of Chicago, 1998), p. 91; see also J. Mayall 'Tragedy, Progress and the International Order', Chapter 3, this volume, pp. 44–52.
12. R. Geuss (2005) 'Thucydides, Nietzsche, Williams', in *Outside Ethics* (Princeton: Princeton University Press), pp. 219–33 at p. 231.
13. W. Shakespeare (1987) *Romeo and Juliet* (Markham: Penguin).
14. Aeschylus *Agamemnon* in *The Oresteia Trilogy: Agamemnon, The Libation Bearers and The Eumenides* (Chicago: University of Chicago Press), line 245.
15. Euripides *The Trojan Women*, trans. Nicholas Rudall (Chicago: Ivan R. Dee, 1999), line 720.
16. Thucydides *History of the Peloponnesian War*, trans. R. Warner (Toronto: Penguin, 1954), Book 7, para. 86.
17. Thucydides, *History of the Peloponnesian War*, Book 6 para. 14.
18. F. Nietzsche (1999) *The Birth of Tragedy and Other Writings*, ed. by R. Geuss and R. Speirs (Cambridge: Cambridge University Press).
19. See I. M. Young (2004) 'Responsibility and Global Labor Justice', *The Journal of Political Philosophy*, 12/4, 365–88, for an account of structural injustice that produces human rights violations in the apparel industry.
20. Euripides *The Bacchae*, in D. Grene and R. Lattimore (eds) (1990) *Greek Tragedies: Volume 3* (Chicago: University of Chicago Press), lines 1390–1.
21. Lebow, *The Tragic Vision*.
22. J. P. Euben (1990) *The Tragedy of Political Theory: The Road Not Taken* (Princeton: Princeton University Press), p. 77.
23. Euben (1990) *The Tragedy of Political Theory*, p. 81.
24. Brown, 'Tragedy, "Tragic Choices" and Contemporary International Political Theory', this volume, p. 83.
25. For liability and social connection models of responsibility in relation to structural injustice, see I. M. Young (2007) *Global Challenges: War, Self-Determination and Responsibility for Justice* (Cambridge: Polity Press), pp. 159–86.
26. P. Baumann and M. Betzler (eds) (2004) *Practical Conflicts: New Philosophical Essays* (Cambridge: Cambridge University Press), p. 1.
27. W. Easterly (2006) *The White Man's Burden* (Toronto: Penguin), p. 255.
28. Quoted in P. Schaber (2004) 'Are There Insolvable Moral Conflicts?' in P. Baumann and M. Betzler (eds) *Practical Conflicts*, p. 281; see also B. Barry (1984) 'Review Essay: Tragic Choices', *Ethics*, 94, 303–18.
29. M. C. Nussbaum (2003) 'Philosophy and Literature', in D. Sedley (ed.) *The Cambridge Companion to Greek and Roman Philosophy* (Cambridge: Cambridge University Press), pp. 211–41 at p. 221. Nussbaum distinguishes between four varieties of tragedy, 'depending on how the gap between the hero's goodness and his fortune opens up': tragedies of 'impeded action', 'involuntary action', 'ethical dilemma', and 'eroded character' (pp. 220–2).
30. Médecins Sans Frontières (2008) 'Food is not Enough: MSF Campaign for Access to Essential Medicines', *Dispatches* (MSF Canada Newsletter), 10/1, 9. See also S. Shepherd, 'Op-ed: Instant Nutrition', *The New York Times*, 30 January 2008.

31. Brown, 'Tragedy, "Tragic Choices" and Contemporary International Political Theory', this volume, p. 77.
32. J. Orbinski (2008) *An Imperfect Offering: Humanitarian Action in the Twenty-First Century* (Toronto: Random House), pp. 362–3.
33. For a cosmopolitan appreciation of hard choices and other tragedies, see C. Lu (2000) 'The One and Many Faces of Cosmopolitanism', *The Journal of Political Philosophy* 8/2, 244–67 at 266–7.
34. D. S. Allen (2000) *The World of Prometheus: The Politics of Punishing in Democratic Athens* (Princeton: Princeton University Press), p. 92.
35. See Euben (1990) *The Tragedy of Political Theory*, and Nietzsche, *The Birth of Tragedy*.
36. Frost, 'Tragedy, Ethics and International Relations', this volume. See also Lebow, 'Tragedy, Politics and Political Science', Chapter 5, this volume, pp. 63–71.
37. Nussbaum (2003) 'Philosophy and Literature', p. 221.
38. Brown, 'Tragedy, "Tragic Choices" and Contemporary International Political Theory', this volume, p. 83.
39. N. Rengger, 'Tragedy or Scepticism? Defending the Anti-Pelagian Mind in World Politics', Chapter 4, this volume, pp. 53–62 (p. 60).
40. N. Kokaz (2001) 'Moderating Power: A Thucydidean Perspective', *Review of International Studies*, 27/1, 27–50.
41. D. Frum and R. Perle (2003) *An End to Evil: How to Win the War on Terror* (New York: Random House), p. 9.

13
The Drama Viewed from Elsewhere

Robbie Shilliam

In their contributions to this volume Mervyn Frost and Ned Lebow (and with qualification, James Mayall and Kamila Stullerova) propose that the agonistic moment of tragedy might be understood as a cathartic one through which crusading forces discover that the pursuit of a particular ethic must not be mistaken for the realization of a universal truth. In various ways, Peter Euben, Chris Brown, and Nicholas Rengger all critique this 'optimistic' viewpoint by pointing to another core aspect of the tragic tradition, namely, the disjuncture it asserts between understanding and action leading to the possibility that knowledge of the self in the world is irreducibly fractured by the contingent character of that world. The debates reveal how pluralistic readings of the tradition of tragic thought can be (a point developed well by Catherine Lu in the previous chapter). However, at the heart of the conversations lie both epistemological and ontological questions about the constitution of 'tragedy' itself: is it an art-form representing life, or is it life itself? And most importantly, can tragedy be filtered into a philosophical form of reasoning mobilized for prescriptive use?

These questions have in large part defined the engagements of contemporary political theory with the notion of 'tragedy'. However, these engagements exhibit a deeper orientation in the way that they approach tragedy as a universal condition/idea that in some way can be brought to bear upon the problem of modernity.[1] The cues for this orientation (but by no means the only ones) are often influenced from readings of Hegel's dialectic (as is the case with Frost) wherein modern world development is produced out of the diremption and then resolution of clashing modes of consciousness;[2] and (as exampled by the contributions from Benjamin Schupmann and Tracy Strong), from readings of Nietzsche's early works that alternatively celebrate the life-force of the

'archaic Dionysian' emotive-poetic against the 'Apollonian' enlightened –
but deadening – vision of analytical reason.[3] Generally, though, one
could say that the attention given to tragedy is part of a wider movement
that places Ancient Greece as a historical reference point, a comparator,
or a symbol, in fine, a *difference* that clarifies for contemporary theorists
the problems and challenges of our modern condition.

In this chapter I use the work of the Nobel Prize winning Caribbean
poet and playwright Derek Walcott to tease out the way in which the
contemporary symbolic association of Ancient Greece with European
modernity allows some but disallows others a meaningful engagement
with the tragic drama. Through his poems and plays Walcott attempts to
find a way to redeem the New World past for its present inhabitants, especially for (but not only) those whose descendents arrived in slave ships,
so that they might become subjects in their own right rather than objects
of European history. Walcott's dramatic explorations of New World subjectification are neither Apollonian nor Dionysian, nor an inter-relation
of the two, but Adamic. By investigating the Adamic form of Walcott's
poems and plays I argue that in order for critical self-reflection on fate,
freedom, morality and wisdom, drama must be enfranchising to the effect
that peoples from elsewhere can be *both* subjects and objects within it.
The symbolic association of Ancient Greece with European – and hence
colonial – modernity falls short of this requisite. Hence, the ethical return
to Ancient Greece via the reading of its tragic dramas cannot be direct but
rather requires journeying beyond one's own city.

Colonial Greece

To begin with, I wish to take a prompt from Peter Euben's musings on
tragedy: contemporary political theorists, Euben notes, are meta-theorists
in a way in which classical tragedians were not meta-dramatists.[4] Contra
tendencies in modern political thought to take tragedy as a universal
category/condition (even if applied to a specific temporal 'epoch'),
issues of fate, freedom, morality and wisdom have always been debated
within and by immediate reference to a temporally *and* geo-culturally
specific context. And as a specific medium for these debates, tragedy is
no different.[5] The origins of the tragic tradition are to be found in the
festival plays of Ancient Greece that paid homage both to the spiritual
mysteries of Dionysus and the political issues of Athens as a city state,
and that encoded both the poetic and the analytical within their public
performances.[6] Deriving their narratives from existing mythical epics,
the tragic plays partook of a 'double reading' by making these epics

speak in indirect or direct ways to contemporaneous issues in Greek life. To this effect, the dramatic roles of the chorus replaced that of the epic narrator with an array of enunciative positions ranging from commentators of the plot, to critics of the plot, to evoking responses to the plot, to participants in the plot. Through this prelocutory and interlocutory mobility, the audience and the actors (and their actions) were connected in the unfolding of the drama and journeyed through the narrative as an inter-related entity that encompassed both subject and object positions. In fine, the drama was not solely composed as a spectacle to be viewed by a dis-embedded onlooker,[7] rather, 'the city turned itself into a theatre watching itself as an object of representation on stage'.[8]

Many political theorists who use the tragic tradition admit that because the original Greek context was so intimately woven into the dramatic articulation and reception of tragedy, the classics cannot speak to us moderns directly. We do not share the same conventions that situated the actors, narrators and audience in relation to each other, nor do we share the same mythical universe within which these related entities pursued the tragic plot. However, these political theorists also argue that classic tragedy consisted of enough ambiguities that allow the originating context to be translated into a contemporary context thus creating new cathartic experiences (if with old words). For example, if compelled to end the plot in the same way, the classic tragedians could, nevertheless, re-narrate the time in-between with different emphases and occurrences. This was possible because tragic plays were not narrated through a single authoritative voice. Rather, the plot often unfolded in secret, behind the scenes (literally off-stage in the *skene*), producing a certain amount of ambivalence in the meaning to be extracted from the narrative.[9] Even within the original dramas, then, the political and social issues of their present were made sense of by a reconstructed relationship to an epic past. It has been argued that the resulting ambiguities and ambivalences of this temporal relationship can serve modern political theory well. They become, in effect, hermeneutical spaces whereby, to use a phrase from Gadamer, a fusion of horizons can take place between the past and the present in order to better glean the specificity that issues of fate, freedom, morality and wisdom take on in the present.[10]

Yet what I wish to point out is that fusing horizons between the past and the present is *not* necessarily the same task as fusing horizons between different geo-cultural contexts, especially when the difference between these contexts has been previously constructed through colonial rule. This is an important point because there exists a strong tendency in many of the contributions to this volume – and in the more general attempt to make tragedy speak to political theory in the Western academy – to assume that membership of one geo-cultural context, 'European' (or perhaps 'Western') Civilization is a universal condition, or if this assumption is not made, to then only talk of those enfranchised within this Civilization. Think, for example, of how the canon of tragic plays and thinkers is usually constructed as quintessentially European: from the Greek to Roman to medieval to Shakespearian to neo-Classical and Romantic; or from Aristotle to Hegel to Nietzsche. Even if this homogenization of tragic tradition through its canonization is critiqued, the critique rarely extends outside of the proscribed canon.

It is true that all translation – inter-temporal and inter-cultural – requires re-shaping the same prelocutory and interlocutory webs of, for example, vocabulary, tone, sound, rhythm, cognitive systems, legal frameworks and cultural reference-points.[11] It is also a truism that 'Europe' is as much as anything else a constructed category of cultural affiliation, indeed, often a hyper-real category in its instantiation as the cultural artefact (European) Civilization. Nevertheless, this constructed character does not make the substantive organizing and segregating effects of European subjectification[12] any less real to those categorized as outsiders to this Civilization. And it is this cultural affiliation – either presumed or assumed – that ultimately manages the construction of traditions of thought via the translation of past works into the present. In other words, the European 'heritage' is the geo-cultural space that allows for a fusion rather than apartheid of horizons. The point is that however tragedy might be problematized or critically reassessed in temporal terms, contemporary thinkers who are unproblematically considered 'European' or 'Western' can proceed by taking their seats as participants in the old theatre. But there are places and peoples in the world that, through colonial rule, have not been allowed such direct affiliation and access.

How, then, is the European drama viewed from elsewhere? And, how is it viewed, moreover, by intellectuals of the (post-)colonial world who have been marked through colonialism as external not simply because of their geographical/geo-cultural location but also because of their temporal disjuncture, that is to say, as belonging to peoples 'outside of history'? It is important to note that for many colonial intellectuals, a linear trajectory of technological and moral progress has at the same time been presented as a singular civilizational stream that has justified violent overflow into the pre-historical matter of existing societies on behalf of a dynamic History.[13] From this perspective, the Greek classics have been transmitted through colonial education as part of a monologue of (European) Civilization.

Those 'native intellectuals' who have attempted to narrate the drama in which they have been caught up, and with resources taught to them rigorously through a colonial education, have been paradoxically denied a subject-position within the rise of Civilization. Instead, these intellectuals have had to make do with *analogy* (via metaphor or simile) as a positional device. However, 'as if it were Greek' has usually implied a chronological inferiority and geo-cultural separation: the mimic is not creative but derivative of an original.[14] In this situation, the whole utility of tragedy as a cathartic art-form – and the general purpose of drama as a medium for critical self-reflection in both personal and public terms – breaks down because apartheid is introduced into the various enunciative positions. The audience does not sit in the theatre of the City, the play is not about their past, and they live in the present only vicariously through alien actors. There is, in other words, a stratification of the prelocutory and interlocutory mobility afforded to those affiliated with European civilization who can journey through the narrative as inter-related subjects and objects of the drama.

To pursue these issues a little further I shall now turn to the work of Derek Walcott. A little justification is in order here regarding this selection. Walcott is not a tragedian (and there is, in any case, more than one form of tragic drama in the postcolonial world),[15] yet he is famous – and partially infamous – for his use of Homeric tropes that he has geo-culturally grounded in the Caribbean. Walcott's most commented upon work, in this respect, is *Omeros*, a book-length poem that combines, among other elements, the Homeric epic of the contest between Achilles and Hector and Sophocles' tragedy of Philoctetes into a drama based upon (and about) St Lucia.[16] Walcott has also written a stage version of the Odyssey for the Royal Shakespeare Company that counterpoints Homeric and Caribbean themes.[17] As noted already, tragedy – in its *world-wide* reception and transmission – has to be understood politically as one aspect of Greek drama with all the civilizational affiliations and segregations that have been condensed into its pages when turned by colonial hands. And it is with regards to this reception and transmission that Walcott, standing elsewhere from European civilization, orients his relationship to the Ancient Greeks.

The Adamic new world

It seems that Walcott, similar to many literary intellectuals of the postcolonial world,[18] is interested in the colonizing of the past by 'History', that is to say, by a Newtonian-causative narrative that proceeds as a series of European subjects acting upon non-European objects. This colonizing process is perhaps especially acute when attempting to document a Caribbean past where the original inhabiting subjects were decimated, where subjects from Africa became legal objects upon undertaking the Middle Passage, and where Indians were introduced as quasi-objects in their capacity as indentured servants. Walcott stands against this colonization of the meaning of the past: 'history makes similes of people, but these people are their own nouns'.[19] For example, Walcott deploys Odysseus as a colonial critique: when asked to provide his name by Cyclops (a totalitarian authority that seems to embody both fascist and colonialist traits),[20] he calls himself 'nobody'. Cyclops is distracted by what he thinks is Odysseus' comic existence, but this merely allows Odysseus to blind the monster. Cyclops shouts 'Nobody has escaped! Nobody blinded me!' Odysseus shouts back 'My name is not nobody! It's Odysseus! And learn, you bloody tyrants, that men can still think!'[21] This passage is redolent of Hegel's *Herr/Knecht* dialectic, however, the importance given to naming, as I shall now discuss, prompts a different understanding of post-colonial subjectification.

In order to retrieve a past for Caribbean peoples that is meaningfully their own, rather than a vicarious one retrieved via metaphor or simile of some other place and time, Walcott promotes an Adamic vision of the New World. This is not an Adamic vision in the orthodox biblical sense whereby Adam is granted (a suspiciously colonial-like) authority to name the world around him, but in the ideographic sense that Adam is endowed with the power to recognize the significance of the given forms that he comes across in his New World sojourn.[22] The Adamic vision of the New World is, in this respect, awesome in the light of its own possibilities rather than being illuminated by the light of European civilization that stands behind the sojourner so as to cast a shadow on that being encountered.[23] To this effect, the past of the New World has a naturalistic basis for Walcott, but not one that is either utopian or romantic (in the German sense). Rather, it is the awesome nature of the New World that constitutes the theatre and makes it resonate as a public space. The drama directs the actors and audience to contemplate the bitter methods that led to their (re-)population of this space, the conditions of possibility that *nevertheless* led them to an awesome subjectification as part of a New World. So for Walcott there is a crucial contrast to be made between dramatizing the past of New World peoples in terms of their subjectification in New World nature, and dramatizing this past in terms of their objectification by reference to European civilization.

In his early work, specifically, in a series of plays on the Haitian revolutionaries, Walcott did in fact use a tragic trope through which to present the fate of Dessalines and Christophe (the first two black leaders of Haiti after independence). These noble heroes had sought to overturn an ordered universe of the slaveholder so as to become the masters of their own destiny; yet the hubris of this act was for them to turn into similar tyrants in the process. Walcott later comments on the harmfulness of this tragic trope for self-reflection by Caribbean peoples because it ultimately represents their past through the narrative of History as 'one race's quarrel with another's God'.[24] For Walcott notes in his reflections of these early plays:

> There was one noble ruin in the archipelago: Christophe's massive citadel at La Ferrière. It was a monument to egomania, more than a strategic castle; an effort to reach [another] God's height. It was the summit of the slave's emergence from bondage ... To put it plainer, it was something we could look up to. It was all we had.[25]

Effectively, Walcott is arguing that a tragic reading of this seminal and novel emancipation struggle makes its protagonists elegiac mimics of an original European drama.

And yet the choice for Walcott, a colonial intellectual versed in the classics as expertly as an Etonian,[26] is not really one of embracing or refuting Ancient Greece. The key issue, rather, is to resist presenting the Caribbean islands as a simile of the Aegean – with elegiac ruins and all – because this would 'humiliate' the landscape of the New World in so far as it robs this nascent public space of its Adamic constitution.[27] There is therefore a fundamental prerequisite for making Greece coterminous, in an egalitarian sense, with the Caribbean: the stage on which the drama takes place cannot be constructed within the narrative of History as the monumental ruins that are invocative of another place.

It is for these reasons that Walcott deems it necessary to construct the stage of New-World drama out of naturalist rather than monumental substances. This sentiment comes out in a quasi-autobiographical discussion:

> The great poets of the New World, from Whitman to Neruda, reject this sense of history. Their vision of man in the New World is Adamic. In their exuberance he is still capable of enormous wonder. Yet he has paid his accounts to Greece and Rome and walks in a world without monuments and ruins.[28]

Hence, we have Walcott's tendencies to use unmarked spaces as the dramatic stage – and we can attribute these tendencies to the fact that these 'landscapes with no tenses' level epochs and empires.[29] In this regard, the sea (viewed, especially, from the shore line of the New World) is a favourite space for Walcott,[30] and *The Sea is History* is exemplary of this mobilization of nature. The short poem works through a biblical narrative from Genesis to the New Testament as well as through a political narrative of renaissance to emancipation to national independence. However, it represents these epochs and events through a set of submarine and oceanic metaphors most of which invoke the multitude of slaves thrown overboard (or who threw themselves overboard) during the Middle Passage, for example:

> Then came from the plucked wires
> of sunlight on the sea floor
>
> the plangent harps of the Babylonian bondage,
> as the white cowries clustered like manacles
> on the drowned women,
>
> and those were the ivory bracelets
> of the Song of Solomon,
> but the ocean kept turning blank pages
>
> Looking for History.[31]

This play on metaphors reveals the absurdity of any attempt at New World subjectification by way of mobilizing the narrative of colonial History. Alternatively, the end stanza points towards an understanding of the time of the becoming of the New World subject as non linear, non analogous to the Old World, non derivative:

> and then in the dark ears of ferns
>
> and in the salt chuckle of rocks
> with their sea pools, there was a sound
> like a rumour without any echo
>
> of History, really beginning.[32]

'The strength of the sea', notes Walcott, 'gives you an idea of time that makes history absurd'. The sea depicts immensity and the colonial narrative of History can only appear as a sail of a ship – an 'insignificant speck' on the rim of its horizon that, instead of linear progression, allows travel in any and all directions (even to – but not *back* to – Greece).[33]

It is important to note, once more, that whatever we might make of Walcott's thoughts they cannot be understood as utopian or romantic:

> It is not that History is obliterated by [the] sunrise. It is there in Antillean geography, in the vegetation itself. The sea sighs with the drowned from the Middle Passage, the butchery of its aborigines, Carib and Aruac and Taino, bleeds in the scarlet of the immortelle, and even the actions of surf on sand cannot erase the African memory, or the lances of cane as a green prison where indentured Asians ... are still serving time.[34]

The purpose of Walcott's drama, then, is not to find a place – socially or naturally constructed – outside of the colonial past. Rather, the purpose is to seek redemption of this past by rendering the meaning of the present not via History as tragic but as a specific kind of sublime experience that neither owes – nor pleads for – an affiliation with European civilization.[35] In sum, the tragedy of colonial History is not ignored or suppressed, but addressed and answered in awe of the possibilities of the New World and the delight of having simply survived the methods by which it was repopulated. Walcott's dramatic explorations of New World subjectification are neither Apollonian nor Dionysian, nor an inter-relation of the two, but Adamic.

Beyond colonized Greece

Walcott's writings can provide provocations for the debate on tragedy in International Relations (IR) theory in the following ways.[36] All the world cannot be compressed into one stage except by a drama the narrative of which follows colonial History. Drama is always also viewed from elsewhere, off stage, out of the theatre, beyond the City. We should not presume that modernity can be represented as a singular epochal drama within which the tradition of Greek tragedy provides a cathartic tool for self-reflection of (European) being in the (Western) world. For in order for critical self-reflection on fate, freedom, morality and wisdom, the drama must be enfranchising to the effect that peoples from elsewhere can be *both* subjects and objects within it. To take this point seriously means to recognize the depth of the contemporary symbolic attachment of Ancient Greece to European colonial history. And to recognize this attachment means that this symbolism cannot be broken solely by making a critical temporal comparison between the European colonial symbolism of Greece and a pre-'European' pre-'colonial' body of Greek tragic drama.

I shall finish by drawing out this challenge by way of the following thought experiment. Firstly, it could be said that, in response to my argument above, the tragedy of theorists of tragedy resides in the fact that there is hubris associated with assuming that a particular geo-cultural context can be expanded into a universal condition. However, this claim would only make of Walcott's writings monumental ruins that celebrate another place and story. Alternatively, and if it is accepted that any meaningful engagement with difference proceeds via the promise of self-understanding, the challenge that faces intellectuals unproblematically enfranchised within the Western Academy is described by Jean-Paul Sartre in his preface to Fanon's *Wretched of the Earth*:

> Europeans, open this book, and enter into it. After a few steps in the night, you will see strangers gathered round a fire, draw closer, listen ... They will see you perhaps, but they will continue to talk among themselves without even lowering their voices. Their indifference strikes at our hearts ...[37]

Paradoxically, the ethical gain of this encounter might lie in loosening the obsession the Western Academic often holds of her/himself as subject, and to imagine herself/himself – for a while – as objects in the drama of someone else's awesome subjectification. For this purpose, the final line of *Omeros* could be turned into an Adamic principle of orientation: Walcott's Achilles, a fisherman, finishes his tasks for the day; 'When he left the beach the sea was still going on.'[38]

Secondly, and subsequently, it is possible to claim that the dialectic of objectification/subjectification discussed in the above paragraph was the *original* purpose of Greek tragedy before Aristotle sought to provide it with a rationalistic framework and before it became subsumed within the colonial narrative of European History. In fact, Walcott says something similar:

> If we looked at them now, we would say that the Greeks had Puerto Rican tastes. Right? Because the stones were painted brightly ... As time went by, and they sort of whitened and weathered, the classics began to be thought of as something bleached-out and rain-spotted, distant.[39]

I have no quarrel with this claim in its descriptive dimension. However, if Western Academics are to pursue it in depth, that is to say, if they are intent on re-discovering a non-colonial, non-colonized Greek tradition of tragedy, then they cannot achieve this by remaining within the city walls. For making the purely temporal journey from past to present and back again gives these walls an elegiac character which (as I have argued above) enfranchises some but presents a barrier to others. In order to return to the Greeks in the contemporary era the Western Academy must take the prompt of the classical Greeks themselves (as well as their Islamic interlocutors):[40] self-reflective theorizing requires geo-cultural travel so that the human drama may be viewed from elsewhere.

Notes

My thanks to the editors, Matthew Trundle and especially Xavier Forde for their comments.

1. On these issues see R. Williams (1966) *Modern Tragedy* (Stanford: Stanford University Press), pp. 32–61; T. Eagleton (2003) *Sweet Violence: The Idea of the Tragic* (Oxford: Blackwell), pp. 18–22, 204–9; C. Rocco (1997) *Tragedy and Enlightenment: Athenian Political Thought and the Dilemmas of Modernity* (Berkeley: University of California Press), pp. 1–7.
2. G. W. F. Hegel, *Phenomenology of Spirit*.
3. F. W. Nietzsche, *The Birth of Tragedy and the Case of Wagner*.
4. J. P. Euben (1990) *The Tragedy of Political Theory: The Road Not Taken* (Princeton, NJ: Princeton University Press), p. 46.
5. See also Williams (1966) *Modern Tragedy*, p. 45.
6. See Eagleton (2003) *Sweet Violence*, p. 9; Euben (1990) *Tragedy of Political Theory*, p. 58.
7. See, in general, C. Calame (2005) 'The Tragic Choral Group: Dramatic Roles and Social Functions', in R. W. Bushnell (ed.) *A Companion to Tragedy* (Oxford: Blackwell).
8. Euben (1990) *Tragedy of Political Theory*, p. 51.
9. R. Scodel (2005) 'Tragedy and Epic', in Bushnell (ed.) *A Companion to Tragedy*, pp. 164–5, 192; Euben (1990) *Tragedy of Political Theory*, p. 57.
10. Seminal examples of this enterprise, broadly stated, are Rocco (1997) *Tragedy and Enlightenment*; Euben (1990) *Tragedy of Political Theory*.
11. On these issues see M. Tymoczko (2002) 'Post-colonial writing and Literary Translation', in S. Bassnet and H. Trivedi (eds) *Post-colonial Translation: Theory and Practice* (London: Routledge); L. Hardwick (2000) *Translating Words, Translating Cultures* (London: Duckworth).
12. My usage of this grammatical term is best associated with Raymond Williams's concept of a 'structure of feeling'. For an expansive discussion see P. Harrison (2000) 'Making Sense: Embodiment and the Sensibilities of the Everyday', *Environment and Planning D: Society and Space*, 18/4, 497–517.
13. See for example, D. Chakrabarty and B. Attwood (2006) 'Risky Histories: Indigenous Pasts, Democracy, and the Discipline of History – A Dialogue between Dipesh Chakrabarty and Bain Attwood', *Meanjin*, 65/1, 200–8.

14. A. Lefevere (2002) 'Composing the Other', in S. Bassnet and H. Trivedi (eds) *Post-colonial Translation: Theory and Practice* (London: Routledge), p. 78.
15. See, for example, B. Crow and C. Banfield (1996) *An Introduction to Post-colonial Theatre* (Cambridge: Cambridge University Press); K. J. Wetmore Jr (2001) *The Athenian Sun in an African Sky: Modern African Adaptations of Classical Greek Tragedy* (London: McFarland & Company).
16. D. Walcott (1990) *Omeros* (New York: Farrar, Straus, Giroux).
17. D. Walcott (1993) *The Odyssey: A Stage Version* (New York: Farrar, Straus, Giroux).
18. For example, A. Nandy (1995) 'History's Forgotten Doubles', *History and Theory*, 34/2, 44–66.
19. Cited in R. D. Hamner (2001) 'Creolizing Homer for the Stage: Walcott's "The Odyssey"', *Twentieth Century Literature*, 47/3, 388.
20. See Z. Giannopoulou (2006) 'Intertextualizing Polyphemus: Politics and Ideology in Walcott's Odyssey', *Comparative Drama*, 40/1, 1–28; I. Martyniuk (2005) 'Playing with Europe: Derek Walcott's Retelling of Homer's Odyssey', *Callaloo*, 28/1, 188–99.
21. Walcott (1993) *The Odyssey*, pp. 71–2.
22. D. Walcott (1974) 'The Muse of History', in O. Coombs (ed.) *Is Massa Day Dead? Black Moods in the Caribbean* (New York: Anchor Books), p. 2; R. Hanford (2000) 'Joseph Brodsky as Critic of Derek Walcott', *Russian Literature*, 349. Commenting on his play *Omeros*, Walcott says, 'what this poem is doing, in part, is trying to hear the names of things and people in their own context'; J. P. White (1996) 'An Interview with Derek Walcott', in W. Baer (ed.) *Conversations with Derek Walcott* (Jackson: University Press of Mississippi), p. 173.
23. Walcott's use of shadow and light to describe the effect of History is quite pronounced. See, for example, White (1996) 'An Interview with Derek Walcott', p. 157.
24. D. Walcott (1999) 'What the Twilight Says', in D. Walcott (ed.) *What the Twilight Says: Essays* (New York: Farrar, Straus, Giroux), p. 13.
25. Walcott (1999) 'What the Twilight Says', p. 13.
26. C. H. Rowell (1996) 'An Interview with Derek Walcott', in Baer (ed.) *Conversations with Derek Walcott*, pp. 124–5.
27. See D. Walcott (1997) 'Reflections on Omeros', *South Atlantic Quarterly*, 96/2, 232.
28. Walcott (1974) 'The Muse of History', pp. 2–3.
29. E. Greenwood (2005) '"Still Going on": Temporal Adverbs and the View of the Past in Walcott's Poetry', *Callaloo*, 28/1, 132–3.
30. Walcott castigates those writers who focus upon shipwrecks on the shore via his critique of deploying elegiac monuments as representations of the New World; Walcott (1974) 'The Muse of History', p. 42.
31. D. Walcott (2007) 'The Sea is History', in E. Baugh (ed.) *Derek Walcott: Selected Poems* (New York: Farrar, Straus, Giroux), p. 123.
32. Walcott (2007) 'The Sea is History', p. 125.
33. White (1996) 'An Interview with Derek Walcott', pp. 158–9.
34. Walcott (1999) 'The Antilles: Fragments of Epic Memory', in Walcott (ed.) *What the Twilight Says: Essays*, p. 81.
35. White (1996) 'An Interview with Derek Walcott', p. 170.

36. It should be made clear that this conclusion might be different if we were to focus on alternative poets and playwrights from elsewhere, for example, the Nigerian Wole Soyinka.

37. J. P. Sartre (2001) 'Preface to the Wretched of the Earth', in J. P. Sartre (ed.) *Colonialism and Neocolonialism* (London: Routledge), p. 141.

38. Walcott (1990) *Omeros*, p. 325.

39. R. Brown and C. Johnson (1996) 'Thinking Poetry: An Interview with Derek Walcott', in Baer (ed.) *Conversations with Derek Walcott*, p. 183.

40. See R. L. Euben (2004) 'Travelling Theorists and Translating Practices', in *What is Political Theory?* (London: Sage Publications), pp. 145–73.

14
Learning from Tragedy and Refocusing International Relations

Toni Erskine and Richard Ned Lebow

Tragedy makes us confront our limits: it reveals human fallibility and vulnerability, illustrates the complexities of our existence, and highlights the contradictions and ambiguities of agency. It shows us that we can initiate a course of action without being able to understand or control it – or adequately calculate its consequences. It teaches us that wisdom and self-awareness might emerge out of adversity and despair. Tragedy cautions against assuming that our own, particular conceptions of justice are universally applicable and should be enforced as such. And, it warns of the dangers that accompany power's over-confidence and perceived invincibility. If an appreciation of tragedy thereby fosters a deeper, more sophisticated understanding of international relations – as we have maintained – how should this influence what we do? How can this understanding guide our actions as citizens or scholars, policy-makers or theorists, witnesses to or students of tragedy?

There are two ways of responding to these questions. The first response concentrates on the lessons that can be taken from tragedy to inform deliberation and decision-making, policy and practice in a way that might mitigate future tragedies. The second response speaks to the academic study of International Relations (IR) and addresses how its assumptions and categories are usefully refocused when viewed through the lens of tragedy. We explore both responses in light of the range of arguments presented throughout the volume and suggest that tragedy not only helps one to better understand contemporary international relations, but can also be valuably prescriptive of how we both view the world and act within it.

Learning from tragedy?

This volume was conceived on twin premises: that tragedy offers useful insights about contemporary international relations; and, that an understanding of tragedy has the potential to reduce tragic outcomes in the future. With the chapter by Nicholas Rengger providing a notable, and eloquent, exception, almost all of our contributors accept the first premise.[1] The second premise, however, is much more divisive. More than one contributor who sees tragedy as a useful vehicle for making sense of international relations, considers the idea that understanding tragedy can serve to avoid or minimize tragic outcomes something of an oxymoron. Hubris is a key cause of tragedy; actors who overvalue their ability to manipulate other actors and their environment endorse initiatives that are likely to produce destructive outcomes the reverse of those intended. The belief that an understanding of tragedy can somehow reduce its likelihood is itself hubristic, they warn, and is therefore likely to promote more rather than less tragedy. Here, we return to the controversial idea that it is possible to learn from tragedy in a way that might somehow mitigate its recurrence and reflect on the concerns and disagreements that this suggestion has engendered among the contributors to the volume.

As we highlighted in Chapter 1, Aristotle maintains that it is not simply the plot lines but also the very form of the drama that is important in terms of the effect that tragedy has on audiences. Tragedy is characterized by a particular structure that provokes an emotional state, which opens people to the possibility of ethical learning.[2] Aristotle attributes the pedagogical power of tragedy to the double perspective it encourages. The *peripeteia*, or major reversal in the fortunes of its principal characters, imparts tension to tragedy because the audience recognizes what is going to happen well before its leading characters do. When these characters confront their fates, the audience experiences a *katharsis*, or release of emotion. The members of the audience are purged of the emotions they have invested in the characters and their situations, which opens them up for reflection and assimilation of the ethical lessons of the play.[3] For example, in *Oedipus Tyrannos*, the audience figures out long before Oedipus does that he has unwittingly killed his father and married his mother. Oedipus' discovery of this awful truth and its consequences for himself and his family overwhelm him. His wife, Jocasta, hangs herself and their children suddenly become pariahs. Oedipus blinds himself with the pin Jocasta used to secure her robe and departs Thebes a beggar. While moved, those in the audience are not overwhelmed the way Oedipus is, as their experience of his fate is second-hand and vicarious. Instead, they have the opportunity to learn from the tragedy that has unfolded before them.

Tragic *katharsis* might be compared to a vaccination in which people are immunized against a disease by being given a small dose of the attenuated pathogen. Being affected but not suffering the way the characters presumably do, theatergoers are in a position to benefit from their experience and may conceivably be 'inoculated' against the behaviour that caused the tragedy. Unlike the characters in a tragedy, they are not destroyed or utterly transformed by the characters' fate. The members of the audience empathize with these characters, but do so at a distance and experience only a mild version of the trauma that engulfs those in the drama. While they are drawn into the tragedy and become emotionally involved with its characters, this distance brings with it the possibility for reflection. For Aristotle, such emotional arousal and reflection encourages learning and makes it possible. We can surmise that Sophocles and Thucydides were drawn to tragedy in part for this reason. Indeed, for ancient Athenians, tragedy not only described terrible things that happened to people and cities – outcomes that they were understood to have brought on themselves, however unwittingly and despite often noble intentions – but was a source of political education. It encoded an approach to life that sought human happiness and fulfillment through self-restraint and integration into the civic life of the *polis*. With respect to contemporary international relations, substantive themes of tragedy such as those that we proposed in Chapter 1 also possess pedagogical value. One might learn from tragedy's depiction of the dangers of hubris and from its account of the self-defeating nature of treating particular conceptions of justice as absolute – and then analyse and modify one's behaviour accordingly.

A tragedy generally presents only a small slice of its hero's life and often ends with his or her death. Among extant plays, the Oedipus cycle is unique in that we encounter the eponymous hero many years later in his old age. The Oedipus we meet in *Oedipus at Colonus* has undergone a transformation. He has reflected on his fate; his blindness has led to vision and he has shed his hubris and become a wise and prudent man. Wisdom, or *sophia*, for the Greeks, and for the aged Oedipus, consists of a holistic understanding of the world and one's place in it. It is a source not only of prudential behaviour but of the happiness and fulfillment that comes from being at one with nature and human society. Real life tragic figures, by contrast, are rarely blessed with this kind of insight. Some historians – with some licence – have portrayed Pericles, Kaiser Wilhelm and George W. Bush as tragic figures and attribute the wars they unleashed in part to their character flaws. Yet, Pericles dies before the tragic consequences of his hubris becomes apparent. The Kaiser and many other Germans denied any responsibility for the tragedy they produced, convincing themselves that they were victims of British perfidy and socialist treachery. And, it seems unlikely that George Bush and his advisors will ever reflect on their behaviour the way Oedipus did. But, like Greek audiences, we can learn something from these tragedies, even if we cannot achieve the kind of wisdom that Oedipus ultimately did. We can progress far enough to become more empathetic, prudent and insightful – and less arrogant and far-reaching in our goals.

For fifth-century BCE Athenians, tragedies were a principal means of producing social knowledge. In today's world, social science aspires to this role. Mainstream IR scholars search for the kinds of regularities that they believe would form the basis of prediction and make social science indispensible to policymakers, corporations, investors and others with a professional stake in international relations. This goal is very much a reflection of the optimism of Western culture, which, ever since the Enlightenment, has demonstrated unwavering faith in the ability of reason to understand, control and reshape the physical and social worlds. Tragedy dramatizes the consequences of hubris – and social science, from this perspective, is hubris in a modern guise. So, too, some of our contributors maintain, the claim that a tragic vision can reduce suffering is itself an instance of hubris. Mervyn Frost, perhaps the most optimistic of our authors about the emergence of global civil society, nevertheless makes a strong case against learning at the outset of his argument. Tragedy, he notes, is often the result of ethical behaviour and the actors in question would have acted the same way even if they had possessed full knowledge of the consequences.[4] Even with perfect foresight, Agamemnon, Orestes, Oedipus and Hamlet would have considered themselves ethically bound to act as they did. Frost poses an interesting, but ultimately unanswerable, counterfactual, because one of the defining features of life is our inability to predict the consequences of our own and others' actions. Kamila Stullerova, in her own contribution to this volume, cites Hans Morgenthau to the effect that the tragic vision rests on this realization.[5]

If foreknowledge does not, or would not, sway the decisions of tragic heroes, how can the form of foreknowledge that tragedy provides possibly influence us? We are notorious for deluding ourselves that all will work out for the best. Psychological research demonstrates that actors committing themselves to risky initiatives routinely deny the possibility that their actions will result in disaster by distorting, rejecting and explaining away threatening information. Motivated bias of this kind is most likely in those tragic situations in which any choice brings inevitable loss.[6] Nevertheless, as Frost argues, tragedy can help us identify ethical problems and face up to these kinds of choices. Moreover, political change in South Africa suggests to Frost that ethical questioning of even deeply embedded political practices can provide the catalyst for transformation.[7] Indeed, in this respect, Frost gestures towards a way in which an understanding of tragedy *can* inform our actions and, in doing so, he challenges his initial statement that tragedy 'cannot have anything to offer those worried about forward-looking questions such as, 'What is to be done?'"[8] Even if actors in a tragedy would have felt compelled to behave in an identical fashion had they, at the moment of decision, possessed knowledge of the tragic outcomes of their choices, we, as witnesses to tragedy, might be motivated to amend the structures within which these agents faced such intractable dilemmas. In other words, we can draw on insights gained from looking back at the types of tragic dilemma upon which Frost focuses in order to variously establish, enhance, reject, redesign or reform the social conditions, institutional frameworks and political structures that shape the particular choices open to us in the future. In this sense, we can learn from tragedy in a way that might reduce further tragic outcomes. James Mayall, in his response to Frost, challenges Frost's optimism about the potential for progress in international society. Nevertheless, Mayall is willing to concede that awareness of tragedy can serve as an antidote to the hubris of progressive thought and the constant temptation to avoid accepting responsibility for well-intentioned actions that go awry.[9]

It is not only we, the contributors to this volume, who do not agree on whether it is possible to learn from tragedy in a way that can positively guide future actions. The tragic playwrights themselves appear to have no uniform position on the ability of humans to learn from tragedy and reduce its likelihood. Aeschylus is by far the most optimistic. One might recall his *Oresteia*, in which one violent deed breeds another, all conceived and carried out in the name of justice. The cycle of revenge, which in the end pits the Furies (*Erinyes*) against Orestes, is finally ended by a court established by Athena. The jury of twelve Athenians is deadlocked and Athena intervenes to cast the deciding vote for Orestes. She convinces the Furies to accept an honoured home beneath the city and henceforth become well-wishers (*Eumenides*). Justice, which took the form of revenge in the *Oresteia* and in Athens, is transformed from a private to a public responsibility. Argument replaces violence as the means by which justice is pursued.[10]

Writing during the Peloponnesian War, Sophocles is less sanguine about the ability of human beings to overcome the worst attributes of their nature through civic life and institutions. He nevertheless authored one optimistic play – *Philoctetes* – in which friendship and persuasion, represented by Neoptolemus, triumph over force and chicanery, as personified by Odysseus. Euripides' plays are bloody and pessimistic and treat learning as largely instrumental and destructive in its consequences. Thucydides was a contemporary of Sophocles and Euripides but lived long enough to witness the final defeat of Athens, the civil unrest that followed and the restoration of democracy in 404 BCE. His account of the Peloponnesian War is generally read as a fatalistic take on power and its exercise, presented most dramatically in the famous Melian Dialogue.[11] Thucydides can nevertheless be read as a more complex and nuanced thinker who thought learning and order possible, but fragile. Elsewhere, one of us contends that Thucydides' Melian Dialogue, when read in context, suggests that Athenian behaviour was more a pathology than the norm.[12] In his chapter, Ned Lebow argues that Thucydides would not have spent decades researching and writing his account and labelling it at the outset 'a possession for all time' unless he thought people had some ability to learn from the past and to control their destinies. Indeed, Lebow draws a parallel to psychotherapy, which assumes that people will continue to act out self-destructive scripts until they recognize this pattern and come to terms with the traumas that drive them. This must be achieved through regression; people must allow themselves to relive painful experiences they have repressed in order to understand how they shape present behaviour. Thucydides' account encourages Athenians and others to relive or experience the trauma of the Peloponnesian War in the most vivid way and work through its meaning for their lives and society.[13]

In their respective chapters, Chris Brown and Peter Euben also engage this debate over the possibility of learning from tragedy and thereby reducing its recurrence. Both advance more moderate claims. Brown agrees that recognition of tragedy 'ought to cause us to act more modestly, to be aware of our limitations and to be suspicious of grand narratives of salvation which pretend that there are no tragic choices to be made'.[14] Euben applauds Lebow's efforts to warn against the self-fulfilling nature of pessimism, but chides him for attempting to square tragedy with rational analysis and faith in progress, a charge Lebow rejects. Euben nevertheless acknowledges that Greek drama was conceived with educational purposes in mind and that tragedy can stimulate learning – but, he qualifies, only if you allow it to master you before you master it. In terms of learning that is particularly salient to contemporary international relations, Euben extracts two political lessons from Euripides' *Bacchae*: single-minded efforts to enhance security are likely to increase disorder and undermine security; and, societies must accommodate the passions that are foundational to politics, as reason becomes part of the problem rather than the solution when it rides roughshod over emotions, or thinks it can.[15] Finally, Euben contends that the tragic insights found in Thucydides are particularly germane to both policy and its improvement.

While this controversy surrounding the potential for tragedy to educate its audience cannot be resolved, it might be clarified by asking if there are different kinds of tragedies with different possibilities for amelioration. In her contribution to this volume, Catherine Lu identifies four types of tragedy: 'tragedies of unmerited suffering', 'tragedies of character', 'tragedies of hard choice', and 'tragedies of moral dilemma'. She contends that each poses different kinds of ethical and political challenges. These four types of tragedy derive from different sources, and this diversity may account in part, as Lu suggests, for the different understandings scholars have of the ability of human beings to reduce the frequency of tragedy.[16] One might argue that 'tragedies of character' can be alleviated by those who have observed in others the tragic outcomes of character flaws – such as hubris, ignorance, and arrogance – and aim to curb these shortcomings in themselves. It is, after all, within our power to cultivate wisdom and exercise restraint. 'Tragedies of hard choice' – for example, those losses resulting from decisions that governments or NGOs must make in distributing limited drugs and health care to populations in which there is widespread need for urgent medical attention – might seem more intractable. This is particularly the case in a world of scarce resources. Yet, even while at first glance this latter category of tragedy may appear more difficult to learn from and mitigate, we cannot ignore that it includes hard choices of our own making, which may be avoided or finessed by more astute political skill and moral courage. Relevant agents are forced to make difficult decisions (in this case, with respect to the distribution of medical aid, so that some people are saved and others allowed to die) when resources are severely limited and need is overwhelming. Yet, although such loss is unavoidable when one is faced with these decisions, the circumstances that create hard choices of this kind are not. In this example, one might note that specific policies and practices perpetuate acute inequalities in the global distribution of resources and wealth, and these in turn provide the necessary conditions for an abundance of hard choices that involve saving only some of the impoverished many. In short, while some tragedies might be avoided through the edification and greater self-awareness of particular decision-makers, others demand broad structural transformation. We have the potential to learn from both – but in markedly different ways. Indeed, if there is, as Lu maintains, a multiplicity of 'tragic visions' that can be invoked to understand and interrogate international relations, then our capacity to draw lessons from tragedy, and limit future tragic outcomes accordingly, may be concomitantly varied.

Refocusing IR assumptions

We have argued that understanding tragedy enables us to better understand international relations – and can even help us to shape policies and practices in a way that might ameliorate future tragic outcomes. Should it not, then, also inform the theoretical tools that IR theorists employ?

One might object to such a proposal on the grounds that tragedy, as an art form, is a wholly inappropriate lens for bringing assumptions within IR into sharper definition. Indeed, in Chapter 4, Rengger makes just such a point as he follows Oakeshott in insisting that life and art must be kept distinct.[17] Tragedy, Oakeshott is adamant, 'belongs to art, not to life'.[18] Although Morgenthau and Lebow explicitly reject this dichotomy, a move that is tacitly approved by the other contributors to this volume, there are, at first glance, good reasons for accepting it. Great art strives to be holistic. Although a shift took place by the late-nineteenth century, classical and Renaissance art, for the most part, conceived of their parts as working together to create an overall whole. Such art does this by having its parts reinforce one another in harmonious ways, or by generating tensions that are – or can be – resolved or transcended, or, if not, that still prompt an appreciation that takes constituent parts into account. This is true of painting, sculpture, architecture, literature, music, opera and ballet. It applies equally to works of a single creator and to collaborative efforts, as in the case of opera and theatre, where performances offer interpretations. They do so convincingly when the plot, acting, singing, staging, costumes and backdrops are outstanding in their own right and help instantiate an overall reading of the work. Politics, by contrast, is an *agon*, a contest whose *dramatis personae* – they are always plural – compete within a conflictual relationship. They are striving to attain different ends, often at each other's expense, as is so often true in struggles over wealth, status or sexual partners. Even when actors cooperate, they retain their autonomy and only join forces because they cannot achieve their ends alone, or reason that they can be reached more efficiently through coordinated action. When political conflict produces harmony it is most often the result of painful compromises.

Given their holistic orientation, traditional artistic frames of reference are likely to impose more order on political behaviour than is warranted. Tragedy, to its credit, attempts to finesse this problem by offering us understandings at the actor *and* system levels. It mimics politics by recognizing and building on *agon*, and emphasizing, rather than downplaying, the autonomy of its actors, the scarcity of the goods they seek – usually honour – and the conflicts this provokes. At the system level, tragedy imposes order on these disorderly and conflictual events by understanding them as part of a repetitive pattern with common underlying causes and outcomes produced by well-defined dynamics. The actors themselves have no understanding of the tragedy of which they are part, and their ignorance creates a tension between the two levels on which tragedies operate. This tension draws us into the drama, and its ultimate resolution provides the basis for lessons about life – *and* lessons about politics.

It is difficult to imagine tragedy not, then, providing a valuable lens for examining fundamental assumptions within the discipline of IR. A central aim of this volume has been to engender debate and discussion about how tragedy can inform our thinking about international relations, and, so, by extension, about the formal frameworks, categories and approaches employed by IR theorists. There are many assumptions within IR that a sophisticated understanding of tragedy might encourage us to qualify or correct, refine or reformulate. The contributors to this volume have touched on a rich array of examples in the preceding pages. Here, we revisit three themes within IR that might be valuably refocused when viewed through the lens (or lenses) of tragedy: causation, moral responsibility, and the role of the emotions.

An alternative perspective on causation: Beyond Humean assumptions

Tragedy is a form of poetry. Aristotle maintained, with tragedy in mind, that poetry can seek a higher truth than history. The latter, he reasoned, describes events while the former has the power to order them in abstract ways to convey profound truths.[19] Lebow suggests that this may be one reason why Thucydides was careful not to call his account of the Peloponnesian War a history.[20] He introduces it in the third person with the phrase *xunegrapse ton polemon*, 'he wrote up the War'.[21] His account is more poetry than history as it presents the war within a tragic format. This required Thucydides to include some events and exclude others, to emphasize some of the events he describes at the expense of others, to present the Corcyraean alliance as a *hamartia*, or great miscalculation, resulting from hubris, and to position and to shape the various speeches in the text to provide signs to readers about the narrative's underlying structure, as the chorus does in a tragedy. If his purpose was to offer an accurate narrative of the war, then Thucydides can understandably be taken to task. But, if his purpose was to provide a deep understanding of its causes and dynamics, then it is a masterful account. Thucydides highlights the importance of agency, accident and confluence, while still directing our attention to underlying dynamics, of which actors were generally unaware, but which appear to have driven their actions and influenced, if not shaped, the consequences of these actions. Unfortunately, ever since Thucydides, serious historians and IR scholars have privileged underlying over immediate causes, thereby neglecting important questions of agency and skewing our understanding of causation. This is not, one might note, generally true for Western culture at large. The reading public prefers biography to history and routinely holds individuals responsible for good and bad outcomes that have more complex causes. Psychological surveys and experiments that study when and how people invoke counterfactuals reveal that they consistently emphasize immediate over underlying causes and agency over circumstance in all but special sets of conditions.[22] Yet, for most of the academy, so-called deep, underlying causes are more compelling and emotionally satisfying.

An appreciation of tragedy teaches us to avoid the modern academy's oversimplification of causation. In Greek tragedy, agency and fate – the latter being analogous, in some respects, to underlying causes or structures – are given equal billing.[23] *Oedipus Tyrannos*, the play that addresses this relationship most directly, is based on the prophecy that Oedipus will kill his father and marry his mother. These predictions come true, but only because Oedipus tries so desperately to forestall them. Further exercise of his free will leads to recognition that he has in fact killed his father and married his mother, provoking her suicide, and his blinding, loss of kingship and expulsion from Thebes. Sophocles' play is open to diverse readings, but any credible one must recognize the harmony as well as tension between the external forces of fate and the role of free will and agency. The concept of fate, as we are invoking it here, is complex and requires unpacking. It comes to Oedipus from the outside in the form of a prophecy. The audience or reader develops an understanding of it as an expression of Oedipus' character; his intelligence, decisiveness, courage and stubbornness prompt the actions that realize the prophecy. This irony encourages speculation, as perhaps Sophocles intended, about the conditions responsible for Oedipus' character traits, or at least favourable to their development and expression. The timing of the play – 429 BCE, two years after the outbreak of the war and during the great Athenian plague that carried off Pericles – has prompted interpretations that Oedipus was intended to represent Pericles and that this was a commentary on the hubris that provoked the Peloponnesian War.[24] We need not necessarily accept such interpretations to understand that character and context are linked at the social – and not just the individual – level, and that great events like the Theban and Athenian plagues and the Peloponnesian War cannot be understood without taking both agency and structure into account. A close reading of Thucydides leads to the same conclusion. Book I indicates a sharp tension between the proximate and underlying causes of war, between the hubris responsible for the miscalculations of key actors in Corcyra, Corinth, Athens and Sparta and the dynamics of city–state competition; they not only interacted to produce a largely undesired hegemonic war, but were co-constitutive.[25] IR scholars on the whole ignore these tensions and relationships, or they resolve them unambiguously in favour of underlying causes, or structures. Scholarly studies of causation have much to learn from Sophocles and Thucydides, and from tragedy more generally.

David Hume grappled with the question of how we can know anything for certain. His solution, which provided the basis for an empiricist epistemology, was to limit knowledge to what our perceptions are capable of transmitting to us. Our ideas arise from experience and are preceded by impressions. The notion of cause is a concept we employ to explain the seemingly 'constant conjunctions' we observe. Causes must be prior to their effects, a temporal relationship that allows us to distinguish between them. Causation is not a characteristic of the world for Hume. It is a mental 'illusion' brought about through the combination of habit and imagination.[26] Humean causation restricts our attention to observable social ontologies, efficient causes and deterministic regularities. This understanding of cause became widely accepted in the nineteenth century by scientists and continues to be accepted uncritically by mainstream IR scholars.[27]

Humean causation facilitated the empirical study of observable features of social life by encouraging researchers to frame hypotheses around variables of cause and effect and to be open about their data, coding and methods of analysis. It is also extremely limiting in its single-minded focus on regularities and lack of interest in unobservable patterns that may be responsible for these regularities and in other behaviour that does not itself manifest in regularity. Humean causation cannot cope with complex causation – situations, that is, in which there are changing relationships among multiple variables. Complex causation is typical of many phenomena of interest to IR scholars, including the origins and development of states, the geneses and outcomes of war, the seeming emergence of zones of peace, the formation, importance and spread of political identities and the causes and consequences of globalization.[28] Attempts to apply Humean causation to these issue areas is difficult in any case because of all of the obstacles that are in the way of identifying and measuring important variables and finding a sufficiently large number of cases that are comparable and independent.

Post-positivist positions are compelling for these and other reasons. Many researchers reject the search for regularities, laws or even generalizations as an inappropriate approach to the social world. IR's constructivists in particular are wary of causal claims, generally preferring to work with the concept of constitution. Sometimes they represent causation and constitution as oppositional, orthogonal or competitive, as Alexander Wendt does.[29] Other constructivists, notably Nicholas Onuf, John Ruggie, and Friedrich Kratochwil, maintain that they are related and ought to be considered in tandem, as rules condition but do not necessarily cause outcomes.[30] Moreover, one of us has recently developed the concept of 'constitutive causation' and uses the relationship between visual frame and political thinking and behaviour to elaborate different ways and circumstances in which constitution has causal consequences.[31]

Milja Kurki describes the quandary post-positivists face when they reject Humean causation in the absence of an alternative model. They must ignore causation, address it in unsatisfactory, and even incoherent, ways, or resort, as many do, to smuggling back in Humean conceptions. Within IR, neo-Gramscians, post-structuralists, feminists and constructivists all confront this problem.[32] Scholars working in these traditions routinely use such concepts as 'influencing', 'producing', 'constraining', 'shaping', or 'enabling' to refer to non-deterministic conditions that appear to make some behaviour more thinkable, acceptable, preferable and likely – and other actions less so. These effects, they understand, invariably depend on the presence of other conditions, whose effects in turn cannot be determined beforehand. In 1948, Hans Morgenthau famously argued that a bipolar international system with nuclear weapons had the potential to be much more peaceful or much more destructive than a multipolar world of conventionally armed great power. The outcome would depend on the moral quality of leadership, and that in turn was a function of agency and the domestic political context in which it operated.[33]

Post-positivist research is interested in identifying patterns of observable behaviour, but even more in discovering reasons for these patterns. To look beneath the surface this way in an open-ended, non-linear world requires us to theorize about unobservables with complex and non-deterministic consequences. This requires narratives that tell non-Humean stories. Tragedy is such a narrative. It is a combat-decorated veteran in what Nietzsche calls the 'mobile army of metaphors, metonymies and anthropomorphisms' that we use to make sense of the world.[34] Tragedy invokes multiple causes and is sensitive to contingency. It constitutes what Hidemi Suganami considers a good causal narrative.[35] Tragedy directs our attention to causes that arise from human nature and the world humans confront, but that are unobservable in nature even though their consequences are visible and significant. Tragedy is avowedly causal without being deterministic. While anchored in deep causes, it not only shows respect for agency, confluence and accident, but it also depends upon them for its effects.

Tragedy, to return to Lu's point, has multiple causes and manifestations.[36] Several other contributors – Frost, Brown and Euben among them – suggest that events and actions work their way through social systems in complex and, by definition, unpredictable ways. Hubris, the cause of tragedy that we have emphasized so far, itself has many causes – although it is most commonly manifested by powerful and successful actors who have come to take their good fortune for granted. Not every powerful and successful figure displays hubris, and not every act of hubris has tragic consequences. Hubris and the catastrophic outcomes to which it sometimes leads are nevertheless important occurrences in social, economic and political life. Despite its obvious drawbacks from a Humean perspective, tragedy offers a more satisfying explanation for a pattern of behaviour than any observable regularities could because it links motives and mindsets to behaviour and outcomes. For the same reason, it allows us to make connections across domains to behaviour and events that are usually studied independently. Tragedy encourages us to make connections among such events as the Vietnam War, Watergate, the collapse of Enron and the Anglo-American invasion of Iraq, all of which may share important causes.

Tragedy offers strong support for the causal role of constitution. Many key actors not only act in accord with understandings of their roles, but may not think of their behaviour as purposeful in the sense assumed by rationalist theories. It is not goal oriented, if by that we mean intended to achieve some external objective. Behaviour appears to them – as ours does to us – as natural expressions of who they are. Much behaviour is attributable to identity. Oedipus is once again a case in point. In the first scene, a priest tells him that the people look up to him as they would a god and expect him to rid the city of its crippling plague. Framing his commitment to rid Thebes of its affliction as a free choice, Oedipus explains that he has already sent Creon to make inquiries of the Pytheness at Delphi. The priest's plea makes it apparent that a king whose office and reputation rest on having saved his city on an earlier occasion – by freeing it of the need to pay human tribute to the Sphinx – could hardly act otherwise.[37] Choice enters the picture again when his search for the plague's cause begins to zero in on the pollution his violation of fundamental taboos has brought to Thebes. Creon, Teresias, Jocasta and the shepherd plead with him to end his search for his origins, but to no avail. In the first encounter, the priest, speaking for the city as a whole, asks Oedipus to do what is natural to his role and character. In the second episode, Sophocles is, in effect, running an experiment. The city wants Oedipus to stop, not to proceed, and to act out of character, which he refuses to do. Sophocles is telling us that Oedipus' single-mindedness is more a function of his character than his role.

Thucydides poses similar questions about role, character and context. He has the Corinthians describe the Athenians as 'addicted to innovation … adventurous beyond their power and … swift to follow up a success and slow to recoil from a reverse and born into the world to take no rest themselves and to give none to others'.[38] Later, writing in the authorial voice, he characterizes them as driven by *polypragmosunē*, literally 'trespass', but widely used in the late-fifth century by critics of modernity to signify a kind of metaphysical restlessness, intellectual discontent and meddlesomeness that found expression in *pleonexia* (envy, ambition, search of glory, monetary greed, lust for power and conquest).[39] By his choice of language and use of stock stereotypes of Athenians and Spartiates, Thucydides is presenting them as representations, respectively, of restless modernity and stick-in-the-mud tradition. This reading suggests that the qualities that made Athenians different were both a cause and expression of modernity. The narrative of Book I provides more evidence that Thucydides considered ambition and restlessness on the one hand and modernity on the other as mutually constitutive and reinforcing. Athenians could not resist the prospect of gain held out by an alliance with Corcyra. Spartiates, moved by shame, envy and honour, could not refuse their allies' request for assistance. If defence of tradition was the 'truest precondition' [*alēthestatē prophasis*] of Sparta's vote for war, embrace of the fifth century version of modernity was the truest condition of Athenian willingness to challenge Sparta.[40]

Tragedy is directly relevant to the constructivist project because of the way it allows us to explore the relationship between constitution and causation via the choices of key actors. Much of the behaviour of tragic figures is determined by their roles, as it was for Orestes, Ajax, Antigone, Creon, the Trojan women and even Oedipus, once he became king. To some degree these roles and the identities they confer are constituted by society. But, they are also chosen. Medea's shifting roles are an obvious case in point. One of the striking features of tragedy, and of politics, is the extent to which actors consistently minimize their freedom of choice with regard to their roles and the performance of these roles. Antigone and Creon do this. They feel hemmed in by their roles and compelled to act in ways which they recognize, or come to suspect, will have dreadful consequences. Sophocles makes it apparent that both protagonists have made conscious choices about their respective roles and framed them in unnecessarily extreme and uncompromising ways. Examples from political life abound; Richard Beardsworth and Tracy Strong point to the foreign policies of the Bush administration and especially its 2003 invasion of Iraq.[41] Constitution has causal consequences, but they are rarely determinate. Rather, they make certain actions more thinkable and attractive and others less so. Choices of which course of action to pursue – even if these choices are understood to be constrained by socially constituted roles and identities – remain with the actors. This final point has important implications for considerations of moral responsibility.

A lens for sharpening questions of moral responsibility[42]

Just as an appreciation of tragedy has the potential to refine how IR theorists approach the notion of causation, so too it promises to add greater depth and nuance to how we address fundamental questions of moral responsibility. While causation represents an important area of enquiry across much mainstream IR theory, questions of moral responsibility have tended to be addressed within a narrower realm of scholarship. These questions occupy a central place within what is referred to as 'normative IR theory', or 'international political theory' (IPT) – a subfield of IR explicitly addressed by Frost, Brown, Beardsworth, and Lu in their respective chapters – and also make important, though less frequent, appearances in recent works within IR that take realist, English School and constructivist approaches.[43] Although there are areas of overlap between accounts of causation and moral responsibility, the two concepts are, importantly, distinct. Enquiries into causation are concerned with how a particular outcome is generated; analyses of moral responsibility distinguish themselves by invoking ethical guidelines and expectations to evaluate or prescribe the acts and omissions of bodies capable of purposive action.[44] Being morally responsible for a particular act or outcome is usefully described as being 'answerable' for it.[45] Moral responsibility is interpreted and invoked in two different, but related, ways: in a forward-looking, prescriptive sense associated with claims to duty and obligation; and, in a backward-looking, evaluative sense linked to claims of blame (or praise) and accountability.[46] Both prospective and retrospective senses are regularly appealed to in ethical analyses of international relations, and often-overlooked intricacies of each are highlighted when viewed through the lens of tragedy.

One might object that invoking tragedy to better understand questions of moral responsibility is hopelessly anachronistic. After all, it would be a mistake to impose upon the ancient Greeks our largely Kantian conceptions of morality and responsibility, tied as they are to notions of free will, intention and autonomous agency. Our contemporary moral consciousness cannot be projected upon Attic tragedies without misrepresenting these dramas, and, perhaps, misunderstanding an important dimension of what makes them 'tragic'. Yet, understandings of human agency and moral responsibility are present in even our earliest examples of tragedy – albeit infused with ambiguity and defined by contradictions. Indeed, this is precisely why tragedy is so useful in interrogating these concepts. As Jean-Pierre Vernant observes, fifth century BCE Athens experienced a 'tragic sense of responsibility', defined by a pull between the emerging idea of autonomous human action, in which agents both decide on and take responsibility for particular courses of action, and the lingering perception that such action remains wholly reliant on supernatural forces beyond the reach and comprehension of these agents.[47] This fundamental tension, Vernant argues, 'brings into question the position of man as an agent and pursues an anxious enquiry into the relationship between man and his own actions'.[48] Shakespearean tragedy attributes less significance to fate than its ancient Greek forbearer and more to the consequences that result from the agent's deeds.[49] Although this means that Shakespeare's tragic dramas thereby appear to be more in line with contemporary conceptions of autonomous human action, their illustration of the limits and mystery of human agency, and their focus on often pathological, character-driven error, is, nevertheless, equally provocative of our understanding of moral responsibility.

In other words, not only do the examples of tragedy explored through-out this volume rest on particular understandings of human agency and responsibility, but they simultaneously call these understandings into question – and thereby encourage those students of IR concerned with ethical questions to challenge and sharpen their own interpretations of moral responsibility in a number of valuable ways.

First, tragedy brings the structures and contexts within which agents must act into clearer focus. While, as we have suggested, studies of cau-sation within IR privilege structure and underlying causes over agency, analyses of moral responsibility have been inclined to do just the oppo-site. Like our understanding of causation, our understanding of moral responsibility stands to benefit from the corrective lens provided by tragedy. In the latter case, work within IR that focuses on ethical issues tends to foreground agency in the attempt to assign moral responsi-bility for particular actions and outcomes. This emphasis on agency is understandable. After all, coherent claims to moral responsibility demand the identification of moral agents: those actors who, by defini-tion, have the capacity to both deliberate over possible courses of action and their consequences and act on the basis of this deliberation, and who are thereby deemed answerable for particular acts, omissions and outcomes.[50] Structures might be part of the causal nexus that leads to tragic outcomes, but only (certain types of) agents can bear the burdens of moral responsibility.[51] When a crisis requires a response, or we want to determine who can be held to account for some harm, perceived injustice or neglect, we quite logically ask which agent should act, or should have acted differently, in light of our understanding of relevant moral guidelines. Within normative IR theory, scholars of a cosmopoli-tan bent defend the duties of individual human agents to respond to, *inter alia*, global poverty, transnational environmental degradation and genocide – and apportion blame to specific actors for both contributing to these crises and failing to respond to them.[52] Moreover, one of us has recently engaged in a similar exercise with respect to the moral respon-sibilities of 'institutional agents', such as states, intergovernmental organizations, and multinational corporations.[53] Identifying agents in international relations that bear moral burdens is an important endeav-our. Yet, by highlighting the impact of powerful realities external to the agent, tragedy cautions that an *exclusive* focus on agency would fail to represent the complexities of human experience.

It is possible to uncover important insights about moral responsibil-ity by revisiting the analogy between the notion of fate prominent in many examples of tragedy and the structures within which agents in international relations deliberate and act. Tragedy reminds us that such agents may ostensibly decide to implement or follow a particular policy, or choose to perform or abstain from specific practices or activities, yet, in fact, have limited scope for deciding or choosing otherwise. This is the case when the wider social, political or economic contexts within which these agents find themselves are action-guiding or disenabling, or when the roles that define particular agents dictate perceived options or constrain decision making. Tragedy thereby raises the possibility that the agent might choose a course of action, but, at the same time, experience a radical circumscription of freedom of choice and be guided by perceptions of necessity. The resulting tension between the influence of so-called structures in determining events in international relations and the prominent idea in contemporary ethical thought that the agent is answerable only for conduct arising from personal choice and the exercise of free will is deeply significant to discussions of moral responsibility. It also raises a host of questions for the IR theorist concerned with issues of moral responsibility. When, and to what degree, can we hold particular agents morally responsible for harm, neglect or wrongdoing if they are constrained or compelled by outside forces, external structures and imposed roles?[54] Are there instances in which agents cannot be held to account (or their degree of retrospective responsibility is diminished) in the context of specific calamitous acts, omissions and outcomes because they could not have acted differently (or their freedom of choice was severely circumscribed)? If there are such instances, do we, nevertheless, have obligations to engage in the sort of social, political and institutional transformation envisaged by Frost in order to create conditions that are less prone to tragic outcomes in the future? An appreciation of tragedy does not answer these questions for us, but it does make us more open to the problems that underlie them – and, crucially, cautions against attempting to analyse agency in isolation from the structures that can variously impede, constrain, enable and compel specific choices and actions.

Second, tragedy highlights themes of contingency, chance, luck and accident, and provocatively suggests that these elements necessarily influence our judgements of moral responsibility.[55] The role of contingency and luck in international relations is generally overlooked by IR theorists.[56] Where its effects *are* acknowledged by those engaged in explicitly ethical analyses, careful attempts are made to ensure that they do not bias our judgements. For example, the accident of where one was born, or one's good or ill fortune in what Ayelet Shachar has called 'the birthright lottery', must not, according to prominent cosmopolitan theorists, colour one's deliberations over principles of global justice.[57]

However, if raw luck unavoidably intervenes in our ethical analyses, regardless of attempts to bracket its effects, then the nature of this intervention demands attention.

Luck, as depicted in many tragedies, poses a powerful challenge to conceptions of autonomous agency. Consider the fortuitous nature of Oedipus' encounter with his father at the crossroads and everything that flows from it. Luck constitutes another category of external influence in international relations that is roughly comparable to the tragedian's fate, while being different from the category of structure already addressed. At the same time, tragedy teaches us that the effects of chance can *inform* both structure and agency. Chance is deeply relevant to sophisticated causal narratives of international relations, as Thucydides recognized when he highlighted the importance of accident and confluence, in addition to agency and structure, in his tragic account of the Peloponnesian War. Nevertheless, acknowledging contingency as not only one aspect of the causal nexus, but as defining of structures, and, particularly, agency, can be deeply subversive of ethical analyses both within and without IR. This is because, in the absence of recklessness or neglect, standard ethical accounts would not hold an agent morally responsible for negative outcomes resulting from forces outside the agent's volition and control. But, if luck is actually partly and unavoidably *constitutive* of agency, then ensuring that our ethical analyses are immune from the effects of luck becomes impossible.

As Bernard Williams astutely observes in his seminal discussion of 'moral luck', elements of chance are difficult to completely extricate from accounts of responsible agency.[58] Williams argues that it is possible to draw from this one of two conclusions: 'that responsible agency is a fairly superficial concept, which has a limited use in harmonizing what happens', or, alternatively, 'that it is not a superficial concept, but that it cannot ultimately be purified'.[59] Tragedy, we suggest, supports the latter conclusion: responsible agency *is* a deeply meaningful concept, but one that cannot be completely protected or removed from the effects of accident, luck and random events. This, indeed, is the conclusion favoured by Williams, who notes that one's 'sense of who one is in terms of what one has done and what in the world one is responsible for' are shaped, at least in part, by chance and the unintended aspects of one's actions.[60] Moreover, in a brief aside, he suggests that acceptance of just this reality is 'central to tragedy' and cites the understanding of agency embodied by Oedipus, who is a victim of chance and the unintended consequences of his own actions, but whose exile and self-mutilation speak to an ascription and acknowledgment of moral responsibility.[61]

In a similar vein, Euben observes that tragedy deems us responsible for what we have done, regardless of whether it was intended, and, moreover, reminds us that 'what we have done *constitutes our character* which in turn establishes the kinds of actions we will and can do'.[62]

Actors in international relations are arguably much less likely than Oedipus to accept moral responsibility for crises and calamities that they did not intend, and that were largely the result of bad luck and happenstance rather than oversight or negligence.[63] Indeed, many actors are disinclined to accept moral responsibility for catastrophes in those clear-cut cases that do result from blatant instances of oversight and negligence. Yet, it is interesting to note that even inadvertent players in tragic outcomes – who unknowingly and without recklessness contributed to them – can feel moved to respond to calls for rectification and compensation. Furthermore, IR theorists interested in normative questions might do well to ask what involvement in those tragic outcomes that owe an overwhelming debt to bad luck does to the character of both individual and corporate players on the world stage – and how the characters of these agents (displayed in policies and postures) then affect their perceived roles and responsibilities in the context of subsequent events.[64] Addressing these questions and reconciling apparent insights about 'moral luck' with ethical analyses in IR is far from straightforward. But, regardless of the rough terrain that comes with traversing previously uncharted territory, these are important routes to explore. Tragedy teaches us that the human condition is too complex, and agency too indeterminate, to allow elements of chance to be purged from ethical consideration.

These first two points might cause some unease among those committed to analysing issues of moral responsibility in international relations – and for reasons that help to account for the tendency among theorists engaged in such endeavours to foreground agency. Indeed, an editorial confession is in order. One of us first approached this project because the suggestion that the concept of tragedy could provide a way of better understanding ethics in international relations both intrigued and worried her. In response to Frost's reflections on the value of tragedy to students of international ethics (elaborated in what is now Chapter 2 of this volume), she initially objected that the invocation of tragedy is deeply troubling from an ethical perspective if harms, injustices and apparent derogations of duty risk being attributed to context and structure, contingency and chance in a way that lets responsible agents off the moral hook. The worry – and even scepticism – arose because suboptimal outcomes could, it seemed, be too easily linked to an amorphous notion of 'fate' (in the form of either external structures or chance) and thereby deemed beyond the control and understanding of responsible agents, who might then be held neither morally accountable nor blameworthy for such outcomes. Would not neglect or wrongdoing on the part of central decision-makers then be overlooked – in a way that would impede and obscure robust ethical evaluation?[65] The concern was that difficult questions of moral responsibility, both in terms of prospectively assigning duties and retrospectively apportioning blame, can be too easily swept under the carpet with the label 'tragic'.[66] However, this scepticism was misguided – at least with respect to the sophisticated understandings of tragedy articulated in this volume. Rather than precluding considerations of moral responsibility by denying or ignoring the role of central decision-makers in contributing to ruinous results, tragedy conversely forces us to rethink our moral judgements in a way that potentially *widens* the net of actions and outcomes for which such agents are deemed responsible. It does this not only by embracing notions of human agency and moral deliberation, but by also simultaneously questioning and reconfiguring them. Agents do not shed moral responsibility when their actions are limited, or even dictated, by external structures; attributions of moral responsibility become compatible with claims to necessity. Moreover, the influence of hard luck means that agents sometimes do what they had not intended – and, as a result, make deeply consequential errors. But, tragedy does not place the effects of chance and attributions of moral responsibility in mutually exclusive categories. Rather, disastrous outcomes, however involuntary and unintended, shape our own ethical evaluations of our actions – and, by extension, inform our characters in ways that informs future action. Tragedy thereby challenges stringent conceptions of moral responsibility that demand arguably unattainable degrees of autonomous action and free choice.

Third, an understanding of tragedy further complicates the conception of agency that IR theorists engaged in ethical debates tend to foreground by drawing attention to agents' pathologies and character flaws and to the often acute limits of human knowledge and understanding. Tragedy neither uniformly nor exclusively attributes crises and calamities to phenomena beyond human control, whether divine powers, natural forces or chance.[67] The same dramas that see tragic outcomes as the work of the gods also attribute disaster to human error arising out of fatal flaws of character – and, indeed, some examples of the genre focus on the latter.[68] If the complicating factors of structure or underlying causes, on the one hand, and accident or chance, on the other, exert *external* influences on agents which affect decision-making and action, and, by extension, raise thorny questions about their degree of moral responsibility in specific contexts, then these character flaws, limited capacities and pathologies might be understood to behave as *internal* forces that raise comparable questions. Tragedy reminds us that concrete manifestations of agency defy any simple, straightforward, idealized conception of rationality, however theoretically eloquent or seemingly efficacious such a conception might be.[69] Moreover, these internal flaws and limitations bring us back to the previous point about 'moral luck'. If some tragedies demonstrate an agent's actions and the negative outcomes of these actions flowing from his or her charac- ter, and if some agents in international relations (whether individual human beings or corporate actors), through good or bad luck, have bet- ter or worse characters or dispositions than others, how does this affect the degree to which the agent in question is morally responsible for his, her, or its own actions?[70]

Finally, tragedy emphasizes the difficulty in making assessments of moral responsibility in the absence of a clear sense of the standards by which actions are to be judged right or wrong, just or unjust, prohib- ited, permissible or required. Not only are judgements of moral respon- sibility affected by external structures and forces, and by the agent's own internal limitations, but such assessments must take into account the evaluative criterion (however grounded and derived) against which judgements are made. What duties are particular agents expected to discharge? Within which moral framework and against whose ethical code do we condemn actions and hold agents to account? Significantly, tragedy highlights to us the potential difficulty in identifying with precision and certainty what such criteria entail. Specifically, it uncov- ers two sets of circumstances in which confusion or tension over the demands of morality occurs: when moral frameworks or ethical codes collide, we are faced with competing conceptions of right, duty or jus- tice, and any viable option is *both* required and prohibited, depending on the moral framework within which it is considered; and, when the norms, shared understandings and values within a single framework are in flux.

The first case is highlighted at the outset of this volume by Frost, and variously addressed by Brown and Lu.[71] We argue in Chapter 1 that this reality of conflicting ethical imperatives serves to teach us that our own conceptions of justice are particular, not universal. In judgements of moral responsibility in international relations, it under- lines the difficult question of how transnational ethical evaluation is possible. Conversely, the second case, dealing with the dynamic nature of norms and values, brings us back to a way in which tragedy itself can speak to circumstances beyond any one particular time or place. According to Jean-Pierre Vernant, the 'tragic moment' of fifth-century Greece was marked by a powerful tension in the social experience of Athenians brought on by the conflict in values between an emerging legal and political thought on the one hand and the ancient religious tradition of the past on the other.[72] In such a context, the moral agent was 'forced to make a decisive choice, to orient his activity in a universe of ambiguous values where nothing is ever stable or unequivocal'.[73] In this universe, 'no rule appears definitively established' and 'even in the course of the play's action, justice itself shifts, twists and is transformed to the contrary'.[74] In this way, tragedy resonates with us in moments of moral upheaval, when previously established values, hitherto accepted worldviews, and erstwhile peremptory norms are openly questioned, challenged and even rejected. One need only look to the recent 'war on terror' and explicit challenges to the prohibitions against torture and preventive war to find contemporary examples of such shifts in seemingly unshakeable shared understandings, manifest in contested international laws and moral norms.[75] In other words, tragedy also reminds us of the problem in assuming that moral norms are in some way fixed. Neither case, we suggest, commits us to resign to relativism or avoid ethical evaluation at the international level. Both, however, remind us that the norms and values upon which we base judgements of moral responsibility in international relations are constantly debated and frequently in flux.

Tragedy at once problematizes and enhances our treatment of moral responsibility in international relations. It does this by highlighting the significance of the external structures within which agents act, revealing the spanner in the works of ethical evaluation introduced by contingency and 'moral luck', forcing us to confront the internal flaws and pathologies that define, and occasionally compromise, human agency and reminding us both of the danger in assuming and the difficulty in discerning a single, clear, unambiguous set of moral guidelines for making judgements and deciding on appropriate courses of action. Tragedy reminds us that the complexities of human existence are incompatible with one-dimensional accounts of either agency or the circumstances within which agents act. An appreciation of tragedy fundamentally complicates considerations of moral responsibility – but in a way that invites IR theorists to address ethical issues with greater nuance.

A more comprehensive view of the emotions

Social science as a whole has given short shrift to the role of emotions. It is undeniably central to psychology, but for some decades this field attempted to subsume emotions to cognition and it is only in recent years that the emotions have become an important subject of study in their own right. Research in neuroscience indicates that emotions are involved in decision-making, generally in a positive way, and from the earliest stage of deciding what information deserves our attention.[76] Political scientists have always recognized emotions as important, but have generally stressed their negative influence on behaviour.[77] The time is long overdue for political science and IR to acknowledge and study the positive contribution of emotions, harnessed to reason, to order and to cooperation. Reason and affect together have a greater potential than either alone to encourage the enlightened and restrained behaviour necessary to preserve *nomos* or reform it to more closely approximate widely-accepted principles of justice.

Tragedy, the application of art to politics, can sensitize us to the positive, not just the negative, role of emotional arousal. This theme is central to Nietzsche, who found the Western emphasis on reason stifling of creativity. As Strong reminds us, Nietzsche found inspiration in Greek tragedy because of the ability of Dionysian art to convince us of the joy of existence. Like music, it exists in a realm that is beyond and prior to phenomena. Language and the concepts its spawns can never capture the cosmic symbolism of poetry and music because language itself is a symbol. It can have superficial contact with poetry and music – it can describe its structure, rhythm, instrumentation and evolution – but it cannot disclose their innermost heart. Art often speaks to us directly, unmediated by language.[78]

We are emotional beings, not computers. Reason always functions in tandem with affect and, together, they can have quite divergent consequences depending on how they interact. Reason combined with positive emotional arousal in the form of affection builds empathy. It encourages us to see others as our ontological equals and to recognize the self-actualizing benefits of close relationships. For Plato, *eros* can be educated by reason and directed towards the good and the beautiful, and even towards the kind wisdom concerned with the ordering of states and families.[79] From Socrates to Gadamer, philosophers have maintained that dialogue has the potential to make us recognize the parochial and limited nature of our understandings of justice. Affection and reason together make us seek cooperation, not only as a means of achieving specific ends, but of becoming ourselves. They bring many of us – individuals and collectivities – to the recognition that self-restraint, or self-imposed limitations on our appetites and spirit, are essential to sustain the kinds of environments in which meaningful cooperation becomes possible.

Reason almost always interacts with affect. Instrumental reason divorced from emotional commitments reinforces people's conceptions of themselves as autonomous and egoistic. It leads them to act in self-ish, if sometimes efficient, ways and to frame relationships with others purely strategically. People are treated as means, not ends in themselves, to use Kant's famous distinction. In these circumstances, the pursuit of self-interest is likely to intensify conflict and undermine or prevent the emergence of communities that enable actors to advance their interests and satisfy their spirit more effectively by means of cooperative behaviour. Modern social science, which welcomes, utilizes and propagates such an understanding of human beings, stands in sharp contrast to traditional philosophy, not only in its assumptions about human beings, but in the kinds of behaviour it encourages and endorses. Ironically, the same social science that worries about the tragedy of the commons frames human beings as autonomous, egoistic actors, encouraging people to behave in ways that bring about this situation. By revealing the positive role of emotional arousal, tragedy encourages IR scholars to rethink the relationship between reason and the emotions.

The way forward?

Tragic plot lines are often highly stylized accounts of fictional aristocrats in archaic times. They nevertheless present and problematize the variously flawed, vulnerable and complex nature of human existence, along with enduring human dilemmas to which people respond in ways audiences have found credible for over two millennia. Tragedy was so central to Athenian culture because it explored these dilemmas and, by doing so, offered lessons about personal and civic life. Although tragedy has survived down to our day it never again played the central role in the political life of a country that it did in Greece. In Elizabethan England it had broad popular appeal but ever since has been relegated to an elite art form. It may have influence on intellectuals, and one might hope through them on political thinking and practice. But, currently, this seems a stretch and such an influence is not readily apparent.[80]

Tragedy today has a limited audience and its potential to help us to understand international relations and refine important categories and concepts in IR is, sadly, untapped. Here Nietzsche was prescient, as Strong points out, because he worried that tragedy could 'die' and deprive us of an invaluable way of understanding the world.[81] The challenging task for IR scholars – whether realists, constructivists or normative IR theorists; whether trained in the social sciences, political philosophy, or some combination of the two – is accordingly three-fold. We must encourage an interest in tragedy among students of international relations, we must use tragedy to better understand ourselves, the world and the theoretical categories we use to interrogate it, and we must devise means of imparting the lessons of an IR theory thus informed by tragedy to policymakers and the wider public. This is admittedly a Sisyphean task, but even limited progress uphill, so to speak, will have important payoffs.

Notes

1. N. Rengger 'Tragedy or Scepticism? Defending the Anti-Pelagian Mind in World Politics', Chapter 5, this volume, pp. 53–62.
2. Aristotle *Politics*, 1341 b35–1342 a20 and *Poetics*, 1450a–b, 1452a1–10, 1453b1–2 in *Complete Works of Aristotle, Volume 2: The Revised Oxford Translation*, ed. by J. Barnes (Princeton: Princeton University Press (1984)).
3. Aristotle *Poetics*, 1450 a–b, 1452 a1–10, 1453 b1–2.
4. M. Frost 'Tragedy, Ethics and International Relations', Chapter 2, this volume, pp. 21–43.
5. H. J. Morgenthau ([1946] 1965) *Scientific Man versus Power Politics* (Chicago: University of Chicago Press), pp. 189, 209; Kamila Stullerova 'Tragedy and Political Theory: Progressivism without an Ideal', Chapter 9, this volume, pp. 112–126.
6. I. L. Janis and L. Mann (1977) *Decision Making: A Psychological Analysis of Conflict, Choice, and Commitment* (New York: Free Press); R. N. Lebow (1981) *Between Peace and War: The Nature of International Crisis* (Baltimore: Johns Hopkins University Press), Chapters 4–5.
7. Frost, 'Tragedy, Ethics and International Relations', this volume.
8. Frost, 'Tragedy, Ethics, and International Relations', this volume, pp. 31–32.
9. J. Mayall 'Tragedy, Progress and the International Order', Chapter 3, this volume, pp. 44–52.
10. Note, however, that the potential for violence and feud nevertheless remain and the transformed Furies can be understood as repressed urges ready to reemerge if the conditions are ripe.
11. Thucydides, *The Landmark Thucydides: A Comprehensive Guide to the Peloponnesian War* (revised edition of the Richard Crawley translation), ed. by Robert B. Strassler (New York: Free Press, 1996), 5.85–113.

12. R. N. Lebow (2003) *The Tragic Vision of Politics: Ethics, Interests and Orders* (Cambridge: Cambridge University Press), Chapter 3–4.

13. R. N. Lebow 'Tragedy, Politics and Political Science', Chapter 5, this volume, pp. 63–71 (p. 69).

14. C. Brown 'Tragedy, 'Tragic Choices' and Contemporary International Political Theory', Chapter 6, this volume, pp. 75–85 (p. 83).

15. P. Euben 'The Tragedy of Tragedy', Chapter 7, this volume, pp. 86–96 (p. 87).

16. C. Lu 'Tragedies and International Relations', Chapter 12, this volume, pp. 158–171.

17. Rengger, 'Tragedy or Scepticism? Defending the Anti-Pelagian Mind in World Politics', this volume.

18. M. Oakeshott (1996) *Religion, Politics and the Moral Life* (ed.) by Tim Fuller (New Haven: Yale University Press), p. 107.

19. Aristotle *Poetics*, 1451 a38–b11.

20. Lebow (2003) *Tragic Vision of Politics*, pp. 73–7.

21. Thucydides, 1.1.

22. N. J. Roese and J. M. Olson 'Counterfactual Thinking: A Critical Overview', in Roese and Olson (eds) *What Might Have Been*, pp. 1–56; D. T. Miller, W. Turnbull and C. McFarland (1990) 'Counterfactual Thinking and Social Perceptions: Thinking about What Might Have Been', in M. P. Zanna (ed.) *Advances in Experimental Social Psychology* (New York: Academic Press), Vol. 23, pp. 305–31; V. Girotto, P. Legrenzi and A. Rizzo (1991) 'Event Controllability in Counterfactual Thinking', *Acta Psychologica*, 78, 111–33; E. P. Seelau, S. M. Seelau, G. L. Wells and P. D. Windschild 'Counterfactual Constraints', in Roese and Olson (eds) *What Might Have Been*, pp. 67–79; H. L. A. Hart and A. M. Honoré (1985) *Causation in Law*, 2nd edn (Oxford: Oxford University Press); D. Kahneman and D. T. Miller (1986) 'Norm Theory: Comparing Reality to the Alternatives', *Psychological Review*, 93, 136–53; D. J. Hilton and B. R. Slugoski (1986) 'Knowledge-Based Causal Attributions: The Abnormal Conditions Focus Model', *Psychological Review*, 93, 75–88; I. Gavanski and G. L. Wells (1989) 'Counterfactual Processing of Normal and Exceptional Events', *Journal of Experimental Social Psychology*, 25, 314–25; M. L. Buck and D. T. Miller (1994) 'Reactions to Incongruous Negative Life Events', *Social Justice Research*, 7, 29–46; C. D. Lundberg and G. E. Frost (1992) 'Counterfactuals in Financial Decision Making', *Acta Psychologica*, 79, 227–44; G. L. Wells, B. R. Taylor and J. W. Turtle (1987) 'The Undoing of Scenarios', *Journal of Personality and Social Psychology*, 53, 421–30; D. Kahneman 'Varieties of Counterfactual Thinking', in Roese and Olson (eds) *What Might Have Been*, pp. 375–96; R. N. Lebow (2011) *Forbidden Fruit: Counterfactuals and International Relations* (Princeton: Princeton University Press), Chapter 6.

23. In the following section, in the context of our discussion of tragedy and moral responsibility, we address the separate category of chance, or luck, which is also external to the agent, and beyond the agent's control, but distinct from structure. Chance, we suggest, can also be seen as roughly comparable to 'fate' in Greek tragedy.

24. B. Knox (1970) *Oedipus at Thebes* (New York: Norton), pp. 61–106. C. Segal (2001) *Oedipus Tyrannus*, 2nd edn (New York: Oxford University Press),

pp. 11–13, suggests that Oedipus was a response to the war and great plague of 429–5 BCE. V. Ehrenberg (1954) *Sophocles and Pericles* (Oxford: Blackwell), pp. 67–9, argues that Oedipus was Sophocles' warning about the consequences of Periclean rationalism. See also F. Zeitlin (1986) 'Thebes: Theater of Self and Society in Athenian Drama', in J. P. Euben (ed.) *Greek Tragedy and Political Theory* (Berkeley and Los Angeles: University of California Press), pp. 101–41.

25. Lebow (2003) *Tragic Vision of Politics*.
26. D. Hume (1955) *An Enquiry Concerning Human Understanding*, ed. Charles Hendel (London: Liberal Arts Press), pp. 27–9, 45, and (1978) *A Treatise of Human Nature*, 2nd edn (Oxford: Oxford University Press), pp. 11, 27, 77, 157, 161–73, 646; M. Kurki (2008) *Causation in International Relations: Reclaiming Causal Analysis* (Cambridge: Cambridge University Press), pp. 33–40.
27. See, for example, G. King, R. O. Keohane, and S. Verba (1994) *Designing Social Inquiry: Scientific Inference in Quantitative Research* (Princeton: Princeton University Press).
28. F. V. Kratochwil (2007) 'Evidence, Inference, and Truth as Problems of Theory Building in the Social Sciences', in R. N. Lebow and M. I. Lichbach (eds) *Theory and Evidence in Comparative Politics and International Relations* (New York: Palgrave Macmillan), pp. 25–54; Kurki (2008) *Causation in International Relations*, pp. 88–123.
29. A. E. Wendt (1998) 'On Constitution and Causation in International Relations', in T. Dunne, M. Cox, and K. Booth (eds) *International Relations, 1919–1999* (Cambridge: Cambridge University Press), pp. 101–17.
30. N. Onuf (1989) *World of Our Making: Rules and Rule in Social Theory and International Relations* (Columbia, SC: University of South Carolina Press); J. G. Ruggie (1993) 'Territoriality and Beyond: Problematizing Modernity in International Relations', *International Organization*, 47/1, 139–74; and F. V. Kratochwil (1989) *Rules, Norms and Decisions* (Cambridge: Cambridge University Press).
31. R. N. Lebow (2009) 'Constitutive Causality: Imagined Spaces and Political Practices', *Millennium*, 38/2, 1–29.
32. Kurki (2008) *Causation in International Relations*, pp. 108–23 on rationalist approaches and pp. 124–46 on reflectivist and constructivist approaches.
33. H. J. Morgenthau (1948) *Politics among Nations* (New York: Knopf), pp. 285–6.
34. F. V. Nietzsche (1999) *The Birth of Tragedy*, trans. by Ronald Speirs (Cambridge: Cambridge University Press), p. 146.
35. H. Suganami (1996) *On the Causes of War* (Oxford: Oxford University Press), pp. 138–44.
36. Lu, 'Tragedies and International Relations', this volume.
37. Sophocles *Oedipus the King*, lines 13–77.
38. Thucydides, 1.70.
39. Thucydides, 6.87.3, uses *polypragmosunē* only once in his text, to characterize Athenians 'hyperactive', but is widely used by others to describe Athens. J. H. Finley (1938) 'Euripides and Thucydides', *Harvard Studies in Classical Philology* 49, 23–68; V. Ehrenberg (1947) '*Polypragmosyne*: A Study in Greek Politics', *Journal of Hellenic Studies*, 67, 46–67; J. W. Allison (1979) 'Thucydides and *Polypragmosyne*', *American Journal of Ancient History*, 4, 10–22.
40. Lebow (2003) *The Tragic Vision of Politics*, pp. 155–59.

41. R. Beardsworth 'Tragedy and Ethical Community in World Politics', Chapter 8, this volume, pp. 97–111; T. Strong 'Nietzsche and Questions of Tragedy, Tyranny and International Relations', Chapter 11, this volume, pp. 144–157.

42. Toni Erskine is very grateful to Richard Beardsworth and Ariel Colonomos for incisive comments on the points made in this section.

43. See, for example, M. C. Williams (2005) *The Realist Tradition and the Limits of International Relations* (Cambridge: Cambridge University Press), N. J. Wheeler (2002) *Saving Strangers: Humanitarian Intervention in International Society* (Oxford: Oxford University Press), and R. Price (ed.) (2008) *Moral Limit and Possibility* (Cambridge: Cambridge University Press) for realist, English School and constructivist engagements with questions of moral responsibility, respectively.

44. Points of contrast, then, are the explicit reference to ethical standards and the overtly evaluative and prescriptive (as opposed to ostensibly descriptive) nature of enquiry found in analyses of moral responsibility, as well as the requirement that those bodies charged with moral responsibility are purposive actors – none of which, arguably, applies to accounts of causation. For an alternative, and extremely valuable, account of the relationship between causation and moral responsibility, see Hidemi Suganami, 'Causal Explanation and Moral Judgement: Undividing a Division', in *Millennium: Journal of International Studies*, 39/3, 717–34. Toni Erskine is very grateful to Hidemi Suganami for fruitful discussions – and constructive debates – on the understanding of causation and the relationship between causal and moral responsibility.

45. As J. R. Lucas highlights in *Responsibility* (Oxford: Clarendon Press (1993)), p. 5, the word 'responsibility' comes from the Latin *respondeo*, meaning 'I answer'.

46. For an overview of both understandings of moral responsibility, specifically in the context of international relations, see T. Erskine (2008) 'Locating Responsibility: The Problem of Moral Agency in International Relations', in C. Reus-Smit and D. Snidal (eds) *The Oxford Handbook of International Relations* (Oxford: Oxford University Press), pp. 699–707, and T. Erskine (2003) 'Making Sense of "Responsibility" in International Relations: Key Questions and Concepts', in T. Erskine (ed.) *Can Institutions Have Responsibilities? Collective Moral Agency and International Relations* (New York: Palgrave Macmillan), pp. 1–16. In the forward-looking sense, we are using 'responsibility', 'duty', and 'obligation' interchangeably to indicate actions or forbearances that one is deemed bound to perform or observe. While we recognize that each concept can also be taken to have a specific, distinct connotation, this is consistent with much contemporary usage.

47. J. -P. Vernant (1990) 'The Historical Moment of Tragedy in Greece: Some Social and Psychological Conditions', in Vernant *Myth and Tragedy in Ancient Greece* (New York: Zone Books), p. 27.

48. J.-P. Vernant (1990) 'Intimations of the Will in Greek Tragedy', in Vernant *Myth and Tragedy in Ancient Greece* (New York: Zone Books), pp. 49–84 (p. 79).

49. A. C. Bradley ([1904] 2007) *Shakespearean Tragedy*, 4th edn (Basingstoke: Palgrave Macmillan), pp. 8–9; 16–20. Interestingly, while Bradley argues that

'fate' does not play a great part in Shakespearean tragedy, he attributes contrary readings of Shakespeare to the influence of Greek tragedy. See Bradley ([1904] 2007) *Shakespearean Tragedy*, p. 19; fn. 12. It should be noted that we are not assuming that the role of fate in ancient Greek tragedy somehow precludes an understanding of consequences as resulting from the agent's deeds. Rather, the combination of agency and fate as factors influencing outcomes is particularly valuable in terms of questioning contemporary assumptions.

50. See Erskine (2008) 'Locating Responsibility', pp. 700–1; and (2003) 'Making Sense of "Responsibility," p. 6.

51. One can also make a distinction between *causal* and *moral* responsibility according to which it makes sense to talk about structures and non-moral agents being *causally* responsible, but not *morally* responsible for an outcome. See Erskine (2003) 'Making Sense of "Responsibility",' p. 16, fn. 29.

52. See, for example, T. W. Pogge ([2002] 2008) *World Poverty and Human Rights: Cosmopolitan Responsibilities and Reforms*, 2nd edn (Cambridge: Polity Press) and S. Caney (2005) *Justice Beyond Borders: A Global Political Theory* (Oxford: Oxford University Press).

53. See T. Erskine (2001) 'Assigning Responsibilities to Institutional Moral Agents: The Case of States and Quasi-states', *Ethics & International Affairs*, 15, 67–85; Erskine (2004) "Blood on the UN's Hands"? Assigning Duties and Apportioning Blame to an Intergovernmental Organization', *Global Society*, 18/1, 21–42; Erskine (2010) 'Kicking Bodies and Damning Souls: The Danger of Harming "Innocent" Individuals While Punishing Delinquent States', *Ethics & International Affairs*, 24/3, 261–85, and the contributions to Erskine (ed.) (2003) *Can Institutional Have Responsibilities? Collective Moral Agency and International Relations* (New York and Basingstoke: Palgrave Macmillan). See also I. Clark et al. (forthcoming (2012)) *Special Responsibilities: Global Problems and American Power* (Cambridge: Cambridge University Press) for a discussion of the special responsibilities of the United States understood as a moral agent.

54. Of course, when considering this question, it is important to remember two points that we proposed in the previous section on causation. First, actors in the realms of both tragedy (such as Creon and Antigone) and politics (such as political leaders who shy away from making difficult decisions in foreign policy) can be inclined to downplay their freedom of choice and exaggerate the role-defined constraints on their actions. Second, even constrained choices remain choices nonetheless. Tragedy highlights the significance of structure in addressing questions moral responsibility, but not in a way that eclipses agency.

55. How the notion of moral luck discussed below complicates conceptions of agency and judgements of responsibility with respect to ethical questions in international relations is further developed in T. Erskine (forthcoming (2012)) 'Moral luck and International Relations', *Millennium: Journal of International Studies*.

56. At the time of writing, we were not aware of any other work that addresses moral luck in the context of international relations. We subsequently learnt of a recent book on preventive war and luck (including moral luck), Ariel Colonomos (2009) *Le Pari de la guerre – guerre préventive, guerre juste?*

(Paris: Denoël), currently available only in French. We are grateful to Richard Beardsworth for this discovery.

57. Examples within normative IR theory include those 'impartialist cosmopolitan' positions influenced by a reworking of John Rawls' idea of the "original position', in which the consequences of contingency and luck are bracketed so that they cannot inform the moral agent's deliberations over global principles of justice. See, for example, C. Beitz ([1979] 1999) *Political Theory and International Relations*, 2nd edn (Princeton, NJ: Princeton University Press) and T. Pogge (1989) *Realizing Rawls* (Ithaca, NY and London: Cornell University Press). For an overview of such Rawls-inspired 'impartialist cosmopolitan' positions, see T. Erskine (2008) *Embedded Cosmopolitanism: Duties to Strangers and Enemies in a World of 'Dislocated Communities'* (Oxford: Oxford University Press), pp. 51–9. The phrase 'birthright lottery', or the idea that political membership and its corresponding rights, benefits and life chances (or lack thereof) constitute circumstances beyond one's control, is taken from Shachar (2009) *The Birthright Lottery: Citizenship and Global Inequality* (Cambridge, MA: Harvard University Press).

58. B. Williams (1982) 'Moral Luck', in *Moral Luck: Philosophical Papers 1973–1980* (Cambridge: Cambridge University Press), pp. 20–39. (An earlier version was published in the *Proceedings of the Aristotelian Society,* Supplementary vol. 50 (1976), 115–36). The literature on 'moral luck' within philosophy is rich and challenging, at odds with standard ethical assumptions within normative IR theory, and ignored across the range of IR approaches that engage to some degree with questions of moral responsibility. A comprehensive account of this literature is beyond the scope of this chapter, but interested readers should also see the following: T. Nagel, 'Moral Luck' (1976) *Proceedings of the Aristotelian Society,* Supplementary vol. 50, 137–51; M. Nussbaum (1986) *The Fragility of Goodness: Luck and Ethics in Greek Tragedy and Philosophy* (New York: Cambridge University Press); and the contributions to D. Statman (ed.) (1993) *Moral Luck* (Albany, NY: State University of New York Press).

59. Williams (1982) *Moral Luck*, pp. 29–30.

60. Williams (1982) *Moral Luck*, pp. 29–30.

61. Williams (1982) *Moral Luck*, p. 30, fn. 2.

62. Euben 'The Tragedy of Tragedy', this volume, p. 88. Emphasis ours.

63. One might note, however, that credit for the unintended positive side effects of an agent's decisions and actions—in other words, credit for the results of good luck—*is* readily accepted by agents, and, arguably, even used to justify questionable acts retrospectively. Retrospective endorsements of military intervention that have unintended humanitarian side-effects are good examples here. See Wheeler's (controversial) argument against 'right intention' being a necessary criterion for intervention to be justified on humanitarian grounds in *Saving Strangers*. Although this vocabulary has not, as far as we are aware, previously been brought to bear on these discussions, this seems an excellent illustration of 'moral luck' as Bernard Williams introduces it.

64. On this point, one might think back to our discussion of Thucydides' representation of the collective characters of Athenians and Spartiates, respectively. Arguably, one could also talk about the characters of particular corporate entities themselves, and how they are affected by involvement in unintended, calamitous outcomes. See, for example, C. Brown,

'"Delinquent" States, Guilty Consciences and Humanitarian Politics in the 1990s', *Journal of International Political Theory*, 4/1, 55–71. Brown argues that the Western powers' roles in particular crises (such as Somalia, 1992–3), their resulting moral censure, and the apparent feelings of guilt and responsibility on the part of state leaders affected the states' policies in future crises (such as Rwanda (1994)).

65. Indeed, one of us posed exactly this question to Mervyn Frost following his presentation on tragedy and ethics at the 2002 International Studies Association (ISA) convention. The discussion that ensued prompted her to commission four short articles, which evolved into the first four chapters of this book.

66. Perhaps this concern was the result of the elision of colloquial conceptions of 'tragedy', commonly invoked in discussions of international relations, and the more specific sense explored in this volume. By saying that something is 'tragic' or 'a tragedy', at least in the colloquial sense, we are simultaneously lamenting some crisis or severe hardship and mourning our inability to act or reverse events in the face of more powerful forces. Yet, when genocide, famine and environmental disaster are described as 'tragic' (as they often are), this label seems either a poor and dangerous excuse for the failure of actors to behave ethically or a concession to apathy. After all, in such cases, there are invariably decision-makers with ample knowledge and resources to have acted differently and avoided or mitigated disaster, who did not simply 'miss the mark' due to forces beyond their control and understanding, but, rather, acted out of negligence, greed or malice. Understood in this way, tragedy seems more an evasion of ethical consideration than any attempt to better understand ethics in international relations. Yet, as one of us learnt (and the other already knew), the evasion of moral responsibility that seems to accompany many reports of 'tragedy' in international relations need not accompany its use in the more specific sense explored in this volume.

67. Martha Nussbaum makes this point in Nussbaum (2003) 'Philosophy and Literature', in D. Sedley (ed.) *The Cambridge Companion to Greek and Roman Philosophy* (Cambridge: Cambridge University Press), pp. 211–41 (pp. 217–18).

68. According to Bradley, Shakespearean tragedies show man to be more the root of his own undoing than a hapless victim of fate. See Bradley ([1904] 2007) *Shakespearean Tragedy*, pp. 18–20.

69. It is interesting to ask what the pathologies and internal limitations of corporate as well as individual agents would mean for questions of moral responsibility. For a discussion of the 'pathologies' of intergovernmental organizations like the UN, see M. Barnett and M. Finnemore (1999) 'The Politics, Power and Pathologies of International Organizations', *International Organization*, 53, 699–732. For the affects of such corporate entities' internal flaws on considerations of their moral responsibilities, see Erskine's account of 'weak institutions' in 'Blood on the UN's Hands?', pp. 21–4, and 'Kicking Bodies and Damning Souls', p. 268.

70. This, of course, goes back to the perplexing questions of whether, and to what degree, we are responsible for our characters.

71. Lu labels these 'tragedies of moral dilemma' in Chapter 12, and describes them as involving 'inescapable moral wrongdoing'. See also Nussbaum's account of 'tragedies of ethical dilemma' in 'Philosophy and Literature', p. 221.

72. J. -P. Vernant (1990) 'The Historical Moment of Tragedy in Greece: Some of the Social and Psychological Conditions', in Vernant *Myth and Tragedy in Ancient Greece*, pp. 23–8 (p. 27).
73. Vernant (1990) 'The Historical Moment', p. 26.
74. Vernant (1990) 'Tensions and Ambiguities in Greek Tragedy', in Vernant *Myth and Tragedy in Ancient Greece*, pp. 29–48 (p. 32).
75. For a discussion of challenges to the prohibition against torture during the 'war on terror', see T. Erskine, *Embedded Cosmopolitanism*, pp. 192–5; for a discussion of challenges to the prohibition against preventive war, see Cian O'Driscoll, *Renegotiation of the Just War Tradition and the Right to War in the Twenty-First Century* (Basingstoke: Palgrave Macmillan (2008)), pp. 27–50.
76. G. Clore (1992) 'Cognitive Phenomenology: Feelings and the Construction of Judgment', in L. Martin and A. Tesser (eds) *The Construction of Social Judgments* (Hillsdale, NJ: Erlbaum), pp. 133–63, and Clore et al. (2002) 'Affective Feelings as Feedback: Some Cognitive Consequences', in L. Martin and G. Clore (eds), *Theories of Mood and Cognition* (Mahway, NJ: Erlbaum), pp. 27–62; A. Damasio (1996) *Descartes' Error: Emotion, Reason, and the Human Brain* (New York: Putnam); G. Jeffrey (1987) *The Psychology of Fear and Stress*, 2nd edn (Cambridge: Cambridge University Press). For a good review of the literature, see R. McDermott (2004) 'The Feeling of Rationality: The Meaning of Neuroscientific Advances for Political Science', *Perspectives in Politics*, 2, 691–706.
77. Important exceptions are G. Marcus, W. Russell Neuman and M. Mackuen (2000) *Affective Intelligence and Political Judgment* (Chicago: University of Chicago Press) and N. C. Crawford (2000) 'The Passion of World Politics: Propositions on Emotion and Emotional Relationships', *International Security*, 24/4, 116–56.
78. Strong, 'Nietzsche and Questions of Tragedy', this volume; Nietzsche (1999) *The Birth of Tragedy*, Sects. 1 and 3; W. Kaufmann (1968) *Nietzsche*, 3rd edn rev. (Princeton: Princeton University Press); H. White (1973) *Metahistory: The Historical Imagination in Nineteenth Century Europe* (Baltimore: Johns Hopkins University Press), pp. 331–74.
79. Plato, *Symposium*, 209 a–b. Plato distinguishes *eros* from *epithumia*, unreasoning or animal desires, which at best can be brought under control.
80. Nevertheless, there may be some hope in the fact that President Obama claims to be inspired by one of the IR theorists influenced by tragedy that we cited in Chapter 1. In a pre-election interview, Obama enthusiastically declared Reinhold Niebuhr to be one of his 'favourite philosophers'. From Niebuhr, Obama described himself taking 'the compelling idea that there is serious evil in the world, and hardship and pain. And, we should be humble and modest in our belief that we can eliminate those things'. D. Brooks (2007) 'Obama, Gospel and Verse', *The New York Times*, April 26, available at http://select.nytimes.com/2007/04/26/opinion/26brooks.html?_r=1, accessed 30 January 2009. Toni Erskine is grateful to Michael C. Williams for drawing her attention to the existence of this interview.
81. Strong 'Nietzsche and Questions of Tragedy', this volume.

Index